SEARCH THE SCRIPTURES WITH AN OPEN MIND

BOB SNIDER

authorHOUSE®

AuthorHouse™
1663 Liberty Drive
Bloomington, IN 47403
www.authorhouse.com
Phone: 1 (800) 839-8640

Published by AuthorHouse 01/26/2017

ISBN: 978-1-5246-6021-5 (sc)
ISBN: 978-1-5246-6022-2 (e)

Library of Congress Control Number: 2017900683

Print information available on the last page.

This book is printed on acid-free paper.

Scripture taken from the King James Version of the Bible.

Dedicated to my wife, Luz Victoria, whose tender loving care made this work possible.

Religion is ninety percent tradition, nine percent superstition, and one percent communion with God.

I want to enjoy the ninety percent, to ignore the nine percent, and to live the one percent.

To do so successfully I must understand one hundred percent

FOREWORD

God played a trick on me. He didn't do it to hurt me, He did it to challenge me.

God put me in the Bible Belt to grow up. Then He gave me an analytical mind, which is good for little else but science. I've spent my entire life responding to that challenge. This work is my final effort to resolve the contradictions and conflicts with which I've had to live.

I want to do the right thing. But, very often, what is so obviously right seems so horribly wrong. Must I live with a double standard, swinging back and forth with each shift of the wandering wind?

No! Truth is truth! When two beliefs differ, both can't be right, and more often than not, both are wrong. It is far more commendable to search for the truth than to stoutly defend a disproven faith or to criticize one who holds a different faith.

I went to a church-supported college, to major in music, hoping to spend my life raising joyous anthems to the Lord and helping others to do the same. The skillful music faculty quickly found that I had absolutely no musical talent. The psychology professor tested my aptitudes and advised me to study science.

My science professor and my religion professor were both nice fellows. They worked for the same religious institution, and they got along well with one another. But each was telling me that the other was lying to me. I asked them about it. The science professor said, "They have their world and we have ours. We never discuss our differences". The religion professor said, "The Bible is not a science textbook". At graduation I could still not reconcile those statements.

As I learned more and more about science, my faith began to weaken. My epiphany came when I was in graduate school.

The cutting edge of physics at the time was the search for an explanation of the recently discovered expanding universe. While pondering that problem, I was jolted by a remembered verse: "And God said, Let there be light, and there was light". Voila! That's what the Big Bang Theory says! So, the Bible is a science textbook, after all.

Another thirty years went by before science could conclusively prove the Big Bang Theory. The Bible had already been telling us about it for thousands of years. There are hundreds of enigmatic statements in the Bible that hint at scientific discoveries to be made much later. Genesis 6:4 says, There were giants in the earth in those days. Neanderthal remains were found there in 1992. Genesis 1:20 says, Let the waters bring forth ... fowl that may fly .... It was proved in 2009 that birds evolved from dinosaurs, amphibians, and fish.

What follows is the story of my search for more of those clues, and my attempts to understand their meanings in the light of the total store of human knowledge.

It's not only science that can enhance our understanding of the Bible. I have used ancient literature, including the sacred texts of other religions, as well as suppressed and prohibited works of the early Christians.

CONTENTS

BELIEFS

There is no disagreement between religion and science,
There are only disagreeable people who need
someone with whom to disagree.

There are three levels of belief

1. Science – belief in that which has been proven,
2. Faith – belief in that which has been neither proven nor disproven, and
3. Superstition – belief in that which has been disproven.

We are born with nothing but faith. As we learn, through experience and education, what has been proven, much of our faith turns to science. Some of it can never be proven, and we must retain that faith indefinitely. If we stubbornly refuse to put aside that which is disproven it becomes superstition.

For example: Belief in God was faith, until His existence was proven. Now it is science. By the same token, atheism was once an alternative faith. Now it is superstition.

The idea that learning (science) is the enemy of faith is nonsense. If an article of faith is weakened by science, it was superstition to begin with. Superstition and ignorance are the twin pillars of tyranny.

GOD?

Si Dieu n'existait pas, il faudrait l'inventer.[1]
— *Voltaire*[2]
(If God did not exist, it would be necessary to invent Him.)

This pithy, slightly humorous, and profoundly meaningful statement begs several questions.

1. Does God exist?
2. Has God been invented, either once or many times?
3. If God does exist, and He has been invented, what does He think of those inventions?

The first question elicits an answer from science. For a long time scientists arbitrarily said "no", without even attempting to verify their answer. Eventually they tried to cap their knowledge with a "final discovery", and were forced to recognize that there is a realm into which the human intellect cannot enter.

The second question is answered by history. And the documented answers would fill several encyclopedias.

The answer to the third question should be obvious, at least to Jews and Christians.

I am the Lord, your God… You shall have no other god before me.

[1] *Épître à l'Auteur des Trois Imposteurs.*
[2] Pen name of François-Marie Arouet. 18th Century philosopher.

PROOF

I am an agnostic, but not an atheist
—Albert Einstein

On May 29, 1919, the shadow of a total solar eclipse moved across the Atlantic Ocean from Brazil to Africa. Scientists on both continents were lying in wait for it. They were unanimous in their desire to get the most accurate observations possible, but their hopes for the result of those measurements varied.

Only during a total eclipse is it possible to see the light from distant stars passing close to the sun. Albert Einstein's controversial Theory of Relativity had predicted that such a ray of light would be bent slightly by solar gravity.[3] That was only one of the astonishing predictions of the Theory. If it could be confirmed, then some credence would also have to be given to the other predictions.

The starlight was deflected, exactly as predicted.[4] Relativity was confirmed! Einstein received a Nobel Prize in 1921.

By all scientific traditions, the Theory of Relativity should have become the Law of Relativity. But scientists, including many of the most prominent, were reluctant.

Why? A well-thought-out and logical theory had been verified by experimental evidence. Wasn't that enough? Not this time. It was up too close and personal. It

[3] Einstein, Albert, *Die Grundlagen der Relitavitätstheorie*, Annalen der Physik, 49.

[4] Dyson, F W, Eddington, A S, & Davidson, C, *A Determination of the Deflection of Light by the Sun's Gravitational Field, ...,*. Philosophical Transactions of the Royal Society - A. 220 (572-582) 291-333.

challenged their cherished faith in the ultimate triumph of mind over matter.

Every previous scientific discovery had exalted the mind of man. It had been going on for centuries, and the expectations of scientists were beginning to approach self-deification. Relativity predicted a limit on human knowledge. The humility to accept such an idea was in short supply.

One of the "predictions" of the Theory of Relativity had already been confirmed, though not recognized, by the Michelson-Morley experiment of 1887. This was an attempt to find the absolute velocity of the Earth through space, without regard to its motion around the sun or past other heavenly bodies. The unacceptable result was that the Earth was apparently stationary, and the rest of the universe revolved around it.

Oh, no! Not again!!

Nicolaus Copernicus

Galileo Galilei

The geocentric model of the Universe had been proposed by Aristotle, and was an official teaching of the Roman Catholic Church. Copernicus, a Catholic canon, developed the heliocentric model, but, fearing the Church's reaction, delayed publishing it until he was on his deathbed, in 1543[5]. It was on the list of prohibited books until 1835. Galileo, using his newly-invented telescope, spectacularly confirmed, and added more detail to, the concept of Copernicus.[6] In 1633 he was convicted of heresy, forced to renounce[7] his work, and imprisoned for the rest of his life. Pope (now Saint) John Paul II, in 1992, formally expressed regret for this injustice, admitting the Church was wrong and Galileo was right.[8]

After three centuries of antagonism between the growing scientific community, which unanimously believed that the Earth revolved around the Sun, and the Church, which insisted that the Earth was unmoving, here was scientific evidence that seemed to support the Church's position.

The Theory of Relativity states that an observer who is part of a system can never receive any information from outside that system. The Universe is finite in space-time. The Infinite exists, but is beyond our reach. We can speak of, but never study nor describe, that which lies beyond. To do so we must use such words as the Infinite, the Unknowable, or the Eternal. Can't someone think of a simple word to. designate such an entity?

The Theory of Relativity was the only viable explanation for the result of the Michel**son**-Morley experiment. It restored the validity of the Copernican Model. But, at the same time it proved the existence of God, more unequivocally than theological speculation ever had.

Even as the proofs piled up, not all scientists accepted Relativity. Despite its rigorous scientific orthodoxy, it had a quasi-spiritual aura, which was hard to stomach. And the

---

5 Copernicus, Nicholas, *De Revolunionibus Orbium.*

6 Gallei, Galileo, *Letter to the Grand Duchess Christina.*

7 Immediately after stating that the Earth was the motionless center pf the Universe, he was heard to mutter "E pur si muove" ("And still it moves").

8 Vatican admits Galileo was right, New Scientist, (1846) 1002-11-07.

public was deeply suspicious of anything so complicated and incomprehensible.

Einstein's popularity was surprising. His genius was considered unprecedented. His modesty and his teddy-bear-like appearance endeared him to many. "Einstein" became a sobriquet for a very intelligent person. Brilliant elementary students were called "little Einsteins".

Albert Einstein visited America in 1833, and was welcomed by a ticker tape parade. During that visit, Hitler seized control of Germany, and Einstein refused to return to his native land. Eventually he became an American citizen. It was a source of great pride for all Americans; even more so when he turned down the proffered presidency of the State of Israel to remain in America.

Relativity had equated space and time. It also equated energy and matter by the most famous algebraic equation ever written:

$$\mathbf{E = mc^2}$$

where "E" is energy, "m" is mass, and "c" is the speed of light. This meant that a miniscule amount of matter could become a huge amount of energy. Einstein, and several Nazi physicists, realized that this could be accomplished by the splitting of certain heavy atoms. Einstein reported this fact directly to President Roosevelt. The race was on!

The mushroom cloud over Hiroshima left no doubt in anyone's mind that Relativity is a fact, no longer just a theory. We have to live with it and all its consequences, whether we like it or not.

We are not the super-beings we have imagined ourselves to be. Our fate is in the hands of a higher power. God exists!

Can science say any more about God? Not by direct observation – that is beyond our ability. But, by examining what He has done, we may discover what He is not. The computer capacity now exists to design a simplified model of the universe, and test its working.[9]

[9] Martin Reese, *Just Six Numbers: The Deep Forces that Shape the Universe.*

It was found in 2001 that if any one of God's arbitrarily-fixed fundamental physical constants were changed, even slightly, life would be impossible.[10] God could have altered any of those numbers in the real world as easily as we can alter them in the cyber world. But he didn't. God is good!

§

Other proofs of God's existence have been taught in theological schools for centuries. While not very convincing to most scientists, they must not be passed over lightly. They involve the widespread belief in God among all cultures, the apparent evidence of his occasional interference in the affairs of men, and the simple question, "If God didn't create the Universe, who did?"

[10] For lack of a better name, some scientists call this the Goldilocks Theory (not too cold, not too hot, just right).

IMAGES

Si Dieu nous a faits à son image, nous le lui avons bien rendu.
--Voltaire

(If God made us in his own image, we have done the same to Him

What does God look like? That's a nonsense question. "Look like" means "to appear similar visually". A visual image is formed when light is reflected from an object through the eyes into the brain. God does not reflect light. He made the light, and put it into our closed universe where it does not affect Him. And light itself is nothing but that segment of the electromagnetic spectrum to which human eyes can respond. Nothing about God is dependent on capabilities of the human anatomy.

Of course the brain can form mental images without any visual input. Each believer has a mental image of the God he worships. And there are almost as many different mental images of God as there are believers.

It is the function of the artist to convert his own mental images into visual form through such media as painting, sculpture, etc. Churches and museums are replete with visualizations of Biblical and other religious persons and events. This forms a significant part of our culture. They are admired and enjoyed by believers and non-believers alike.

But few artists would dare a representation of God Himself.

Michelangelo dared! His painting *God Imparting the Breath of Life to Adam* forms part of the mosaic ceiling of the Sistine Chapel. Many persons view it in awe and ecstasy. It undoubtedly inspires a prayerful reverence. But is it God? Is it even a reasonably accurate rendition of God's true image?

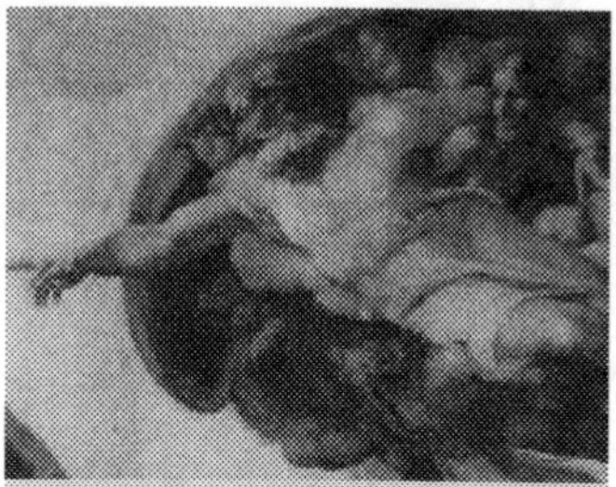

Michelangelo's God

Michelangelo's God is a white male human, aged but strong, with flowing long white hair and beard, blue-grey eyes and a "Roman nose". There are living persons who look much like that, especially in Italy. But most of us look quite different. And weren't we all made in the image of the same God? Even Adam in the painting might be questionable. He has a white skin, though the Garden of Eden was in Africa.

§

Is God male? Ask that without warning, and most people will say, "yes". But give them a few minutes to think about it, and many will change to "I don't know", or even "no". The idea of God's masculinity originated in sexist societies long ago, but is now sustained by habit and tradition. It is difficult to change because of an inadequacy in English and many other languages. It is impossible to refer to a person or a personified entity without using a gender-specific pronoun. And masculine is the default gender.

Attempts to solve this problem have been rare, sometimes humorous, and always ineffective. Mary Baker Eddy is said (probably apocryphally) to have counseled a distraught woman, "Talk to God, my dear. She will understand". And John Wayne, the epitome of American he-manliness, in his last interview with Barbara Walters, referred to God as "He or She".

The Catholic Catechism says that God is a spirit without sex or race, but that, for convenience, is designated by a masculine pronoun. Most Protestant churches (major exception – the Mormons) take the same attitude, but have made no formal statement. In Islam the male is supreme, whether human or divine. But Islam prohibits the making of images of any person or human-like being. That is why their mosques and other establishments are filled with intricate geometrical designs. Radical Islamists sometimes destroy great works of art containing personal images.

§

Christianity arose within a white society. The concept of a white God must have hindered missionary efforts among people of other races. Most of the non-white Christians today are descended from slaves of white masters.

Portraits of a white Christ decorate many African-American churches. Yes, this is historically accurate. But any implication that His Heavenly Father is also white is false, misleading, and unfair'

The artist Paul Gauguin, disgusted with French chauvinism and stuffiness, spent some of his life in the South Seas. His *La Orana Maria* ("Hail Mary" in Tahitian) is a Polynesian Madonna.

Hail Mary! — by Gauguin

The Holy Mother and her Child are shown in a typical Polynesian pose, wearing typical Polynesian clothing, and, above all, with typical Polynesian physiognomy. The worshippers are typical Polynesians. Gauguin's powerful message: The love of Jesus Christ is not just for those who adopt European culture; it is for everyone, in his own culture.

Gauguin was bitterly criticized in France. He was accused of treason, heresy, and even pornography. But his presentation of the Gospel in a new and meaningful context must be given some of the credit for the thatched-roof churches that now dot the South Pacific and for the Christian Islanders who saved the lives of many allied servicemen during World War II.

§

What language does God speak? That's a silly question. But some of the answers it has gotten are even sillier. Believers have done ridiculous thing in order to speak to God "properly".

The Council of Nicaea wrote the Nicene Creed and decided which books would be included in the Bible. Their work had to be approved by the pagan Emperor Constantine before Christianity could become the official religion of the Roman Empire. The books selected had been written in Hebrew, Aramaic, and Greek. All were translated into the debased Latin of the common people, and the Vulgate Bible came into use. The Mass was only in Latin until well into modern times. It was widely believed, but never proclaimed, that God spoke Latin.

Protestant reformers generally did not disagree with Catholic theology. (Martin Luther was among Copernicus's severest critics.) Their objections were to clerical corruption and to the use of an incomprehensible language. They promoted translation of the Bible into vernacular languages. The first widely-used translation in each language became a quasi-religious icon itself. Conservatives stoutly resisted updating as the language itself changed.

The King James Version[11] of the Bible and Shakespeare's plays were produced about the same time, and written in the language spoken at that time. Together they raised the literary standing of the English language itself, and strengthened it against future changes. Nevertheless, by the early Eighteenth Century, the words "thee" and "thou" had dropped out of the spoken language. They were still used in the liturgy, and by persons

[11] The King James Bible is meant for use by Protestants, but the Douai Version, used by Catholics, was created about the same time, and its language is almost identical.

showing off their religiosity. (It is amusing to note how many of those persons fail to distinguish the grammatical difference between the two words.)

Ninety percent of the Bibles stocked in a large modern bookstore are the King James Version. Newer versions are available of course, but few people want them. Those new versions are much more understandable and meaningful, and they have been more carefully and accurately translated from even more ancient texts. The New Revised Standard Version is approved for use in both Orthodox and Catholic churches, and by all major Protestant denominations. Many churches have adopted it as their official Bible, but most parishioners of those churches still prefer King James. Habit and tradition are more important than wisdom and understanding! In the Bible Belt several fundamentalist preachers have insisted that prayers be said in Sixteenth Century English because "that's the language God speaks".

§

The above comments undoubtedly display a strong deist tendency. Deism is belief in God with no encumbrance from dogma or religious authority. Deism and atheism are antonyms. A deist can conscientiously associate himself with any monotheistic religion, but he cannot assume that followers of that religion will accept him. Deism began as a system of faith. Now, in the light of modern science, it requires only acceptance of a proven fact. By the same reasoning, atheism is no longer a faith, it is now a superstition.

Deism arose in Western Europe during the Enlightenment of the Seventeenth and Eighteenth Centuries, in response to both the increasing understanding of natural phenomena and the brutality of the religious wars and inquisitions. Many prominent persons were deists, and the philosopher Voltaire was their spokesperson.[12] Deism flourished during the American and French

[12] Theism differs slightly from Deism. It accepts that God still intervenes in the operation of the Universe, sometimes in answer to prayers. The philosophy of this work is cautiously theistic.

Revolutions. Several Founding Fathers, including Thomas Jefferson[13] and Benjamin

Franklin, were deists. Albert Einstein was a deist. A recent expression of deistic thinking came from Oprah Winfrey. When interviewing a professed atheist, she said, "You're not really an atheist. You adore Nature, and you love humanity. That's what Cod is."

Perhaps the last word should be reserved for the Algonquian Indians. They called God "Manitou", which translates into English as "Great Spirit".

[13] Jefferson's personal credo: "I have sworn eternal enmity to every form of tyranny over the mind of man".

COSMOSOS

The heavens declare the glory of God, and the firmament sheweth his handiwork.
— Psalm 19:1

During the 1920s Edwin P Hubble, using the new Mount Wilson Telescope in California, discovered that certain stars, known as Cepheid Variables, dimmed and brightened alternately, and that the period of change was proportional to the absolute brightness of the star.[14] From the observed frequency of the fluctuation he could calculate the energy emitted by the star. And, since the apparent brightness decreases with distance, he could then compute the distance to the star.

The Universe was much larger than astronomers had thought! But that wasn't all. Hubble studied the chemical makeup of those stars by looking for characteristic patterns in the spectra of their light. The patterns were there, but not exactly where they were supposed to be. They were moved toward the red end of the spectrum, some more than others. (Due to the Doppler Effect, waves are apparently shortened if their source is approaching, lengthened if it is receding.) Then he noticed that the magnitude of the Red Shift was proportional to the distance to the star. This had two important consequences. It provided a method of measuring the distance to any star. And

[14] Absolute brightness can be calculated from the apparent brightness and the distance to the star. The distances to a few nearby stars had already been determined by triangulation from opposite sides of the Earth's orbit.

it proved that the Universe is expanding.[15]

§

Astronomers had their work cut out for them. They could now create a three-dimensional map of the Universe, a much larger Universe than they had ever imagined. But they also had to explain why that Universe was expanding.

Edwin Hubble

§

One of Einstein's original equations had predicted an expanding universe, but he couldn't believe it. He introduced a "fudge factor" to keep the Universe constant. Now Hubble had proved it was expanding. The two scientists met in person, and humbly accepted the result of their joint effort. The world for his grievous error, and in doing so he became even greater.

But why was the Universe expanding? Theories came thick and fast. Everybody wanted to get in on the act. Ideas ranged from the sublime to the ridiculous. By the 1950s all but two of those ideas had been shot down by either experimental evidence or better thought-out theories. The Big Bang Theory and the Continuous Creation Theory were still standing. Which would prevail?

And God said, "Let there be light". And there was light.[16]

That's a better description of the Big Bang than any scientist ever wrote. Slowly evidence accumulated favoring the Big Bang as the explanation of the expanding universe, and the Big Bang Theory is now scientific

[15] Hubble E, *A relation between distance and radialvelocity among extra-galactic nebulae,* Proceedings of the National Academy of Sciences (1929) 15(3) 169-174.

[16] Genesis: 1,3

orthodoxy. The Biblical account of the Beginning is confirmed!

> As satisfying as it is, the Bible only partly describes the Big Bang. God revealed more than that to some ancient patriarch, who had neither the language nor the worldview to record its full meaning. Legends told by his various descendants included different parts of the Revelation.
>
> The Quran says: ... *the heavens and the earth were joined together before We (Allah) tore them apart.*[5] Thus the Bible states that the Universe began with a gigantic explosion, and the Quran adds that everything in the heavens and the earth came out of that explosion.

The road to this conclusion was rocky. The concept of the Big Bang was developed by a thought experiment. Hubble's expansion was mentally reversed and traced back to a time when the entire Universe was crammed into one infinitesimally tiny speck. That time turned out to be 13.83 billion years ago. Scientists dealing with such vast expanses of time and space called themselves cosmologists. The science of cosmology became a recognized branch of astronomy. And that touched a tender nerve.

Every religion has its cosmology. Some are simple and straightforward, others quite elaborate. None is based on any known facts, and even the traditions they maintain were not established until long after the events described. Several of the major religious cosmologies contain elements surprisingly similar to facts established by science. The Bible starts with an allusion to the Big Bang. The Hindu Cosmology is the only one that includes a time scale of the same order of magnitude as that found by science. Both Hindu and Chinese cosmologies suggest the possibility of multiple universes, which is also now being considered by quantum mechanics, on the cutting edge of physics. If we accept that the Genesis story is divinely inspired, can we not also give God credit for helping the Hindus and the Chinese get something right?

Final confirmation of the Big Bang Theory came with discovery of the Cosmic Background Radiation. The "empty space"

[17] Quran: 21,30

between the stars looks black to the human eye, even when seen through an ordinary telescope. But, with extremely sensitive equipment, a very faint radiation can be detected. It corresponds to a temperature of a tiny fraction of a degree above absolute zero. This is the "echo of the Big Bang", what is left after billions of years of expansion and cooling. [18]

The Bible says nothing about the long period after the Big Bang and before the condensation of the Earth's atmospheric water. But we find:

...All (the heavenly bodies) go along, each in its own rounded path.[19]

This truth was discovered by Copernicus in the Sixteenth Century, but was denied and officially suppressed by the Church until the late Twentieth Century.

§

[18] Aaronson, Steve (Jan 1980), *"The Light of the Creation: An Interview with A A Penzias & Robert W Wilson'*, Bell Wilson, Laboratories Record, 12-18,

[19] Quran: 21,31.

The Book of Genesis divides the process of Creation into six days. What is a "day"?

The Bible clearly separates the day from the night. A day, then, was the period from sunrise to sunset. The length of that period varies with the season and with the latitude. In the very high latitudes the day can vary from zero to several months in length. Today we generally consider the day to be 24 hours long.[20] That is defined as the time interval between two apparent transits of the sun through the same azimuth. But the Earth's period of rotation is about four minutes shorter than that. Are we talking about a solar day or a sidereal day? It doesn't matter. Both are getting longer. For billions of years the rotation has been very slowly decelerating due to tidal forces and the unbalance caused by extra snow and ice in the winter hemisphere. Twice a year astronomers make very careful measurements, and decide whether to add a "leap second" in order to keep our clocks in sync with Nature. 25 leap seconds

[20] Division of the day into hours, minutes, and seconds was invented by Moslems in the Eleventh Century,

have been added during the past 42 years. So the year is now about one half second longer than it was a century ago, and the day is correspondingly longer. When the Earth was first formed, it was whirling much faster. And before it was formed there was no such thing as day or night.

God does not do a "day's work" in response to such slippery concepts as those that restrain human beings.

We have another definition of "day" in such phrases as 'George Washington's day" (most of a century), the 'Romans' day" (several centuries), or the "dinosaurs' day" (millions of years). These are only a few of the "days" God might use. Who are we to say which He chose?

§

God's work on the second "day" was altering the almost finished Earth into a very special condition so that it could sustain life. The Milky Way Galaxy, the Solar System, and at least the frame of the Earth had to have been created on the "first "day". The "first "day" of Creation was by far the longest; about nine billion years. The number and variety of accomplishments during that period are awe-inspiring. Cosmologists are just beginning to hammer out the details, and many things are still unclear.

The most controversial and most interesting time was an extremely short period, less than a billionth of a second, right after the Big Bang. Physicists are trying to work out what happened during that brief moment. None of the theories advanced are widely accepted. Some of the best actually require violations of sacrosanct physical laws.

Physicists didn't enact those laws, they only discovered them. God is in charge. When and in what order He established the rules under which the Universe runs may be inaccessible to us.

Much of our knowledge originated as an answer to "Why …..?" And the answer to such a question was sometimes met with "OK, that's so, but why is it so?" A series of "why" questions is often very enlightening, but if pursued far enough will inevitably end with "because God said so, that's why!" There are some scientific laws and fixed numbers that must be accepted, however reluctantly, without question.

By the end of that initial instant of the first day of Creation, God had ordained the Law of Gravity, the Laws of Motion, the Laws of Thermodynamics, and other laws, and had fixed the Speed of Light, the Gravitational Constant, the Elementary Charge, and other constants, possibly including the value of π.

For approximately the next 381,000 years the Universe was a soupy plasma of energy and matter, indistinguishable one from the other. Then matter, almost entirely in the form of hydrogen atoms, separated. Gravity pulled it toward tiny irregularities in density, and the first stars were born. Extreme pressures and temperatures in the centers of stars caused nuclear fusion, which converted hydrogen and helium into heavier elements. When a star exhausts its nuclear fuel it may explode,. or it may cast off its outer shell while the core collapses into a neutron star or a black hole. In either case vast clouds of dust and gas are spread through surrounding space. These clouds contain a variety of atoms and molecules, but still consist primarily of the lighter elements. Density irregularities form centers around which second, third, and later generations of stars can develop. The atoms in each generation undergo fusion into even heavier atoms.

Within a few billion years all the chemical elements in the periodic table were present in the Universe, and all the things with which we are familiar, including our own bodies, could be created. As Carl Sagan so eloquently put it, "We are made of star stuff". More prosaic astronomers call clouds of that star stuff "dust". And the Bible is talking about the same thing when it says, "Dust thou art, and to dust thou shalt return." No linguistic trickery is involved. It's very straightforward.

Our star, the sun, condensed out of a vast nebula within the Milky Way Galaxy about 5.5 billion years ago. The rest of that swirling cloud then formed into three concentric regions of celestial objects. Each of those objects followed its own peculiar orbit around its governing star. The outer region, the Oort Cloud,[21] contained millions of small objects, including minor planets and comets. The middle region was the home of the giant gas planets, Jupiter, Saturn, Uranus, and Neptune. In the inner region were dozens, probably hundreds of small rocky planets, whose orbits were very eccentric and often intersecting.

[21] AKA The Kuiper Belt

Earth was born when several of these tiny planets smashed together. Some of them may have already been partly molten, and the impacts generated more heat. The magma helped them stick together, though some broken off pieces may have been flung out into space. The larger it grew, the more strongly the Earth attracted nearby objects. After about 100 million years of impacts there were only four significant planets left in the inner Solar System: Mercury, Venus, Earth, and Mars. Relatively minor impacts continue into the present day.

Energy from the impacts plus increasing gravitational pressure from the growing mass kept the Earth in a mostly molten state. Heavier metallic, mostly iron, materials gravitated toward the center of the sphere. Rocky materials arranged themselves in concentric layers, with the lightest (granite) on the outside. Slowly the planet cooled, and the outer portion became a crust.

Late in the Impact Period the Earth was struck a glancing blow by another planet about one tenth its size. Most of the outer crust was torn off, the other planet disintegrated, and each of the pieces went its own way. Many fell back into the Earth and were absorbed. Some flew out into space. Others went into orbit around the Earth, where they coalesced with the broken-off pieces of crust, and formed the Moon.

The remaining outer crust, some 25 to 30 percent, was all on one side of the planet. The surface of the Earth consists of a number of "plates", oceanic plates and continental plates, which are in constant, though extremely slow, motion relative to each other.

This imbalance made the rotation very unstable and wobbly. The wobbles put intense pressure on that single continent, which scientists call Pangaea, eventually causing it to break up into smaller continents. Each continent drifted in response to forces from the Earth's wobble, convection currents within the core, solar and lunar tides, and its own inertia. At least once Pangaea reassembled itself in another configuration and then broke up again. The continental drift is still going on today, and will be examined in more detail when we get to our discussion of the origin of mankind.

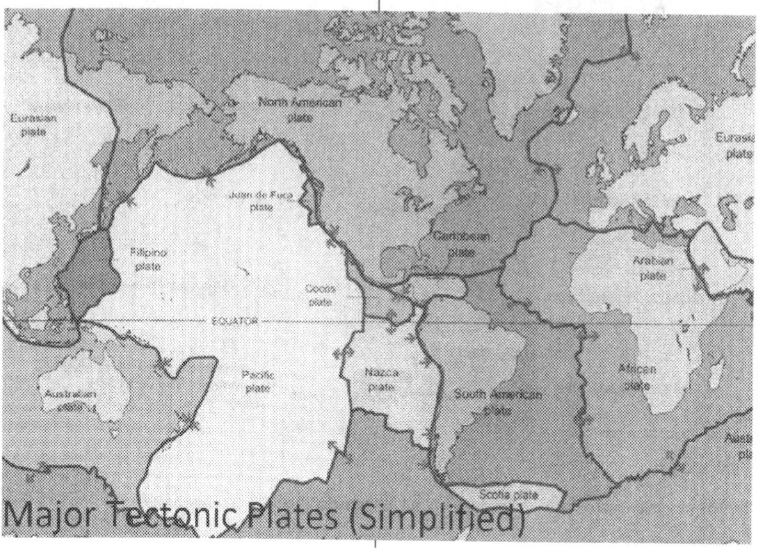

Major Tectonic Plates (Simplified)

The Theory of Continental Drift was proposed in 1912 by Alfred Wegener. It was promptly ridiculed by most scientists. Wegener died in disgrace in 1830.[22] But, during the 1950s, new studies of paleomagnetism showed that several continents had once been far from their present locations. And the discovery of mid-ocean rifts and sea-floor spreading in the 1960s left no doubt that Wegener was right.

Alfred Wegener

§

As the Earth-Moon system settled into stable orbits, inertial forces tried (futilely) to restore the Earth's symmetry. The remaining outer crust fractured into continents, which began drifting toward an unattainable perfect balance. In effect, granite continents float on an underlying layer of basalt, which also forms the crust under the oceans. The plates move around often bumping into each other. When two continental plates came together their abutting edges would be pushed upward into mountain ranges several miles high. An oceanic plate being forced under a continental plate would drag the edge f that plate down with it, creating a trough several miles deep.

The continuing breakup of the African Plate is of special interest to us. Fossils of nearly all the early hominids, which existed before the creation of humans, are found primarily in and near the African Rift valleys. The slow deepening and widening of those valleys, the rising of mountains along their edges, and the drainage systems of lakes and rivers which occupy them must be studied if we are to make any sense out of the second chapter of Genesis.

[22] His reputation has been restored. The *Alfred-Wegener-Institut fûr Polar und Meeresforshung* opened in Bremerhaven in 1981.

§

The lighter elements, which are the most abundant in the Universe, could not be held by the Earth's gravity, and quickly escaped into space. Vast quantities of gasses trapped within the molten planet bubbled to the surface and formed the primordial atmosphere. Nearly all the helium and much of the hydrogen then escaped. But hydrogen is chemically active and some of it formed bonds with other elements to create molecules heavy enough to be held to the Earth. The atmosphere consisted mostly of nitrogen (N_2), ammonia (NH_3), methane (CH_4), carbon dioxide (CO_2), and water (H_2O). The water was all in the form of vapor, the planet was still too hot for liquid water. But there was enough of it to literally fill the oceans.

He solid Earth was fully formed 4.4 billion years ago, but crustal movements, ("plate tectonics") continued to alter its form up to the present. To go on from here, we must look at the second "day"

WATERS

L'acqua è la forza trainante di tutta la natura.
— Leonardo da Vinci
(Water is the driving force of all nature.)

And God said, Let there be a firmament in the midst of the waters, and let it divide the waters from the waters. And God made the firmament, and divided the waters which were under the firmament from the waters which were above the firmament: and it was so. And God called the firmament Heaven. And the evening and the morning were the second day. And God said, Let the waters under the heaven be gathered together unto one place, and let the dry land appear: and it was so. And God called the dry land Earth; and the gathering together of the waters called the Seas: and God saw that it was good.[23]

[23] Genesis 1:6-10.

This is one of the most difficult parts of the Bible to understand. Translations +differ wildly, and even the best, most carefully thought out, is poor. If we're going to make any sense at all of it, we'll have to go all the way back to the original Hebrew text and try, if we can, to understand the mind-set of the people to whom God made this revelation.

Before attempting to understand the individual words, let's try to discern what the overall text is about, so we can put it into context. The last sentence clearly describes he origin of the oceans. "Gathering together" must be the runoff of liquid water from the land through rivers and streams into the ocean. Those processes constitute the last half of the Hydrologic Cycle! The previous sentences must be an attempt to describe the harder-to-visualize first half of the Cycle, evaporation, condensation, and precipitation

It is interesting to note that the word "waters" is always in the plural. Could that be a recognition that water occurs in more than one form? It would be millennia before scientists found that there were three states of matter; solid, liquid, and gas; and that water was one of the few substances that could easily exist in all three states on the Earth.

Conversion of water from one state to another is the essence of the Hydrologic Cycle. It is the source of the energy that drives the atmospheric and oceanic circulations that produce climate and weather.

Firmament" comes from the Latin "firmamentum", which is a literal translation of the Greek "στερεομα" (stereoma – solid surface or strong structure). The original Hebrew word was "צ'קר" (raqiah – stretching out or expanse). Why is the meaning of the translated words so different from that of the original divinely inspired word?

The translation from Hebrew into Greek, the Septuagint, was made about 300 BC at Alexandria, Egypt, for a community of Jewish businessmen who had become so thoroughly absorbed into the Hellenic world that they could no longer use their own language. They had enthusiastically adopted Greek art, science, and language, but wanted to keep their own religion. The translators were more familiar with Greek science than they were with the ancient divinely inspired story.

Greek science was all theory. Nothing was checked out by observation or experiment. Aristotle's Μετεορολογικα (things above) appeared about the same time as the Septuagint. It described weather phenomena and celestial bodies, as though they were all of the same nature. In Aristotle's view the sky was a solid vault onto which the stars were affixed like tiny gems. The sun, the moon, and the planets rotated around the Earth just below the vault, and the clouds orbited at a lower level. And that view had to be incorporated into the translation. Στερεομα was Aristotle's vault.

"Heaven" comes from Anglo-Saxon "heofan", which means either "sky" or "the abode of God". Nearly every Indo-European language has a word with that same double meaning (e.g. German *Himmel* and Spanish *cielo*). But the original Hebrew "שמים" (shanayim) meant only "sky". Translators of the New Revised Standard Version finally chose to use that word, though they still use "dome" where King James says "firmament".

Seen in a historical context, the formation of the firmament was the first step in creating the Hydrologic Cycle. The process began as the solid Earth cooled to the boiling point of water. Liquid water started to condense out of the atmosphere. With further cooling, most of the water fell to the surface, and the precipitation was both liquid and solid.

§

The science of hydrology has travelled a rough road against religious opposition. God's original revelation of its basic principle was received by a people whose language could not handle its subtleties. Those who expanded and translated the story often had other axes to grind. And that's too bad. It could have saved much grief. The ancient Egyptians had extensive hydraulic systems. And so has every civilized society. Agriculture, water supply, navigation, and flood protection all depend on hydrology. But for centuries it was done only by rule-of-thumb. Science could have made these operations much more efficient, and avoided wastage of our most precious natural resource.

§

Another segment of Scripture has proven an anathema to hydrology. Ecclesiastes 1:7 says,

"All the rivers run into the sea; yet the sea is not full; unto the place from whence the rivers come, thither they return again."

Bernard Palissy

That verse has been taken by many to mean that rivers receive their water from a supernatural source. That part of the Hydrologic Cycle is only partly visible, but it is no less real.

It was only in the Sixteenth Century that Bernard Palissy in France was able to prove that rainfall on a river valley supplied all the water flowing in the river.[24] He was convicted of heresy, and died in the Bastille. But the problem has still not gone away.

[24] Perrault, Pierre, *De l'origine des fontaines.* (1685)

Hydroelectric and flood control projects of the Tennessee Valley Authority disrupted the lives of many residents of the Bible Belt. Perhaps it was resentment as much as religion that turned them against hydrologists and hydraulic engineers. Colleges in the area still shy away from the teaching of hydrology for fear of boycotts.

When the "second day" ended, about four billion years ago, the active young Earth had all the necessary building blocks and was ready for God's gift of life.

LIFE

And God said, Let the Earth bring forth.....
— Genesis 1²

On the[25] first and second days God had created something directly, with the command "Let there be ....". On the third day, and again on the fifth and sixth days, He commanded the Earth to produce something. He had already created and formed the Earth, given it the necessary raw materials, and ordained the rules under which those materials could be processed into living creatures.

Not all scientists agree on the definition of life, or on the number of "kingdoms" in the living world. Some say viruses are alive, some say they are not. Some say fungi are plants, others say they constitute a separate kingdom. We shall ignore viruses as irrelevant to our discussion. And we shall consider only two kingdoms of life, which is in accordance with common parlance. (We all consider mushrooms, which are actually fungi, to be vegetables.) As working definitions;

(1) a living thing (a) ingests nutrients from its environment, (b) responds to stimuli, and (c) reproduces;

(2) a plant ingests inorganic material;

(3) an animal ingests plants and/or other animals;

(4) a chemosynthetic plant is energized solely by chemical action; and

(5) a photosynthetic plant is energized by both solar

[25] Each of God's three commands to create life began with these words.

radiation and the chemical reactions catalyzed by it.

The Solar System is ablaze with ultraviolet radiation. Ultraviolet rays are deadly to every form of life. Life is possible only behind an ultraviolet shield. There are two natural substances that can capture ultraviolet light and convert it into harmless forms of energy: (1) ozone, and (2) a deep layer of liquid water.

As the oceans deepened and cooled, more and more solar radiation was absorbed in their upper layers. The bottom waters were safe havens from ultraviolet rays, but they were also dark, too cold for incipient life, and devoid of the complex chemicals needed to form organic molecules.

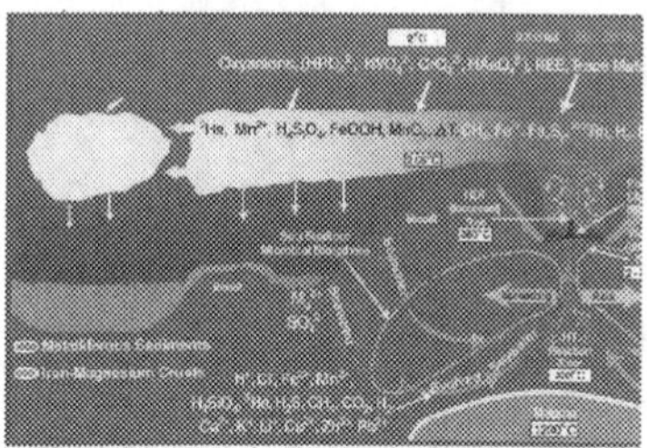

Where the Earth first brought forth life

This is a file from the Wikimedia Commons. Information from its description page there is shown below.

But there were holes in the bottom of the sea. Where crustal plates came together and plunged downward toward the molten core of the planet, gaps between the plates allowed magma to surge up, laden with phosphorus, carbon, and other useful elements. These intensely hot hydrothermal vents, or "black smokers" warmed the surrounding sea water and mixed it with a rich soup of prebiotic chemicals.

When God said "bring forth plants"[26], about 3.76 billion years ago, the ocean was ready.

Water around the hydrothermal vents was very turbulent, with a strong thermal gradient between the extremely hot effluent and the cold surrounding bottom water. Each of these effects led to a large but variable electrical field. And there were chemical attractions among the many different atoms and molecules churning around. Collisions and adhesions were frequent. Organic molecules formed and took part in the general chaos.

---

[26] Different versions of the Bible use the word "vegetation" or give the names of several specific plants. All this is interpreted as saying God ordered the creation of plant life, aprocess that is still going on.

Impacting molecules merged into larger conglomerations. Some impacts were brought about by random motions. Some of those motions were helped along by electrical gradients, others by chemical attraction. As the object grew larger (it was still microscopic in our frame of reference) a membrane might form around it. The membrane controlled intake and excretion of materials. If it grew large enough it might split into two almost identical units. It was now eating, responding to external forces, and reproducing. It was alive!

Robert Ballard, in the submersible *Alvin* discovered exotic life forms that could live without sunlight in 1978 in the depths of the Galapagos Trench. In 2004 Colleen Cavanaugh proved that such microorganisms could be produced from inorganic chemicals found in the deep sea, responding to natural physical forces.[27] (In 2013 similar organisms were found in rocks under the sea bed. What, if any, era relation these have to the Creation story is unknown.)

This first chapter in the story of life lasted about a billion years. Single-celled creatures spread and diversified, but remained in favored locations deep in the sea. Toward the end of the period some of them developed more complex systems of inner membranes, including nuclei which could perform special functions. Ribonucleic acid (RNA) appeared in the nuclei of some cells. It had the power to control reproduction and insure that daughter cells were accurate copies, strong enough to continue the line.

Discoverers of the Earth's First Life	

Living things moved out from their original home into more dangerous waters, and a few of them were tough enough to survive. They were leaving their food supply. Some moved into thin layer in the upper waters where some sunlight penetrated but most of the ultraviolet had

[27] Cavanaugh's organisms reproduced 0nly a few generations before dying out. God's similar creatures have reproduced billions of generations, down to and including us.

been eliminated. Within a few of them was found the chemical chlorophyll. Chlorophyll is a catalyst that enables plants to manufacture their own food from carbon dioxide and water. Those substances are plentiful throughout the oceans and even on the land. Life was no longer confined to its original food source. It was ready to explode into myriad forms and take over the entire Earth.

But first God had to prepare the sunlit Earth to welcome life. He did that on the "fourth day".

SKY

My blanket…I can't be without it!
—Linus Van Pelt[24]

The[28] language of the Biblical account of the "fourth day" is very confusing. These verses include redundant repetition, as though the writer were seeking words that had not yet been coined to describe a very complex process that God had revealed to him.

The subject is "light newly-placed in the sky". It is plain that these lights mark the division between day and night, and mark the progression of the seasons.

The sun and the moon are not named, but they are obviously the sources of the light. From a casual perusal of these verses, one might conclude (and many have) that God created the sun and the moon at that time. But that's not what it says! It says, "…***let there be lights in the firmament of the heaven*** (the sky)".

The sun and the moon had been created on the first day, and were already emitting and reflecting energy (light). But the living organisms that had been created on the third day were in the depths of the sea, where they could not utilize, or even perceive, that light.

"Day", "night", and "seasons" were meaningless to them. This is the situation that God corrected on the fourth day. He brought His creatures up into the light, gave them new powers, and created the sky to nourish and protect them.

Light is the portion of the electromagnetic spectrum that can be perceived by human eyes.

[28] Character in the *Peanuts* comic strip, by Charles Schultz.

The sky is not a physical object, but an optical illusion that exists only in the mind of a living thing that sees it. Thus, God's work on the fourth day was not the creation of new celestial bodies, it was giving the life forms He had already created the ability to multiply, diversify, and fill the planet that He had made for them.

The waters of the second day and the plants of the third day would not have been possible if God had not already created the sun, and probably also the moon. The third, fourth, fifth, and sixth days were devoted to the creation of the biosphere. God didn't take "time off" on the fourth day to work on a different project. Each of those four days was a step in the continuous process of filling the Earth with life.

Photosynthetic plants soon came to dominate the upper layers of the ocean. Their metabolism, driven by chlorophyll, consisted of taking in water, carbon dioxide, and other nutrients, combining them chemically to form their own body tissues, and releasing pure oxygen as a waste product. Most of the oxygen escaped into the atmosphere. A chain reaction was thus established. The more oxygen the atmosphere held, the faster plants could proliferate and spread, and the faster even more oxygen was released,

Richard Willstätter

Discovery of the structure and function of the chlorophyll molecule in 1915 earned Richard Willstätter[29] a Nobel Prize. It was only then that scientists could work out the oxidation of the atmosphere and the development of the ozone shield.

Atmospheric oxygen naturally takes on the molecular form

[29] Willstätter refused to develop poison gasses in World War I, but earned an Iron Cross for developing defenses against poison gasses. He fled Nazi anti-Semitism in 1939, and died in Switzerland.

O_2. When such a molecule is struck by ultraviolet radiation it is torn apart into atomic oxygen (O+O), and absorbs the radiant energy. Atomic oxygen is unstable, and quickly absorbs even more ultraviolet energy, to recombine as ozone (O_3). Ozone is poisonous to most life forms, but as the oxygen component of the air increased and deepened, the ultraviolet-absorbing layer of ozone moved up into the high atmosphere, leaving the lower layers full of life-sustaining pure oxygen. The ozone shield was discovered in 1830 by Sydney Chapman.

Sydney Chapman

What is the sky, and why is it blue? It is an optical illusion caused by the selective scattering of light in the blue segment of the solar spectrum. Just as ozone molecules absorb ultraviolet energy, molecules of oxygen and nitrogen cause photons of blue light to bounce. Oxygen (O_2) has a molecular weight of 32, nitrogen (N_2) has a molecular weight of 28. Molecules within that range of weight have a diameter about equal to the wave length of blue light. Shorter wave lengths come straight in between the air molecules, longer ones push them out of the way. But blue light bounces all over the sky, making it appear blue. The apparent color of the sun is a mixture of all the colors that come straight through. It contains no blue – that comes from all directions. Of course the sky could exist only after living things had developed organs sensitive to light.

Cyanobacteria began releasing significant amounts of oxygen about 2.4 billion years ago. It was about 600 million years ago that the ozone shield became able to protect life over the entire Earth.

The Oxygen Catastrophe (2.4 – 2.1 billion years ago) caused the first great mass extinction, killing off most of the species then existing, leaving those most fit to survive on the reforming Earth. Most of the survivors were now true (though very primitive) plants. Oxygen removed most of the greenhouse gasses from the atmosphere, triggering the first, longest, and coldest Ice Age.

Microbes that did not have chlorophyll needed a new food supply after they had drifted away from the original hydrothermal source. Some of them developed the ability to absorb (eat) their photosynthetic neighbors, who were full of carbohydrates and other nutrients. Thus began the first food chain. These protozoa then developed other abilities useful in obtaining food. Though they couldn't use the sunlight to process their food, it could help them find it. Their outer membranes developed light-sensitive spots which could direct them toward food.

When the fourth day ended, 544 million years ago, the sun was shining down though a blue sky, bringing life-sustaining energy to the abundant plant life that filled the upper layers of the ocean and was beginning to spread onto the continents. Ultraviolet radiation at the Earth's surface had been reduced to a tolerable level. And there were living things in the ocean that were not plants. They were not exactly anything else either. What was God going to do with them?

ANIMALS

And God said, Let the waters bring forth abundantly the moving creature that hath life, and fowl that may fly above the earth in the open firmament of heaven.
—Genesis 1:20

And that is exactly what happened on the fifth day of Creation. The only self-moving beings were protozoa, which quickly became true animals, multiplied, developed into many forms of sea creatures, and then moved up onto the land in the form of amphibians and reptiles. Near the end of the fifth day some of the small dinosaurs sprouted feathers, became birds, and took to the air.

Some of the pores through which protozoa had absorbed their food developed into feeding tubes or mouths, and then became full-fledged digestive systems. Cilia, which had propelled them toward food, and sometimes away from predators, became fins, tails, or even legs. Light-sensing spots became eyes, at first very rudimentary, but eventually of remarkable complexity.

Early on the fifth day sexual reproduction appeared among both plants and animals. Two parents each contributed to the genetic makeup of the offspring. Differentiation could now take place at a much faster rate, and the number of species multiplied rapidly. New forms found new environmental niches, and took advantage of newly developed food sources. The largest and strongest species moved to the tops of lengthening food chains.

Portions of the outer membranes (skins) of soft-bodied animals hardened into shells. Mollusks and shellfish spread through the oceans. Some free-swimming forms internalized hard tissue, developed skeletons, and became fish, the first vertebrates.

Some fish developed air-sacs (primitive lungs), and lived in shallow coastal waters, learning to breath air. Their fins lengthen and strengthened as they pushed themselves along the bottom, and finally they dragged themselves right up onto the land. Amphibians could live either on land or in the water, and from them came the reptiles.

Reptiles spread over all the continents, taking advantage of the lush vegetation that was waiting for them. Some of them became carnivores, and many grew to enormous size. The second half of the fifth day was the Age of Dinosaurs.

There was one more major category of animals to appear on that day. Some of the small dinosaurs grew feathers. Their forelimbs developed into wings, and they learned to fly. By the end of the day the sky was filled with true birds.

The fifth day of Creation came to a crashing end – literally. Sixty-six million years ago the Chicxulub Asteroid, most recent of the great imparters, struck the Yucatan Peninsula, punching a 110-mile wide hole through the earth's crust.[30] Magma spewed out, the shock set off earthquakes, volcanoes, and giant tsunamis around the world. Dust and debris, much of it ablaze and/or poisonous, filled the atmosphere.

Most of the earth's vegetation literally burned up. Sunlight was cut off from the surface for several years, depriving both plants and animals of their food. When the air cleared, several years later, the dinosaurs were extinct.[31] So were 76% of all the species that had been living. The devastation was more complete on land than in the oceans.

---

[30] Luis Alvarez and his coworkers hypothecized an asteroid impact in 1981 from a worldwide layer of iridium. The crater was discovered about the same time by explorers for Petróleos Mexicanos, but was not published until 1992,

[31] Except for a few flying dinosaurs, not yet completely converted into birds.

God had his work laid out for the next day.

HOW GOD CREATED LIFE

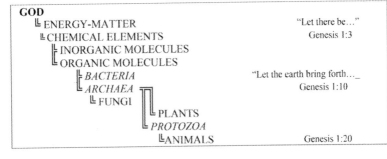

GOD
- ENERGY-MATTER — "Let there be…" Genesis 1:3
  - CHEMICAL ELEMENTS
    - INORGANIC MOLECULES
    - ORGANIC MOLECULES
      - *BACTERIA* — "Let the earth bring forth…_ Genesis 1:10
      - *ARCHAEA*
        - FUNGI
        - PLANTS
        - *PROTOZOA*
          - ANIMALS — Genesis 1:20

THE DIVERSIFICATION OF ANIMALS

ANIMALS
- INVERTABRATES
  - FISH
    - AMPHIBIA (Frogs, etc.)
      - REPTILES (Including dinosaurs)
        - BIRDS
          - MAMMALS
            - RODENTS, CARNIVORES, etc.
              - PRIMATES
                - LEMURS, MONKEYS, etc.
                  - HOMONOIDS
                    - APES
                      - AUSTRALOPITHECUS
                        - PARANTHROPUS
                        - HOMO HABILIS
                          - HOMO ERECTUS
                            - HOMO NEANDERTHALIS
                            - HOMO DENISOVA
                            - HUMANS

As the earth recovered its green mantle, providing a much richer food supply,. mammals multiplied, grew, and diversified. There were horned animals, both large and small, many of which were eventually domesticated (cattle, etc.).

MAMMALS

And God said, Let the earth bring forth the living creature after his kind, cattle and creeping things, and beast of the earth after his kind,...Let us make man in our image...

And the devastated, partially incinerated Earth responded. It brought forth a new kind of animal, an animal that did not lay eggs. It gave birth to living offspring. The Age of Mammals had begun. Cattle, creeping things, beasts of the earth, and man are all mammals, and the Bible says they were all created on the Sixth day.

Most numerous and most diversified of the mammals were the rodents (creeping things). With their strong teeth and tough digestive systems they could survive where others couldn't. They took over what was left of the vanquished dinosaurs' environmental niche.

As the earth recovered its green mantle, providing a much richer food supply,. mammals multiplied, grew, and diversified. There were horned animals, both large and small, many of which were eventually domesticated (cattle, etc.).

1.

Some mammals became dissatisfied with a vegetarian diet, and began to eat other animals. Carnivores include bears, cats, and dogs. They varied considerably in size.

There were some small animals we know as primates early on the sixth day. They fed mostly on insects. Catching crawling insects was not a problem, but flying insects was another story. They tried hard but rarely succeeded, until a few of them managed to struggle up small trees. This worked so well that they gradually grew fingers to hold on better to the trees. By 25 million years ago there were animals with full-fledged hands on the ends of all four legs. Some of them even had prehensile tails for more support and stability in grasping tree limbs.

By the time they had learned to move freely around in the tree tops they had discovered fruit, a more nourishing and delicious diet. The animals grew larger and developed many new forms.

Jumping from limb to limb is a more efficient way to move in the treetops than crawling along the limbs, but that requires excellent eyesight. The eyes of most primates moved from the sides to the front of their heads. Two eyes facing the same direction provide binocular vision and depth perception. (Side-facing eyes give a wider field of view for detecting predators – a protection now provided by altitude.)

Processing the binocular images and calculating the force needed to jump to a distant limb required a lot of brain power. Individuals who lacked sufficient intelligence risked, and often suffered, death in falls. Those of lower intelligence were weeded out, and the entire population slowly developed larger brains.

Six million years ago the continent of Africa cracked, and the Great Rift Valley began to open up. (It will eventually become another ocean.) Mountains, which were thrust up in the area, blocked air currents causing the climate to change. The jungle east of the Rift became a semi-arid grassland with only scattered patches of trees. Primates west of the Valley continued their idyllic way of life, but those to the east had to adopt new habits – or die.

Food was now scarcer, but more varied. The creature had the ability and versatility to deal with it. He had to walk upright to see over the tall grass. His spine was already used to the vertical position. The fingers on his feet were now useless, and they became shorter and less flexible. To compensate for his limited field of vision, he travelled in groups with many pairs of eyes on the lookout. Such group protection required close communication among members of the group. They developed audible vocal signals which eventually became language.

There were many plant materials that could be eaten, but they were small and hard to gather. Cutting or digging was often necessary. The fingers of the hands became even more dexterous as they made tools for these tasks.

A major new source of food was the animals that grazed on the grasslands. But they were hard to catch, hard to kill, and hard to butcher. It required organized group effort, strategy, tools, and weapons. All these were developed and improved. The new hunters had become a formidable force, capable of doing great harm to the environment.

It was time for God to act again.

And God said, Let us make man in our own image…male and female created He them...

This time God did not say, "Let there be" to create something out of nothing. He did not say "Let the earth bring forth". He is making something to resemble Himself. That something is the same in both male and female. It cannot be a physical body, males and females are physically quite different. Their physical bodies already existed. What He made now was spiritual, like God Himself, connected directly to the Almighty Creator Spirit.

The body of the cleverest, proudest, most powerful, and most selfish animal on the planet, containing a bit of God's own spirit to keep it under control, is a human.

"DAYS"

For a thousand years in thy sight are as yesterday when it has past, and as a watch in the night.
—Psalms 90:4

THE "DAYS" OF CREATION

DAY	BEGAN Years ago	M AJOR CREATIONS	BIOLOGIC ERA	GEOLOGIC PERIOD
1	13,820,000,000	Energy-Matter, Space-Time, Stars, Chemical elements, Galaxies, Planets		Pre-Earth
2	4,400,000,000	Clouds, Precipitation, River systems, Oceans		Hadean
3	3,760,000,000	Life, Plants	Archaean	Pre-Cambrian
4	2,400,000,000	Photosynthesis, Oxygen, Ozone		Pre-Cambrian
5	544,000,000	Invertebrates, Fish, Amphibians, Reptiles, Birds	Paleozoic Mesozoic	Cambrian Ordovician Silurian Devonian Mississippian Pennsylvanian Permian Triassic Jurassic Cretaceous
6	66,000,000	Mammals, Humans	Cenozoic	Tertiary Quaternary

7	200,000	Culture Civilization	During this "day" God rested. allowing the Universe to run according to the phyaical laws He had ordained.

MANKIND

Our Heavenly Father invented man because he was disappointed in the monkey.
—Mark Twain

By the end of the sixth "day" God had made the earth and all the heavenly bodies. He had worked the earth into approximately its present form and had filled it with a myriad of living beings. His last creation was mankind.

The last part of Genesis 1 and the first of Genesis 2 show the start of mankind as a perverse free-will creature. Both the Scriptural and the scientific information are ambiguous. The traditional story of Adam and Eve relies as much on assumptions as it does on the Bible. And it varies from one religion to another.

Let's start with a careful examination of what Genesis actually says.

1. God had already created male and female in his own (spiritual) image. The humans involved are not named. Now He determines whether that spirit can control their baser instincts, and the appropriate punishment when it does not.

2. The individuals punished are named Adam and Eve. Neither of those words is a personal name in the ancient Hebrew language. They are common nouns, meaning "a man" and "helpmate".

3. The Bible does not say that they were the only people in the world at that time. It says that their sons found wives, one of them in a "far country".

4. It does not say that all humans are descended from Adam and Eve, `though science can prove that they are.

5. Typically, no date or place is given, though there are some hints as to the location. Science can help with both where and when.

Many theologians state that Cain's wife was Awad. and Seth's wife was Azura. Some state, and nearly all imply, that both men married their sisters. The Bible says no such ting! This questionable information has been traced to the Book of Jubilees, which is not accepted as holy scripture by any modern church.

It is not probable that God would subject people newly-created in His own image to a practice so likely to produce defective offspring

§

The story of Adam's rib is simply a false translation, made intentionally millennia ago to "keep women in their place", and perpetuated by a tradition honored by the dominant males of many cultures.

The ancient Hebrew word "עלצ" ("tslea") meant "side", "corner", "flank", "chamber", or "half". Nowhere else in the Bible is that word translated "rib". In most of the contexts it refers to one of two equal halves. Genesis quotes Adam, "This is now bone of my bones, and flesh of my flesh". Eve was definitely made of more than just Adam's rib. The Bible says so!

This story is analogous to the Greek myth that Athena sprang out of the forehead of Zeus. The proud Athenians were justifying their dominance over the other Greeks.

An early rabbi named Joshua changed "side" to "rib". His explanation for doing so is still extant – the rib is the only organ that a man can give up without losing some of his control over his wife.[32] This is a very rare, almost unique, occurrence. An early translator left us a written explanation of why he chose the word he did,

[32] Katherine Bushnell, *God's Word to Women,* Paragraph 43, (1921). Christians for Biblical Equality, Minneapolis

The tradition of Adam's rib was firmly established among the English people long before the King James Bible was translated. Even the New Revised Standard Version continues the same error. Not all modern cultures hold so firmly to this outmoded and unnecessary tradition. "Côte" means either "rib" or "side" in French.

§

Discovery of deoxyribonucleic acid (DNA) by Watson and Crick in 1953, and sequencing of the human genome in the late 20th Century provided a powerful new tool for finding the genetic history of individuals, families, and even nations. It is used in court cases, genealogical studies, and in histories of entire species.

The mitochondrial component of DNA is more stable and easier to trace through eons of time than other components. But it is inherited only from the female line. Samples of DNA from many populations all over the world were tested to find the most recent common ancestor in a direct matrilineal line. The "mitochondrial Eve" lived between 140,000 and 200,000 years ago. Is she the same person as the Biblical Eve? Not necessarily. She could have been or, she could have been a descendant of the Biblical Eve in an all-female line.

Patrilineal lines of descent are harder to trace. It can be done, using the Y-chromosome. The procedure is more cumbersome, and gives less precise results. The "Y-chromosomal Adam" lived between 120,000 and 306,000 years ago.[33]

The Y-chromosomal Adam and the mitochondrial Eve would not necessarily have lived at the same time, and would definitely not have been parents of the same children. Each had descendants through both male and female lines. But the overlap in the two calculations plus the fact that fossil data fall within the same time frame, gives confidence that we have a reasonable approximation of the timing of the events in Genesis 2. It is estimated that God created

[33] ikipedia, *Mitochondrial Eve*.

homo-sapiens-sapiens about 200,000 years ago and that He tested them in the Garden of Eden about 195,000 years ago.

Analysis of the variability in modern human DNA shows us that early humans multiplied to a population of many millions, and then were nearly wiped out by some kind of catastrophe. It also shows that humans interbred with earlier forms of hominins before those became extinct. It shows that, for more than half of human history, all people were black, and that the other races developed as mutants from black ancestors.

§

The Leakey family, who had gone to East Africa as Christian missionaries, made a study of the many fossils found there. After rewriting the history of the Genus Homo, with fossils unearthed in Olduvai Gorge, they finally found actual human remains along the lower Omo River, just north of Lake Turkana, which occupies much of the main Rift. The oldest human fossils known were found in the lower Omo River Valley of Ethiopia in 1968. In 2004 the rock strata in which the fossils were found were dated by potassium-argon technology to 195,000 ±5000 years ago. [34] These people were no more than a few generations removed from their ancestors Adam and Eve. The Biblical story of the first human family had been confirmed by anthropology!![35]

[34] *Fossil Reanalysis Pushes Back Origin of Homo sapiens,* Scientific American, February 2005.

[35] Anthropology can be a dangerous profession. Richard Leakey lost both legs in the crash of his sabotaged aircraft. Then a "Christian" official removed him from his work facility to stop his "heresy". His colleague Dian Fossey was murdered by poachers while trying to protect endangered hominoids.

A layer of volcanic ash just underneath the fossils was dated, by another method, to 196,000 years ago. This almost perfect correspondence of dates determined by four entirely different methods gives unusual confidence in the accuracy of the results.

Our best cues to the location of the Garden of Eden are found in Genesis 2. Those clues add up to the description of a river system. But river systems change with time, and over 200,000 years vast changes can occur. We now know how far back in time to study those changes

RIVERS

There's a land where the mountains are nameless,
And the rivers all run God knows where.
—Robert Service[36]

The[36] whole history of mankind has taken place during the Pleistocene Ice Age.[37] That portion of the Pleistocene can be divided into several stages:

STAGE	YEARS AGO	RAIN FALL	SEA LEVEL
Riss[38] Glaciation	200,000-130,000	Heavy	Low
Inter Glacial	130,000-72,000	Light	High
Würm Glaciation	72,000-12,000	Heavy	Low
Inter glacial	12,000-present	Light	High

Adam and Eve lived during the early part of the Riss Glaciation. Rainfall was heavy, rivers carried large volumes of water and eroded their valleys, lake levels were high, and they readily found outlets to the sea. But sea levels were 200 to 400 feet lower than at present, and rivers extended out across some of what is now submerged land before reaching the sea. During interglacials the opposite was true. Lake levels were lower. Some lakes had no outlets, and became salty. Rivers diminished to a trickle, some stopped flowing, leaving only a few small salty lakes to mark their former courses. The ocean stood near its present level, and the lower portions of some river valleys were flooded.

Alteration of the topography can also bring about vast changes in the flow of rivers. And we

[36] From *The Spell of the Yukon.*

[37] It is not known whether man could survive a non-ice age; he's never tried it. Global warming may be bringing the Pleistocene to an end.

[38] European nomenclature is used for glaciations.

are dealing with an area of very active geology.

The Rift valleys are continuously widening, and generally deepening, while the highlands along their sides are rising. The new crust being created in the rifts is very thin, and portions of it may be raised or lowered several hundred feet by the churning magma underneath. These processes seem to take place randomly, and very close attention is necessary to ferret out the details.

Much of man's early story involved events that took place on or near the Arabian crustal plate. That plate had broken off from the African plate about six million years ago, and has been moving slowly northeastward and northward ever since. Over the last 200,000 years significant changes have occurred;

The Arabian Plate is completely surrounded by active fault zones. Each is altering the terrain in its own way.

The Arabian Shield is an area of hard granitic rock which has been slowly rising for millions of years. The Red Sea Rift is a sharp crack right across the middle of it, a diverging fault, whose valley is already filled with salt water. It will eventually become an ocean. Mountains on both sides of the Rift are still rising.

The Gulf of Aden Rift is also a diverging fault. It is spreading a little faster, but its sides are rising more slowly.

The Zagros Fault, along the coast of Iran and northward east of Iraq, is converging. The Arabian Plate is plunging downward (subducting) under the Eurasian Plate. The Zagros Mountains are rising, and the eastern part of the Arabian Plate is being dragged downward. This movement, togethler with the rising sea level, has allowed the ocean to spread into the Persian Gulf, which was formerly dry land.

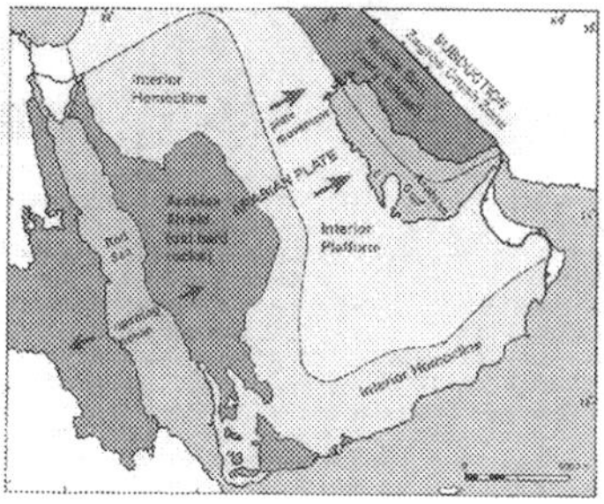

In the north the Bitlis Suture is also a convergent fault. Here the two plates are simply ramming against one another at the same level, causing the Taurus Mountains to rise.

Finally, the Dead Sea Rift, which includes the Jordan Valley and the Gulf of Aqaba, is a slip strike fault (analogous to California's San Andreas Fault). One plate is simply sliding past the other, with little effect on their elevation. This fault, like all the others, is associated with earthquakes and volcanoes,

The northeastern side of Arabia has been subsiding for millions of years, while the southwestern side has been rising. The accumulated difference in elevation over 200,000 years could easily have reversed the slope of the land, and the direction of some rivers flowing across it.[39]

§

Scholars have been searching for the Garden of Eden ever since the Torah was first published. And they have found it in hundreds of places as, diverse as Chinese Turkestan and Missouri. Most of them are obviously wrong. But a few may be right. Each has done his best with the resources available to him. Some have analyzed those resources a little more meticulously than others. Some have obviously been prejudiced in their choice of resources. New resources have come to light from time to time, and more may still appear.

The earliest, and by far the most important, of those resources is the Bible. The Book of Genesis mentions four rivers that were connected with the river that ran out of Eden. We must be dealing with a single river system, a main stream plus its tributaries. The Bible does not say that those rivers would still be connected thousands of years later, but they were connected at the time of Adam and Eve. Nor does it say that they would forever bear the same names. Only one of those names, the Euphrates, can be found on today's map. The Hiddekel is said to be east of Assyria, a good clue which is confirmed by the

[39] The lack of a precise figure for this rate of change is admittedly the weakest link in this analysis of Eden's river system.

Prophet Daniel who mentions the Hiddekel in a context that shows clearly he is talking about the river we now call the Tigris. The Gihon "encompasseth the whole land of Ethiopia". Ethiopia at that time was all the land back from the west shore of the Red Sea and south of Egypt. To get a river in this area connected to the Tigris and Euphrates, we are going to have to find some major geological changes in the landscape. The Pishon River "encompassleth the whole land of Havilah". That doesn't help much. Nor does the mention of precious minerals – they can be found in many places. There is no "Land of Havilah". There were two individuals named Havilah mentioned in the Bible. One was a grandson of Ham, and presumably shared his curse, being banished to an unknown distant and undesirable place. The other, many years later, was descended from Ishmael, and lived somewhere in southern Arabia.

And a river went out of Eden to water the garden; and from thence it was parted and went into four heads.

The river went out of Eden, so all four of the other rivers were downstream. The "parting" cannot refer to water flow; it must refer to the appearance of the system on a map. The "head" is not where one river joins another, but the source of the river, at its opposite end, usually high in some mountains. The rivers are numbered, strongly implying that they are listed in the order of their confluence with the rest of the system. We now have all the information needed to draw a schematic (not to scale, and not necessarily properly oriented) of this river system.

→Eden→Pishon→

↑

Gihon←

↑

Hiddekel←

↑

Euphrates

This scheme will not work in nature unless the terrain is arranged so that all the rivers run downhill. It is not so arranged at present. These rivers are in a region of intense plate tectonic activity. Rapid changes (on a geological time scale) are to be expected. To reconstruct the terrain that controlled the flow of these rivers, we must look at geologic processes over the past 200,000 years.

§

We will start with the Euphrates River. It can be found on today's map. The terrain over which it runs has been relatively stable. The only significant changes have been near its mouth. It now shares a delta with the Tigris River at the head of the Persian Gulf. The delta is constantly being changed by sedimentation and erosion, and has been alternately lengthened and shortened by changes in sea level. The intricate web of channels through the delta makes it possible to consider either of these rivers a tributary of the other.

The Hiddekel River is easily identified as the Tigris. It is not hard to make the Euphrates a tributary of the Hiddekel, as Genesis implies. But we must also make the Hiddekel a tributary of the Gihon, which "compasseth Ethiopia". Is that possible?

It is if we can find a channel from the Delta region through which a river could have run downhill in the general direction of Ethiopia and emptied into another river which we can identify as the Gihon.

The LandSat satellite, in 1983, discovered a broad, deeply eroded valley, which had been covered by drifting sand, running across Arabia from the Hejaz Mountains to the Tigris-Euphrates Delta. Geologists, using ground penetrating radar and other tools, determined that a major river, which they named the Kuwait River, had flowed northeastward through this channel from 50,000 BC to 6000 BC.[40] This is a major new tool in our search for Eden. But on close analysis we see that it was too recent, and it flowed the wrong direction.

[40] James A Sauer, *The River Runs Dry,* Biblical Archaeology Review, Vol 24, #4, pp 42-54.

Discovery of the Kuwait River caused a flurry of excitement among Biblical scholars, and brought forth several new theories of Eden's rivers. Most of them put the Pishon River through that newly-found valley, and placed Eden at the head of the Persian Gulf. But that makes the rivers flow into Eden, not out of it. It arranges the rivers in the wrong sequence. And it cannot account for the cherubim at the east gate of Eden or the Land of Nod farther east. In all these respects it disagrees with Genesis. And it totally ignores the fossil and genetic data.

It is an observed fact that northeastern Arabia is sinking and that southwestern Arabia is rising. The same process extended back to 200,000 years ago could have reversed the slope of the land. A river flowing through the valley at that time would have flowed the opposite direction. The Hejaz Mountains, which now line the east shore of the Red Sea, were much lower, and the valleys through them were not yet filled with the congealed lava that blocks them today.

The Hiddekel River, encountering higher ground which had not yet subducted, turned right and crossed the mouth of the Euphrates, receiving the water from that stream. The combined flow continued southwestward across Arabia, through the now hidden valley, to fall into the Red Sea Rift. There it joined the Gihon River,

The Gihon received the waters of the Hiddekel, and "encompassed Ethiopia". It occupied the Red Sea Rift, which at that time was entirely above the glacially-induced low sea level. Headwaters of the Gihon were in the Golan Heights. It flowed through the Sea of Galilee and the Jordan River to the basin of the Dead Sea. That basin was then occupied by a large freshwater lake which had an outlet to the Gulf of Aqaba. It continued the entire length of the Red Sea Rift to the "Triple Rift Junction".

The Triple Rift Junction, also known as the Afar Triangle, is the thinnest part of the Earth's crust. The Red Sea Rift separates the Arabian Plate from the African Plate. The Gulf of Aden Rift separates the Arabian Plate from the Somali Plate. And the Great Rift separates the African Plate from the Somali Plate. The three plates have been pulling away from each other for six million years. At the present time the Red Sea Rift is widening 15 millimeters per year, the Gulf of Aden Rift by 16 millimeters per year, and the Great Rift by 5 millimeters per year. The oceanic rifts were two to three miles narrower 200,000 years ago than they are now. The continental rift was only slightly narrower.

Of even greater importance is the rise and fall of sea level over geologic time periods. During most of the past 200,000 years sea level has been substantially lower than it is now, often by several hundred feet. This means that at the time of the Garden of Eden both the Red Sea and the Gulf of Aden were dry land, with a river running down the middle of each of them.

The Gihon River encountered, and emptied into, the Pishon at the Triple Rift Junction. The other two branches of that Junction were occupied by segments of the Pishon River. The Pishon at that time drained much of the Great Rift Valley, including many lakes and tributary rivers. The Pishon, now including the water received from the Gihom, continued eastward across what is now the bottom of the Gulf of Aden. The valley it occupied is still found at the bottom.

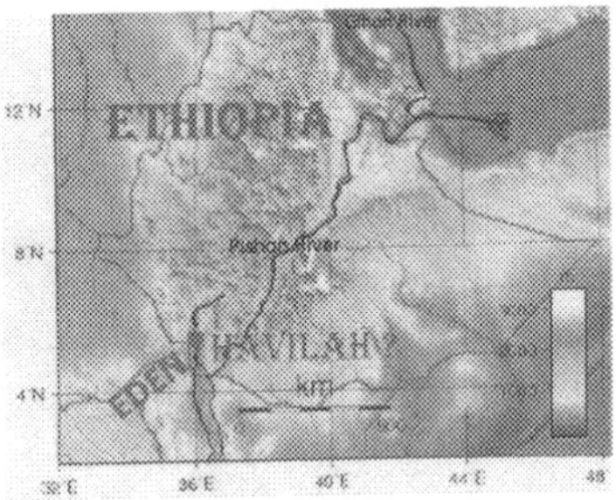

The Great Rift Valley is replete with hominid fossils, both human and non-human. The earliest confirmed human remains are found along the Omo River a short distance above its outlet at Lake Turkana.

The upper portion of the Rift Valley extending northeastward across Ethiopia from the north end of Lake Turkana is now mostly dry, containing only a few small salty lakes to mark the former course of a great river. Through the lower part of that Valley flows the Awash River, all that remains of the once mighty

Pishon. The Awash now ends in an evaporating lake in the Afar, but its former valley continues across the jumbled terrain of Djibouti, where it once received its tributary the Gihon, and across the seafloor into the Gulf of Aden.

What else is found at the north end of Lake Turkana? The mouth of the Omo River, just above which anthropologists have found the earliest human remains. Geologists have dated the rocks in which those remains were found to the same time that volcanologists have dated the ash layer underneath them. And geneticists have found that the most recent common ancestors of all living humans lived at precisely that same time.

Lake Turkana has a complex geological history. It has occupied a portion of the Rift Valley for millions of years. But its size and the flow of water through it have varied greatly. During glaciations it is large, containing fresh water, standing at a high level, and emptying into an outlet stream. During interglacials, such as now, it is smaller, lower, containing noxious chemicals (it is now alkaline), and without an outlet.

During the Würm Glaciation Lake Turkana had an outlet to the northwest into the Nile. It had no outlet during the Riss-Würm Interglacial. During the Riss Glaciation its outlet was to the northeast through the Great Rift Valley.

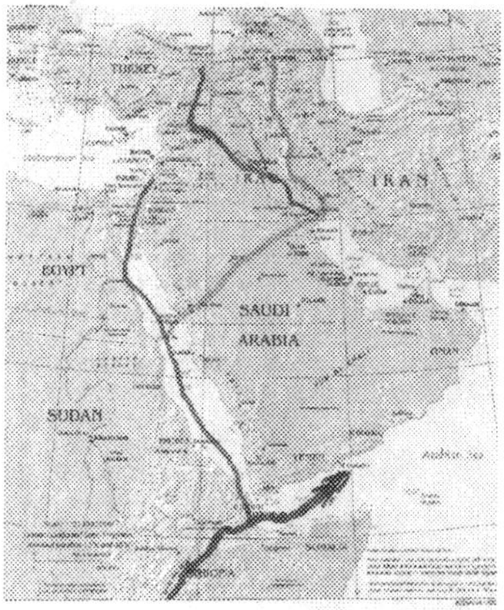

The Rivers of EdeN (Modern names added)

HE RIVERS OF EDEN	
BIBLICAL NAME	MODERN NAME
Garden of Eden	Omo National Park, Ethiopia
A river ran out of it	Omo River
East gate of Eden	Northeast corner of Lake Turkana
Pishon River	Lakes Turkana, Shala, Abijatta, Ziway, Koka. Awash River. Lake Abhe. Gulf of Tadjoura, Gulf of Aden.
Land of Nod	Awash Valley
Land of Havilah	?
Gihon River	Sea of Galilee. Jordan River. Dead Sea. Gulf of Aqaba. Red Sea.
Ethiopia (or Cush)	Northern Ethiopia. Eritrea
Hiddekel River	Tigris River. Wadi Batin. Valley through Hejaz Mountains.
Assyria	Central Iraq
Euphrates River	Euphrates River

EDEN

Banish me from Eden when you will;
But first let me eat of the fruit of the tree of knowledge!
—*Robert Ingersoll*[41]

There are four ways in which humans differ from apes::[41]

1. They have souls,

2. Their bodies are mostly free of hair,

3. Women suffer birth pangs, and

4. They speak.

Each of these changes is discussed in Genesis. The soul was provided by God near the end of the Sixth Day. Upon their expulsion from Eden, Adam was to "eat bread in the sweat of thy face". And Eve was to "bring forth children in sorrow".

Man is the only animal that sweats, or needs to. The great effort required to catch the food now available to them caused men's bodies to overheat. Those with less hair had a much better chance of avoiding heart attacks. The hair follicles, no longer used, changed to sweat glands, and evaporation further cooled the body.

Human females are the only animals that suffer pain in giving birth. The greater intelligence needed for cooperative hunting, language, and tool making caused the brain and its encompassing skull to grow so large that great strain was put on the tissues of the birth canal.

(See the chapter on "Speech" for the beginning of human language.)

[41] *The Works of Robert Ingersoll,* Vol. III.

Dominion over God's earth and all its creatures comes at a price.

Expulsion of Adam and Eve from Eden deprived them of their easily accessible source of delicious food. There was still plenty of food, but it was scattered over a very broad area, in varied forms, and hard to gather ad prepare.

§

The first person to leave this area was Cain, after the murder of Abel. He went eastward to the Land of Nod. That would be down the Pishon (now Awash) River to the Danakil Depression. That area is now desiccated and far below sea level. At that time it was well watered and supported a large population. But the region is geologically very unstable. Both the floor of the depression and the highlands surrounding it can be lowered or raised, and have been many times. On several occasions the sea has poured into the valley, only to evaporate centuries later when the highlands rose again. (Salt mining supports the present sparse population.)

It was apparently one of these floods that forced the Nodites to migrate farther eastward about 125,000 years ago, in the first significant human migration out of Africa.

The third son of Adam and Eve was Seth. He and his family remained near the original homeland; though, as their numbers increased they must have spread into surrounding territory. Eventually, some 100,000 years later, a large group of Seth's descendants migrated northward into the Near East. Most of the persons mentioned by name in the Bible were descended from Seth.

Adam and Eve had other sons and daughters. Nothing more is said of them. They must have migrated westward and southward to fill the rest of the African continent.

As the human population grew to become a well-established part of the earth's ecologic system, they remained within a few hundred miles of the Garden of Eden. There were hominids of other surviving species that far outnumbered them.

Europe, the Near East, Central Asia, and the north coast of Africa were all home to Neanderthals. Recent DNA studies show that many Neanderthals had light colored skins (All humans at that time were black), and some had red hair.

The recently discovered Denisovans shared some territory with the Neanderthals in Central Asia, and probably occupied much of East Asia, though no other sites have identified. (Denisovan DNA exists in all Far Eastern people, down to and including the Australian aborigines.

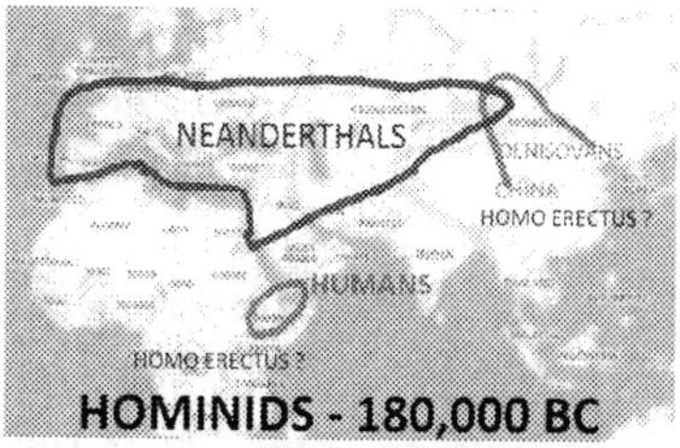

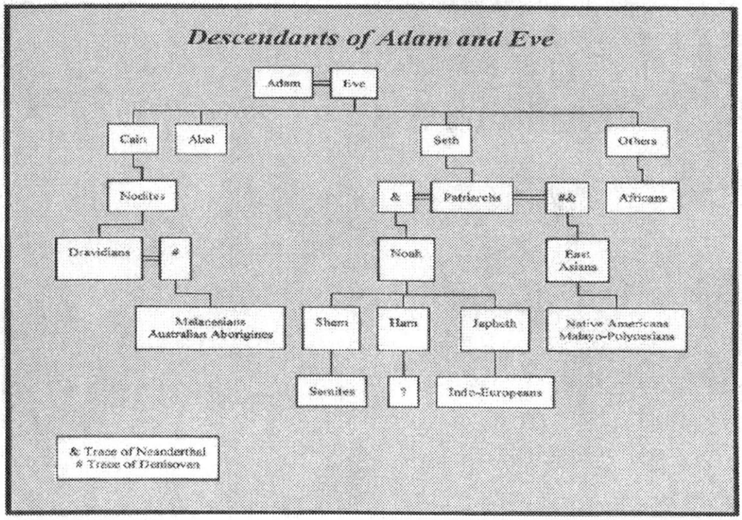

NOD

It is a capital mistake to theorize before you have all the evidence, It biases the judgment.
—Sir Arthur Conan Doyle[42]

In today's culture the "Land of Nod" is just a humorous expression for drowsiness. But such a land is mentioned in the Bible, albeit cryptically. Theologians have dreamed up metaphysical ideas to tell us that no such physical place actually existed; that it is just a punitive spiritual condition. And preachers use those ideas as threats to sinners[42].

We shouldn't laugh at the Bible. And we shouldn't look for ego-serving fantasies to explain away its mysteries. We should very carefully read what it actually says, and search for outside clues to verify it, and possibly fill in more details.

[42] From *A Study in Scarlet.*

The Land of Nod features prominently in the Book of Enoch, and its inhabitants are called Nodites. We find two men named Enoch in the Book of Genesis. Enoch[1] was the son of Cain and the grandson of Adam.[43] Enoch[2] was seventh in the line of patriarchs descended from Adam through Seth.[44] He was the only one of the patriarchs of whom it was said, "he walked with God".

The meaning of this phrase is not clear. It may have indicated that he was the first to believe in only one God, though his people would continue to be polytheistic for millennia to come. Or it may mean that he was chosen to lead his branch of the people out of Africa into Asia, Archaeological

[43] Genesis 3: 17-24.

[44] Genesis 5:18-24.

data suggests that event took place about two thirds of the way along the time line from Adam to Noah.

Enoch[2] was has been said to have been the author of the Book of Enoch,[45] but that is very doubtful. It speaks of times and places with which he could hardly have been familiar. Only fragments of the original text have been found. They are written in a mixture of Hebrew and Aramaic, and have been dated to between 300 and 200 BC. The Septuagint had already been translated, and it did not include Enoch. No portion of the text is known to exist in either Greek or Latin. Many Jews and early Christians were familiar with Enoch, but it was rejected, and ordered to be destroyed by the Council of Nicaea.

i. The only extant ancient complete texts of the Book of Enoch are written in Ge'ez, an extinct language spoken in the Horn of Africa at the time of Christ. It is part of the Bible used, even today, by the Ethiopian Orthodox Church and the Eritrean Orthodox Church. Fragments of its text, in Hebrew and Aramaic, were found among the Dead Sea Scrolls. A slightly abridged English version, said to have been translated from an unknown ancient language by Joseph Smith, is accepted by the Church of Jesus Christ of Latter Day Saints (Mormons) as divinely inspired scripture.

The Book of Enoch tells the story of Enoch[1] and his descendants. It agrees with Genesis that Cain built a city named Enoch in the land of Nod, which was well to the east of Eden. Four more generations of Cain's descendants are listed. Then the Book of Enoch goes on to state that the family grew to be a great nation before a natural catastrophe made their land uninhabitable. They then migrated to the north and east, and found a new homeland which they named Dalmatia.[46]

[45] Scholars have identified three ancient texts, all called Books of Enoch. 2 Enoch and 3 Enoch are both very short, and include nothing pertinent to our discussion. Book of Enoch here refers to what many scholars call 1 Enoch.

[46] This is entirely different from, and has nothing to do with, the modern province of Dalmatia, which is the coastal region of Croatia.

That homeland was what is now the bottom of the Persian Gulf. All of human history up to that time had taken place during a glacial period, and sea level had been well below what it is now, often by several hundred feet. The Gulf was a lush valley through which flowed the combined waters of the Tigris and Euphrates, all the way to its then-mouth in the Gulf of Oman, with a couple of small freshwater lakes in deeper sections of the valley. It was one of the choicest areas of the earth for human habitation.

But just beyond the river's end the ocean was slowly rising as it received the water from the great melting glaciers. About 6000 BC it overtopped the sandbar at the river's mouth. The river reversed its flow, bringing salt water into the lakes and fouling the water supply for the crops and the people. The lakes continued to rise slowly, drowning the farmland and flooding many people out of their homes. By 4500 BC the ocean was near its present level, and Dalmatia was submerged.

The people forced out of their land fled to higher ground, eventually becoming packed into a small peninsula, which later became the island now called Bahrain. Population density forced them to adopt a quasi-urban lifestyle, and they named their city Dilmun.[47] The small amount of cropland remaining, plus the resources of the sea, was insufficient to support the population. So they created a colony around the new mouths of the Tigris and Euphrates Rivers.

The final portion of the Book of Enoch tells of preparation to build a huge monument to the former glory of Dilmun and Dalmatia. After much discussion it was finally decided to put that monument on the mainland colony rather than on the island. To follow the story from here on we must return to the Book of Genesis. But some archaeological data is needed to establish the connection between the two ancient texts.

The Epic of Gilgamesh, which dates to 2100 BC, and is considered the world's oldest written literature, tells of the Sumerian hero-king's travels. On a visit to Dilmun, he heard tales of the former idyllic life in Dalmatia.

The design of some stamped seals found in the lowest layer at Tell Eridu seems to have originated in India. This suggests the possibility that the Nodites were related to the Dravidians.

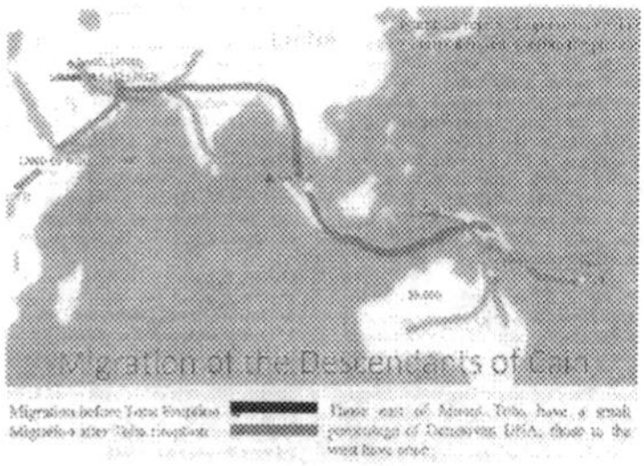

EXTINCTION

Extinction is the rule. Survival is the exception.[48]
—Carl Sagan

The span of time from Adam to Noah was the Age of the Patriarchs. Archaeology tells us that, for almost half that time all humans still lived in tropical Africa and subsisted by hunting and gathering. Toward the end of the Age some of them were moving gradually northward into areas where the art of agriculture was being developed. The Bible gives no dates or places, but mentions certain individuals who lived during this time.[47]

The Bible lists fantastically long lives for these patriarchs. Human fossils from that age and location are from individuals who rarely survived their fourth decade. There are several explanations for this discrepancy. The art of writing was still far in the future. These tales were handed down by oral tradition for dozens of millennia before they could be written down. And in their original homeland there are neither temperature variations nor length-of-daylight variations to mark the seasons. No type of calendar had been invented, and there was no system of numbers capable of counting higher than the number of human digits.

§

By 73,000 BC humans had occupied all of Africa, the south coast of Asia, and part of the East Indies. Their population had grown to reach several million. Their predatory and wasteful lifestyle was taking its toll on the environment of the areas they had settled. Several of their prey animals had already been hunted

[47] *The Varieties of Scientific Experience: A Personal View of the Search for God*

to extinction. Something was bound to happen.

In 72000 ±3000 BC Mount Toba on the island of Sumatra exploded. It was the greatest volcanic eruption of the last two million years. It ejected 100 times as much material as did Mount Tambora n 1825, the greatest eruption in recorded history. For six years the atmosphere was filled with ash, producing continuous winter throughout the world. A mini-ice age lasted for 1000 years.

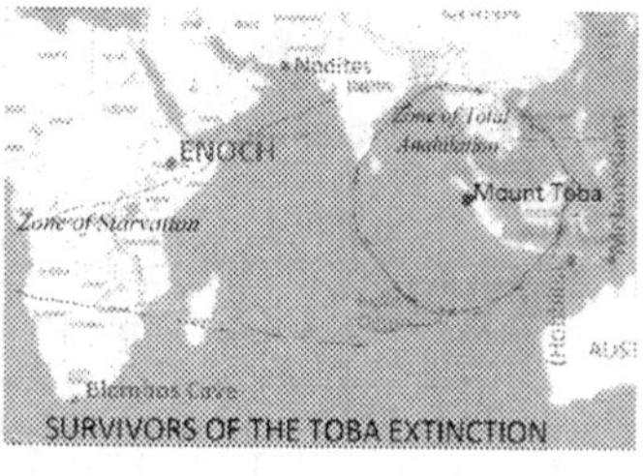

SURVIVORS OF THE TOBA EXTINCTION

The human population, and most other living things within several hundred miles of Toba, died instantly. During the next few years nearly all the remaining humans perished of starvation, disease, or exposure. A large percentage of plants and animals also died, but the toll on them was not as great as it was on humans. Even the Neanderthals had a little better survival rate. This is not considered one of the Great Extinctions. It affected primarily humanity.

Genetics offers several ways to calculate the number of surviving individuals. One of those methods suggests that only 40 women of child-bearing age survived. At the other extreme is a calculation of 15,000 total individuals. The most likely number seems to be about 4000 survivors. All humans now living are descended from them.[48]

The survivors would have been the strongest members of those few groups which had access to unusually well-protected refuges near to a food supply which had not been destroyed. There must have been many such groups at first. Most of them soon became extinct. A few survived. Only one site has been identified definitely as the home of survivors of the eruption of Mount Toba.

[48] Stanley H Ambrose, *Late Pleistocene Human Population Bottleneck, Volcanic Winter, and Differentiation of Modern Humans*, Journal of Human Evolution, 1998,34, 623.

Blombos Cave lies on the shore of South Africa, about 100 feet above present sea level. It contains detritus from several periods of human occupancy. The most recent, about 71,000 BC, was smaller (only 80 to 100 individuals) but more sophisticated than its predecessors. Their diet consisted almost entirely of shellfish – the earlier people had eaten a wide variety of plants and animals, but all those had disappeared. It was not necessary, nor completely safe, to leave the cave except for a brief period at low tide to harvest the shellfish that were abundant in the intertidal zone. This cave contains the earliest known art. Sea shells were used not only as utensils, but also as decorations.[49] There were also geometrical figures painted on the cave walls.

Though no other sites have been found, circumstances indicate that there had to be at least three more groups of survivors, and there may have been many more. The presence of dark-skinned people today in and east of New Guinea, and also in southern India shows that there must have been small groups of survivors just east and just west of the zone of total destruction by Mount Toba,

The largest group of survivors was in Ethiopia. Archaeologists have found no trace of their homes at that time, but in succeeding years there is evidence of migration from Ethiopia to the Near East along the Red Sea Basin, with possibly another group going by way of the Nile Valley. It is these people and their descendants whose story we can find in the Bible.

A casual reader of the Bible might say that the writers did not know about, or ignored, this terrible human catastrophe. But let's take a closer look.

By use of several different scientific procedures we have reliable dates for Adam, for Noah, and for the Mount Toba eruption. We find that the eruption occurred about two-thirds of the way along the time line from Adam to Noah. The

[49] C S Henshilwood, *Holocene History of the Southern Cape, South Africa: Excavations at Blombos Cave...*, 2008, Archaeopress.

Bible gives only a list of names and ages during that period. Few other details are given, but at about the two-thirds point we find

And Enoch walked with God: and was not: for God took him.[50]

None of the other patriarchs is singled out for such distinction. All the others simply "died". What did Enoch do that was different?

Theologians have wrestled with that question, and come up with several interesting, but unverified, answers. The commonest is that Enoch was taken directly to Heaven without ever dying. One version says that he took a large number of followers with him. Another story says that he led his people to a place similar to the Garden of Eden, from which their ancestors had been expelled. The Epistle of Jude,[51] in the New Testament, has some more information:

...clouds they are without water, carried about by winds; trees whose fruit withereth, without fruit, twice dead, plucked up by the roots; Raging waves of the sea, foaming out their own shame, wandering stars, whom is reserved the blackness of darkness forever. And Enoch, the seventh from Adam, prophesied of these, saying, Behold, the Lord cometh with ten thousands of his saints.[52]

That's a pretty good description of a volcanic winter. Mormon theology states that Enoch founded the righteous City of Zion in the midst of an otherwise wicked world. There is only one other example of "walking with God" in Genesis: Noah, who led a small group of survivors away from an environmental disaster, which had destroyed all their neighbors. Could Enoch have done the same?

[50] Genesis 5:24.

[51] Jude, the step-brother of Jesus, was quoting from the Book of Enoch (See NOD above). His letter was accepted as part of the Bible, though his source was not.

[52] Jude 12-1

One more passage in Genesis gives a hint to what Enoch might have done. After the story of Enoch but before Noah's flood Genesis 6:4 says "***And there were giants on the earth in those days***". Anthropology tells us that humans first encountered Neanderthals as they moved from Ethiopia into the Holy Land, soon after the Mount Toba near-extinction.[53]

Enoch was their leader.

§

The tale of Noah is another story of mass extinction, on a more limited scale. The same thing happened on an even smaller scale at Sodom and Gomorrah. Is extinction a normal part of earth's history? What does science have to say?

Biologists identify five great historical mass extinctions. The sixth is in progress now.

1. 445 million years ago a radiation imbalance in the atmosphere caused the earth to become a giant snowball, and 71% of all species perished.

2. 371 million years ago an unknown factor again destroyed 71% of life.

3. 252 million years ago a combination of causes destroyed 83% of all living things. Animals with shells were particularly hard hit.

4. 200 million years ago volcanism destroyed 76% of life, notably the large amphibians.

5. 66 million years ago an asteroid impact destroyed 76% of the earth's species, including the dinosaurs.

6. Species are disappearing faster right now than they did during any of the "great extinctions".[54] The obvious reason is man-made pollution. Who knows where this will end?

All the great extinctions took place before the first man was

[53] Theodora Sutcliffe, *When Neanderthals Replaced Us,* Discover, June 2016, 64-66.

[54] Richard Leakey, *The Sixth Extinction: Patterns of Life and the Future of Humankind.*

born. The Bible mentions a couple of regional human extinctions, and makes a very vague reference to an almost complete worldwide extinction.

Useful estimates of the earth's human population are available for the last two millennia. It grew at a rather steady rate of 0.1% per year, until the beginning of the Industrial Revolution, and then accelerated. With the onset of modern medicine the growth rate exploded.

Using that first rate of increase, it is calculated that the progeny of one couple can increase to 100 million persons (the world population at the time of Christ) in about 15,000 years. Two conclusions follow from this: (1). Noah's flood caused only a regional extinction, and (2). We have another proof of a cataclysmic event like the explosion of Mount Toba.

Both science and the Bible tell us that near extinction of humans, on varying scales, has occurred several times. Those responsible for managing the global warming crisis must be very aware of this fact.

Even as this is being written, a controversy continues over the meaning of a recent discovery. Hominid fossils were discovered in 2003 in Liang Bua Cave on the island of Flores in Indonesia. They appeared to be from a species never seen before, and were named *homo floresiensis.* The creature was distinguished primarily by it short stature, about three feet six inches, and by its small braincase. Popular media dubbed it the "hobbit". By dating the geologic layers in which the fossils were found, it was determined that the hominids had existed from about 75,000 years ago to about 13,000 years ago. They would have co-existed with *homo sapiens,* who are known to have been in that general area during part of that period. Unfortunately it has not been possible to extract DNA from those fossils, so their position on the family tree of Man remains conjectural.

Two theories are contending for acceptance: (1) They are a separate species, not in the same line of descent as modern humans. (2) They are a sub-group of *homo sapiens*, who suffered a genetic deformity. To decide, we must consider: (1) Was there another species present from whom they could have been descended? (2) What was the probability of a mutation which could have deformed, but not killed them?

Artifacts were found deeper in the same cave, at about the 94,000 year level, but there was no indication of who had made them. A stone axe of a type made by *homo erectus* was found on Flores, but it couldn't be dated. Java Man, one of the best preserved fossils of *homo erectus*, lived between 1.8 and 1.4 million years ago. The species became extinct between 500,000 and 200,000 years ago. Later species descended from them lived in Africa and Eurasia, but are not known in Indonesia. *Homo sapiens*, migrating from Africa, reached the Flores area about 100,000 years ago.

Correspondence of the Mount Toba eruption and the first appearance of *homo floresiensis* is too close for coincidence. Flores is actually within the range of instant total annihilation from that blast. The following scenario is hypothesized.

A small group of humans was, by dint if good luck, inside the cave when the eruption occurred, and had enough food to sustain them until they could emerge. They found their island almost lifeless and covered by poisonous radioactive dust. Most of those who survived the blast soon starved. The few that were left passed severely damaged genes to their children. Their deformed progeny managed to carry on for 60,000 years until they perished for lack of genetic diversity. People of another race, who eventually repopulated the island, called them "ebu gogo", and considered them evil spirits.

THE GENUS *Homo* BEFORE AND AFTER THE TOBA SUPERERUPTION				
AREA	ETHNICITY	ESTIMATED POPULATION BEFORE	ESTIMATED POPULATION AFTER	CAUSE OF DEATHS
Eastern East Indies	Nodites Denisovans	1,000,000	800	Starvation
SE Asia Western East Indies	Nodites	10,000,000	None	Blast Heat
India	Nodites	8,000,000	None	Radioactive fallout Starvation
Persian Gulf Area	Nodites	2,000,000	500	Starvation
East Central Africa	Humans	20,000,000	2,000	Radioactive fallout Starvation
Rest of Africa	Humans	8,000,000	700	Starvation
Europe	Neanderthals	200,000	7,000	Starvation

RACES

Infinite diversity in infinite combinations,
Symbolizing the elements that create truth and beauty.
—Commander Spock[55]

Homo-sapiens-sapiens is the only species of hominid on earth today. There are three major races distinguished primarily by skin color. There are other bodily characteristics associated with each race, and there is considerable variation, even in skin color, among individuals within each race.[55]

Race has been a hot-button issue throughout recorded history. In the 1960s an elderly black woman was asked why her white neighbors were so violently resisting school integration. Her answer: "Everybody's got to be proud of something. If you ain't got nothing else to be proud of, you can be proud of your white skin."

There is no scientific evidence or tenable interpretation of Holy Scripture that can support ideas of racial superiority. But such feelings have biased both scientific and religious attitudes toward racial differences

§

Johann Friedrich Blumenbach, in 1805, published the first pseudo-scientific treatise on race. He believed the first humans were white, and lived in the Caucasus area. He considered the Georgians the most beautiful people on earth. In his theory, the other races developed when groups wandered off and degenerated due to bad health habits or poor nutrition. His classification was based on physical appearance and culture. He classified the

[55] From the *Star Trek* television series, created by Eugene Roddenberry.

races, in order of perfection (in his opinion), by both color and supposed place of origin.

1. White Caucasian
2. Yellow Mongolian
3. Brown Malayan
4. Black Ethiopian
5. Red American

Blumenbach was wrong on the number of races, and on the original home of mankind. But it is uncanny how he found the correct sources for the three of his races that do exist. His racial classification was taught in many schools well into the Twentieth Century, and some of his race designations are still used informally in law enforcement.

Another commonly used racial classification. scheme is allegedly based on the Bible. It assumes that Noah and all his ancestors were white, that all people except Noah's family died in the Flood, and that each of the three races now existing consists of the descendants of one of Noah's sons. Semites, who are white, are descended from Shem, so all white people must be descended from Shem. Black people must be black because they carry the curse of Ham.[56] That leaves Japheth who, by default, must be ancestor of the yellow race. There are variations in this system. Many groups of people who were unpopular at the time have been included among the descendants of Ham,

§

The genetic material to produce the three races was already present on earth when Adam and Eve were in the Garden of Eden. When God created the first man there were still several other species of hominids on the Earth. Neanderthals were thriving in southern Europe, the Near East, and central Asia. Denisovans, of whom we still know very little, must have occupied much of East Asia. Smaller groups of more primitive species were still holding on in eastern Asia, western and southern Africa, and perhaps other places.

All these older species became extinct, probably without

[56] The Book of Mormon states flatly that a dark skin is a curse from God.

descendants, except the Neanderthals and Denisovans. They were once believed to have suffered the same fate. But their DNA has now been extracted from fossils, and sequenced. Comparing it to the DNA of living humans, it is found that all Europeans and all East Asians have a small amount (1% to 4%) of Neanderthal blood; East Asians, Melanesians, and Australian Aborigines have similarly small traces of Denisovan blood; but black Africans, African-Americans, and Dravidians have neither.[57]

The consequences of this finding are:

1. There was some limited interbreeding between humans and Neanderthals. And between humans and Denisovans,

2. Humans, Neanderthals, and Denisovans are not separate species, but sub-groups of the same species.

3. Most of the black race is descended 100% from the earliest human ancestors. The other races are descended about 98% from those same ancestors, but also have a few Neanderthal and/or Denisovan among their ancestors.

4. Adam and Eve were black, as were all their descendants down to a certain time, at least until they had started to migrate out of Africa.

§

In 2010 fossils of a previously unknown species, which was then named *homo denisova*, were found in a cave in Siberia near the Chinese border.[58] It was possible to extract DNA, but analysis and comparison to DNA of living groups is still incomplete.

[57] An increasing number of anthropologists now designate them Homo-sapiens-neanderthalensis, Homo-sapiens denisova, and Homo-sapiens-sapiens.

[58] Maggie Fox, *Possible new human ancestor found in Siberia*, Reuters, 24 March 2010.

The fossils of Peking Man were the most recent example of *homo erectus*. He lived at about the same time as Adam and Eve. It is possible, though improbable, that he may have interbred with humans. The fossils disappeared during the Japanese occupation of China prior to World War II, and before DNA was discovered.

§

Melanin is the pigment that darkens human skin. The more a person has the darker his skin is. The function of melanin is to control the penetration of sunlight into the skin. If there is too little the body will have inadequate vitamin D. If there is too much skin cancer may result. A suntan is the body's automatic, but temporary, adjustment to an increase in sunlight. It is not inheritable. In any large group of people, the person whose melanin is best suited to the environment will live longer and have more children than those who have either too much or too little. When the group moves to a different environment, its average skin color, over a long period of time, changes appropriately.

§

Migration of humans out of Africa into Arabia, started about 125,000 years ago.[59] At first they tried to keep within the warm climatic zone to which they were accustomed. They spread along the south coast of Asia, and had reached well into the East Indies by the time of the Mount Toba eruption. Most of them died instantly at that time. But there were at least three pockets of survivors.

The easternmost group, not far from the Hobbits (*homo floresiensis*), who also survived, later spread across New Guinea into the Melanesian Islands and southward into Australia by 55,000 years ago.

Another group of survivors was somewhere between the Persian Gulf and the mouth of the Indus River. Once the environment had recovered they

[59] Some, or all, of these people may have been descended from Cain. See NOD, above.

spread in both directions. One group created Dalmatia, which is now the bottom of the Persian Gulf. They were last heard of at the Tower of Babel. Soon after that they disappeared, probably absorbed into surrounding peoples. The other group went down the west coast of India, and eventually spread over the entire Subcontinent. Later, invading Aryans pushed them into the southern part of India.

The people of Blombos Cave, and perhaps a few other groups much like them, spread to cover most of Africa. All sub-Saharan Africans and African-Americans are descended from them.

Perhaps the largest group of survivors was in Ethiopia. But there couldn't have been many more than a few thousand of them. Like all other humans at that time, they were black. But before they got entirely out of Africa their skins were much lighter toned. The primary cause of this change was a mutated gene, but it was greatly accelerated by very unusual environmental conditions. And later on it got a little additional boost from hybridization with the lighter complected Neanderthals.

Most mutations are caused by radioactive damage to a gene. They occur entirely at random, though they are most numerous in the presence of a large number of radioactive particles, such as those found in the effluent from a very active volcano. The majority have little effect on the individual's health or reproductive potential. But if one produces a change that makes a better adjustment to the environment, it will persist and spread through the population.

One person in Enoch's group suffered a mutation that destroyed much of his ability to produce melanin. Before the eruption, that would have harmed his health. But living through several years of darkness, followed by many years of diminished sunshine, made it a very useful change.

The "founder effect" is well known to geneticists. A useful mutation which appears in a small population will spread much more rapidly than one which appears in a larger population.

This is due to the more limited supply of potential mates. Within eight or ten generations the entire group would have been white.

White humans, now with a little Neanderthal blood, reached Europe from the Caucasus region 35,000 years ago, and had spread across the continent to Iberia by 30,000 years ago. They swept the Neanderthals before them, eventually driving them to extinction. Warfare no doubt killed many Neanderthals, but the principal reason for their demise was that the humans simply took away their food supply.

Our DNA shows that there was some interbreeding between humans and Neanderthals, and that hybrid children were sometimes adopted by human families. There is evidence that a few of those hybrid children were adopted into Neanderthal families. Lascaux Cave, in southwestern France, was found in 1940. It contained a Neanderthal skeleton so crippled by arthritis that its owner must have lived for several years without having been able to walk or eat unless someone else was helping him. These people had a sense of moral responsibility. A nearby burial contained artifacts obviously intended for use in the next world. These people believed in an afterlife. They had souls, which could only have been inherited from human ancestors. The last full-blooded Neanderthal died in Gibraltar about 28,000 years ago.

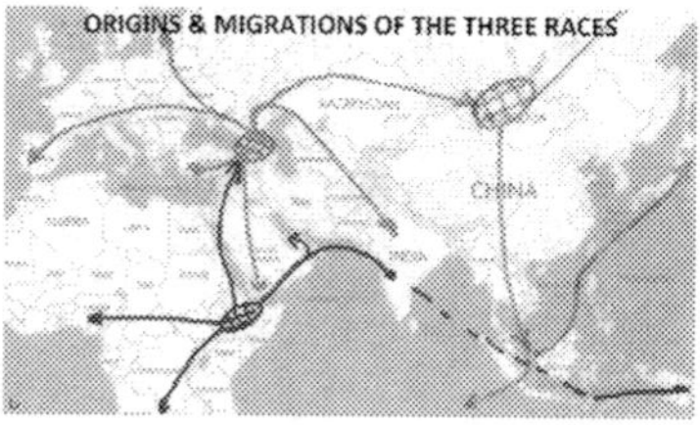

§

The yellow race appeared in Mongolia about 45,000 BC. It is descended primarily from the white immigrants to that area, with some additional genetic input from the Denisovans and possibly others. Its primary migration has been to the south into or across China. (The Great Wall was built to minimize damage done to Chinese civilization by the continuation of such migration.)

The first great population of East Asians was established in Sundaland. Sundaland no longer exists. It was the bottom of the Sunda Sea and the adjacent islands and peninsulas.

Sundaland was a lush tropical area capable of supporting a large human population. It has done so twice. Between about 100,000 and 72,000 BC it held about half the humans on earth, all black. They were wiped out by the Toba eruption. By about 40,000 BC the land had recovered its fertility, and was ready for the massive immigration of East Asians coming down from the north. It again became densely populated until about 10,000 BC, when rising sea levels, associated with the end of the last Pleistocene glaciation, began to submerge most of it.

For tens of thousands of years the two most numerous peoples in the world were the Chinese and the Sundanese. They were from a common origin, but a mutation among the Chinese gave them differently shaped teeth. Thus, from linguistic studies and fossilized teeth we can follow the migrations from Sundaland.

As much of Sundaland turned into islands, the people developed the art of navigation. Today their descendants inhabit islands from Madagascar to New Zealand to Hawaii. All the people of Southeast Asia and many of those of southern China are also descended from the Sundanese, as are the Taiwanese, the Ainu of northern Japan, and the Athabaskan, Tlingit, and Navajo Indians of North America.

§

All living humans are related, and all are descended from Adam and Eve. The African race is descended from the original humans, with no genetic additions from other sources. The European race was an offshoot of the African race about 71,000 years ago. It developed its distinguishing characteristics during a long migration from Ethiopia to the Caucasus. Some 20,000 years later the East Asian race developed from a group of white people who had migrated into Mongolia.

GENETIC HERITAGE OF THE RACES			
GROUP	HUMAN	NEAND.	DENIS.
Black 1	Y	N	N
Black 2	Y	N	Y
White	Y	Y	N
Yellow	Y	Y	Y

Ironically, the largest group of the Black Race is the only group in which the science of genetics has <u>not</u> found proof of ancient miscegenation.

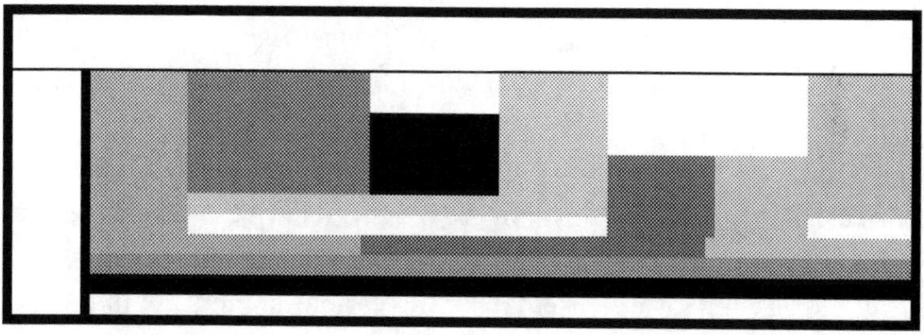

SPEECH

不知道詞彙的力量，它是不可能知道更多

……………………………—Confucius

(Without knowing the force of words, it is impossible to know more.)

The Bible is a compilation of stories. They are all now in written form. But many of those stories tell of events that happened long before the art of writing was developed. Those stories were passed along by oral legends until it became possible to write them down. A few of the events may have occurred before people learned to talk. When did that happen? And how did they preserve their earlier history? Finally, important events took place before there were any people to observe them. Only God could have preserved a record of those events.

When, where, and by whom some books were accepted as parts of the Bible, and others were rejected, is discussed below in the chapter labeled "BIBLE". This chapter, and the chapter on "WRITING" examine the sources of the information that the various authors put into those books.

There are three ways an author could have gotten some or all of the information he put into his book:

1. He might have been an eyewitness to the event,
2. He might have been divinely inspired, or
3. He might have used an oral legend passed down from earlier generations.

Of course that legend could have originated with either an eyewitness or a divinely inspired person.

§

Not all the oral legends on which Biblical Scripture was based could have originated as eyewitness accounts. The earliest events mentioned took place before there were any humans to observe them. These had to have been divinely revealed. And we cannot be sure that the earliest humans had language capable of telling the stories that we read in the Bible. What can science say about that?

There are several theories of the origin of speech, none of them universally accepted. The truth is probably a combination of many of them. Some words originated one way, others another way, in response to the needs of the moment. Languages grew gradually as their speakers required more words to handle the greater needs of their increasingly complex lives.

The use of language requires two biological adaptations: (1) the intelligence to understand it, and (2) the vocal apparatus to produce it. Many animals have one or the other of these, to a small degree, which enables them to emit simple vocal messages. But only humans have enough of both to produce full-fledged language. Animal vocalizations tell little more than their emotional state, and are usually accompanied by gestures.

§

Whales and dolphins exchange vocal information with other members of their species. Sound carries farther in water than in air. Whales even have different "languages" in different parts of the world. A whale transplanted from one ocean to another will, at first, be confused, but will soon learn the meanings if the new and unfamiliar sounds he is hearing.

Some birds, notably parrots, can be taught to mimic human words, but they attach no meanings to the sounds.

Among non-human primates, the vervet monkey comes the closest to actually speaking. He has a vocabulary of about twenty words, mostly referring to food sources or to predators. When a human reproduces a vervet word, nearby monkeys react appropriately.

Many apes have the ability to understand language, but they cannot produce it. A well-trained ape will obey the commands, even complex commands, of his human trainer. Gorillas, bonobos, orangutans, and chimpanzees can be taught to communicate with their human trainers and with each other in a sign language similar to that used by the human deaf community. Gorillas and chimpanzees can send and understand computer messages, using simplified software. Adult chimpanzees have been observed teaching their young to use the sign language that they learned from their human trainers.

§

Scientific ideas on the origin of human speech are sketchy and not very informative. Observations are few and indirect. Fossils can be studied to see if anatomical features of the speech organs are present. It is believed that the creation of symbolic art requires a brain capable of processing language. Studies of Neanderthal remains show that at least some of them had vocal organs barely meeting the criteria for speaking. Symbolic art was found in their cave at Lascaux, France. Of course the Neanderthals had been in contact with, and had probably interbred with, humans for thousands of years by the time that art was produced. It is unlikely that most Neanderthals had sophisticated language.

The symbolic cave art at Blombos Cave in South Africa is twice as old as that of Lascaux. It was made by *homo sapiens.* It is possible that Neanderthals and humans learned to talk about the same time, not long after the humans appeared, and not long before the Neanderthals disappeared.

Estimates of the date that people began to talk vary wildly and have large margins if error. A very loose average of those dates would be somewhere around the time of Adam and Eve.

§

There was little need for talk in the Garden of Eden. There were no dangers to avoid, and everything they needed was within arm's reach. But when they were ejected from the Garden the situation changed drastically.

They were now meat eaters, and their food had to be caught. The trees were gone, they were on the savannah, surrounded by tall grass and shrubbery. Their prey animals hid among the foliage. It took great effort and cooperation to find them and to run them down. The hunters could not communicate by gestures because they were often out of sight of each other. And that same foliage also provided cover for large predator animals, many of which savored human flesh. It was of vital importance to notify their companions of the presence and movement of animals: it was a matter of life and death that they be informed what kind of animal was present.

Life was dangerous. It could continue only by survival of the fittest. Those who could make, and understand, a distinctive sound which would unambiguously identify each type of animal survived. Those who couldn't do so died.

The Bible tells us of the first words, expressing something more than mere emotion, uttered by a human being:

And out of the ground the Lord God formed every beast of the ground, and every fowl of the air; and brought them unto Adam to see what he would call them, and whatsoever Adam called every living creature, that was the name thereof.
--Genesis 2:19

§

Several organs of the human anatomy must work together to reproduce speech. The lungs expel the air which will carry the sound waves. The vocal cords, deep in the throat, tighten and loosen alternately to produce the compressional waves that create the sensation of sound. These waves are given pitch and resonance as they flow through the upper nasal cavity and the oral cavity, which are shaped by the surrounding muscles to produce the vowel sounds. Consonants are interruptions or brief restrictions in the flow of air, brought about by holding the lips, the teeth, the tongue, the hard palate, and/or the soft palate in appropriate configurations.

Linguistic scientists have identified 145 distinct sounds (phonemes) that the human vocal organs can make. Each language has its own group of sounds selected from among those available phonemes. Nearly all English speakers use the same group of 44 phonemes.[60] When we speak for a long time in other languages, native speakers of those languages can quickly identify us by the way we mispronounce their phonemes that are not in our language. And we notice immediately the way that they mispronounce the two phonemes that we spell "th", which are not used in most other languages.

Pronunciation of certain phonemes puts a strain on tender vocal organs. We don't notice it, because using those sounds repeatedly for many years has toughened those organs. With enough study and practice, we can learn to speak a foreign language like a native. But we can't do it continuously for a long time without pain. A long series of French nasals will give us a headache, German gutterals will cause a sore throat, and the Spanish /rr/ might lead to a bleeding tongue. Native speakers have no trouble with those sounds because they were making them as small children while their vocal organs were still growing. It is well known that a child can learn a second language much more easily than an adult.

[60] The /r/ phoneme in English is weakening. It has already disappeared in some southeastern states. Among worldwide English speakers, only the Scots still pronounce it properly.

LEGENDS

I believe that legends and myths are largely made of truth.
—J. R. R. Tolkien

The first five books of the Bible are called the Pentateuch, or the Books of Moses. It was once believed that they were actually written by Moses. Most scholars now believe that they appeared, in some form, about the time of Moses, but only a minority believes that he actually wrote them himself.

§

Some Hebrews in Moses' time were familiar with Egyptian hieroglyphics. In fact, both Joseph and Moses had been mentioned in them, under other names. But they did no writing in their own language until they had borrowed an alphabet from the Phoenicians, several hundred years after Moses' death.

The first manuscripts in the Hebrew language appeared about 1100 BC. They are mostly short segments of ancient legends, written in an almost unintelligible script. Most of them, with improved formatting, eventually made their way into the Torah.

Early Christian writings were largely eyewitness accounts, and they were all written in Greek. Writers of the Synoptic Gospels, Matthew, Mark, and Luke, were with Jesus, and their stories are contemporary. The Gospel of John was compiled from a number of tales, which had been preserved, in either oral or written from, for two or three generations before they were assembled. Most of the epistles make some reference to current events, and many mention Old

Testament events. The source of the ancient information is often not known, but it is still valuable, and should not be dismissed lightly.

§

The principal questions in authenticating these oral legends are:

1. Through how many generations did they have to be repeated before they could be written? And

2. How reliable are the repetitions?

The scientific study of pre-history is a relatively new discipline. Results so far must be considered tentative and speculative, but the few general ideas that have begun to emerge are worthy of our attention.

Pre-history was long considered the province of literature. Every society has its legendary heroes. They appear in stories ranging from fairy tales to epic sagas. They are told and retold so many times that no one doubts them. Still, no one quite believes them either.

Did King Arthur really live? How about Goliath? Or Romulus and Remus? Was Helen of Troy a real person? If we can't fully believe the tales of Paul Bunyan and John Henry, then what are we to make of them?

These legends tell us something about who we are, how we got here, and how we distinguish right from wrong. Without them we would be much poorer. We realize that they cannot stand the harsh light of an infallible lie detector, but they are not just pure fiction. We are not trying to deceive anyone when we repeat them. There is an element of true history in every legend. Can we find it? Or should we even try to find it?

§

A study by Reid and Nunn[61] found that the legends of Australian aborigines accurately described changes in landforms that had affected the lives of their ancestors 10,000 years earlier.

[61] The /r/ phoneme in English is weakening. It has already disappeared in some southeastern states. Among worldwide English speakers, only the Scots still pronounce it properly.

The legends did not give any indication of the time of the events, and they ascribed the changes to the influence of supernatural beings.

§

Dislocations of World War II rendered many people unable or afraid to keep contemporary records, but provided a large number of survivors whose stories could be checked against each other and against actual records.

Gassend[62] found that events reported generally conformed to the facts, but the numbers were usually inflated, and that most persons "adjust" their narratives to enhance their own or their group's apparent strength, cleverness, or morality.

O'Neill[63] found that narrators interviewed more than once tended to change their stories according to their mood at the time, and according to their understanding of the interviewers' expectations.

If we can't fully believe all the legends repeated in the "Word of God", any mental reservations we might harbor should tend in the direction of these findings.

§

One example has been found of a story that was preserved through many years by two separate societies, one literate and one illiterate. Now they can be compared.

"What happened to Chirikov's men?" was a long-enduring mystery. Aleksei Chirikov was captain of the smaller vessel in Vitus Bering's fleet of 1741. Known to be a poor navigator, he was ordered to keep in sight of the flagship, But they became separated in a storm. Chirikov wandered on aimlessly, until he sighted land. He sent a boat with several sailors ashore to find food, fresh water, and, if possible, directions. They didn't return. So he sent a second boat ashore. They also failed to return.

[62] Reid, Nick & Patrick Nunn, *Ancient Aboriginal StoriesPpreserve Memory of a Rise in Sea Level,* Conversation 21 Jan 2013.

[63] Gassend, Jean-Luc, *Operation Dragoon: Autopsy of a Battle, 2015.*

He managed to find his way back to his home port, where he filed a written report of the event.

Fast-forward two centuries. In 1959 Congress passed the Alaska Statehood Act. It required, among other things, that the new state government do everything possible to preserve the native oral history. A Tlingit elder told a story of two boatloads of white men coming ashore on Yakobi Island, near the now-abandoned village of Apolosova.[64] Perceived as invaders, they were robbed and killed. Their clothing and other possessions were described, as was the ship from which they had come.

Russian archives are silent on the location and on the fate of the men. The Tlingit legend omits the date and the origin of the men. In many other details the two stories are identical. Neither narrative is complete in itself. Together, and only together, they tell the whole story. In this case, at least, the oral legend, which had been maintained for over two-hundred years, was as accurate as the written record.

§

An excellent proof of the accuracy of information transmitted through many centuries of verbal retelling is in the Hindu Scriptures. (See CURSE, below.) It is remarkable that the Mahabharata and the Matsya Purana still told the same story that we find in Genesis, after five thousand years of being handed down orally through the generations of two widely separated societies. Many Christian scholars refuse to read the sacred books of other religions, for fear of heresy. They are missing a marvelously uplifting verification of the validity and accuracy of their own Scriptures!

§

These studies show that events told in legends are likely to be true. Dates, when given, are unreliable. Numbers may well be exaggerated. Names may be changed. The ethnic group and the god(s) of the teller may be aggrandized.

[64] O'Neill, Gilda, *Lost Voices, Memoeries of a vanished way of Life,* Arrow 2006.

FLOOD

Until he extends his circle of compassion to all living things,. man will not find peace.
—Albert Schweitzer

The span of time from Adam to Noah was the Age of the Patriarchs. Archaeology tells us that, for over half that time, all humans still lived in tropical Africa and subsisted by hunting and gathering. Toward the end of the age they were moving gradually northward into areas where they developed the art of agriculture. The Bible gives no dates or places, but mentions certain individuals whose names can be associated with unusual events.[65]

The Bible lists fantastically long lives for these patriarchs. Human fossils from that age and location are from individuals who rarely survived their fourth decade. There are two explanations for this discrepancy. The art of writing was still far in the future. These tales were handed down by oral tradition for dozens of millennia before they could be written down. And in their original homeland there are neither temperature variations nor length-of-daylight variations to mark the seasons.

§

In 2000 Robert Ballard[66] found the remains of an ancient habitation on the bottom of the Black Sea, 310 feet below the surface near the confluence of two drowned river courses, about ten miles north of Synope, Turkey. This had been a populous community,

[65] Dihle, John, *The Mysteries of Yakobi Island,* The Juneau Empire, 23 April 2015

[66] The undersea explorer who found the wreck of the Titanic.

which subsisted mostly by animal husbandry, but also had some primitive agriculture. Circumstances described below suggest that Noah and his family may well have been members of that community. From a boat floating directly above the site the only land visible is the summit of Mount Ararat. Several miles further out Ballard found an ancient shoreline, now 550 feet below sea level. The sea bottom in this area was once very densely-populated.

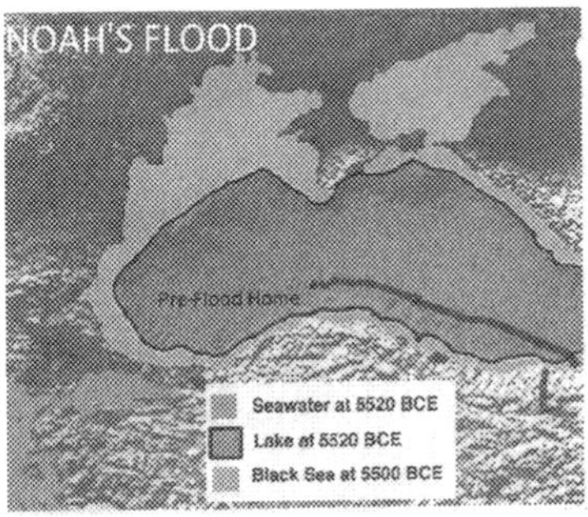

Geologists William Ryan and Walter Pitman, in 1997, published the results of their work on post-glacial sea level changes.[67] At the maximum of the Pleistocene Ice Age, about 20,000 years ago, so much water had been taken from the oceans and locked up in the continental ice sheets that sea level, including the Mediterranean, was 400 feet lower than it is now. The rocky sill between the Black Sea and the Mediterranean was above water, and the two seas became separated. Much of the water in the Black Sea evaporated and could not be replenished. It had become an enclosed salty lake, like the Caspian Sea and the Dead Sea. The surface dropped far below sea level, and more than half the bottom became dry land. Rivers flowed across that newly exposed land, and it and, supported a large human population.

About 5600 BC the rising Mediterranean spilled over the sill, eroding a channel \through the Bosporus, and suddenly filling the basin of the Black Sea. Hydraulic engineers calculated that the first wave would have spread in a tsunami-like fashion, after which the water would have continued to rise gradually for about forty days to reach sea level.

Anyone who received no advance warning of this catastrophe would

[67] New York Herald, May 4, 1855

have had little chance of survival. It was a mass extinction of a human culture. The entire world, as they knew it, was flooded.

§

Noah had his family and many animals on the Ark. The most valuable component of wealth in that age was livestock, and Noah wanted to save as many of his animals as possible. But it is unlikely that he had elephants or giraffes. And certainly there were no kangaroos or unicorns. The only way he could navigate the Ark was by keeping land in sight, and he prudently headed straight for the only land he could see – Mount Ararat.

And the Ark rested … on the mountains of Ararat. — *Genesis 8:4*

Note that the Bible says "mountains", not "Mount". The 16,854 foot peak of Mount Ararat is an excellent navigation marker, but an impossible landing place. The mountains of Ararat consist of two high peaks and a number of smaller hills resting on a broad plateau. Noah could have landed anywhere in that area. They couldn't go back, the entire world they had known was gone.

Headwater tributaries of both the Euphrates and the Tigris Rivers run down the south slopes of Ararat. The earliest written records of the Semitic people are found in the valley shared by those two rivers.

THE MOUNTAINS OF ARARAT

The Bible lists many descendants of each of Noah's three sons: Shem, Ham, and Japheth. Each was the progenitor of several ethnic groups. Ham had been cursed by his father, and his descendants were scattered in many rather small groups. Shem was ancestor of the Semites, and Japheth of the Aryans. After a list of his descendants, little more is said of Ham. The rest of the Old Testament is basically a history of the Semites, though it is noted that several of them had Hamitic wives. Japheth's family is not mentioned again by name in the Bible, but their distinguished history is known from other sources.

CURSE

The negro is damned, and is to serve his master till God chooses to remove the curse of Ham.
—Brigham Young[66]

Deeply entrenched tradition holds that many supposedly inferior nations, and all dark-skinned people are descended from Ham. Nonsense!! The Bible says no such thing. There isn't a shred of scientific evidence to support the idea. Both Biblical and linguistic evidence are weak, ambiguous, and subject to misinterpretation, accidental or intentional. Arab slave traders and their American customers used this idea to justify their nefarious commerce. It was one of several scriptural passages that Hitler used to justify the Holocaust.

The story of Noah, and indeed most of the Old Testament, were written by the escendants of Shem. Japheth's descendants wrote up their version of the story. Compare the two versions.

THE BIBLE	**THE HINDU SCRIPTURES**
Genesis 6:13 *And God said unto Noah, The end of all flesh is come before me; for the earth is filled with* *violence for them; and behold, I will destroy them with the earth.* Genesis 7:16-17 *And they that went in, went male and female of all flesh, as God commanded him, and the Lord shut him in. And the flood was forty days upon the earth.* Genesis 9:20-27 *And Noah began to be an husbandman, and he planted a vineyard; and he drank of the wine and was drunken; and he was uncovered within his tent. And Ham, the father of Caanan, saw the nakedness of his father, and told his two brethren without. And Shem and Japheth took a garment and laid it upon both their shoulders, and went backward and covered the nakedness of their father, and their faces were backward, and they saw not the nakedness of their father. And Noah awoke from his wine, and he knew what his younger son had done to him. And he said, Cursed be Canaan, a servant of servants to his brethren. And he said, Blessed be the Lord God of Shem, and Canaan shall be his servant. God shall enlarge Japheth and he shall dwell in the tents of Shem; and Canaan shall be his servant.*	From the Mahabharata *The progeny of Adamis and Hevas became so wicked that they were no longer able to exist peacefully. Brahma therefore decided to punish his creatures, Vishnu ordered Vaivasvata to build a ship for him and his family. When the ship was ready, and Vaivasvata and his family were inside with the seeds of every plant and a pair of every species of animal, the big rains began and the rivers began to overflow.* From the Matsya Purana *1. To Satyavarman excellent in virtue, that sovereign of the whole earth, were born three sons; the eldest Shem, then Sham, and thirdly Jyapeti. They were all men of good morals, excellent in virtue and virtuous deeds, skilled in the use of weapons to strike with, or to be thrown; brave men, eager for victory in battle. But Satyavarman, being continually delighted with devout meditation, and seeing his sons fit for dominion, laid upon them the burdens of government, Whilst he remained honoring and satisfying the gods and priests, one day by act of destiny, the king having drunk mead became senseless and lay asleep naked. Then was he seen by Sham, and by him were his two brothers called. Having recovered his intellect, and perfectly knowing what had passed, he cursed Sham, saying, "Thou shalt be the servant of servants." And to Jyapeti he gave all on the north of the snowy mountains; but he by the power of religious contemplation, obtained supreme bliss,*

The Semites travelled southward from Ararat. Their story is well recounted in the Bible. Many of the tribes mentioned, besides the Israelites, were Semitic. More recent Semitic peoples are Phoenicians, Carthaginians, Sicels Maltese, Arabs, and Jews.

The Hamites also traveled southward, but became scattered. There is no particular ethnic group that can be proven Hamitic. Nor can any Hamitic languages be definitely identified, though many theories have been published.

Japheth's descendants, whom scientists call Indo-Europeans[68], are best identified by linguistic studies. The broad extent of their territory is illustrated by the words "Erin" (Ireland) and "Iran", both of which are derived from "Aryan". The earliest form of Indo-European identified was spoken on the east shore of the Black Sea about 4300 BC. They had reached Eastern Europe by 3300 BC, India by 2500 BC, and Western Europe by 1500 BC. The Hittites and the Mittani, mentioned in the Old Testament, were Indo-European, as were the Greeks and Romans of the New Testament.

§

We owe it to ourselves to read very, very carefully the verses describing the "curse of Ham", and to try hard not to read into them what is not actually there. Many persons have done exactly that, with tragic and long-lasting consequences. Before analyzing what the Bible says here, let's look at what it does not say.

God did <u>not</u> curse Ham, or Canaan, or anyone else. The curse was uttered by Noah, after he had been awakened from an embarrassing condition in which he had been sleeping off a hangover. He lashed out irrationally, and condemned the descendants of a man who was not present, and was, in no way, involved in any abuse he may have suffered. Is God, or anyone trying to do His will, responsible for enforcing such a curse?

[68] Scientists have known for almost a century that early Indo-Europeans called themselves Aryans, but they refuse to use that word because of its Nazi connotations.

The Bible says unequivocally that the descendants of the person cursed (the Canaanites) were white.

It does not say that Ham had any descendants living in Africa. It was centuries later that historians put the names of Ham's other sons on certain countries in North Africa. There is no evidence, from any source, that those sons or their descendants ever lived in those countries. At any rate, those sons were not cursed. And, further, the inhabitants if those countries are, and always have been, white.

Interpretations of the Curse of Ham, claiming that God has condemned dark-skinned people to perpetual servitude, first appeared within a few decades after the completion of the Torah. Different versions have come out frequently ever since. New ones now show up often on the Internet. The number of permutations, and the range of ideas they include, is mind-boggling. They disagree wildly in detail. That is not surprising; none of them are based on fact. Their contents are controlled only by the writer's imagination. But they all have one feature in common: every one of them gives the ethnic group to which the interpreter belongs a divine right to exploit, abuse, and disempower members of another group.

Unfortunately many of those interpreters have been clergymen, from whom we should be able to expect better.

The interpreter is, in effect, placing a curse where God did not. There are no black people who are descended from Canaan. But Jesus was a descendant of Canaan.[69]

Proclaiming the so-called Curse of Ham is not only denying the Word of God; it is cursing Our Savior!

[69] The Book of Joshua says that Rahab was a Canaanite, the Book of Luke lists Rahab as an ancestor of Jesus. See GENOCIDE and NATIVITY, below.

BABEL

Это слишком легко, виновать человек когда он вне пользу и заставить его взять на себя вину за чужие ошибки.[71]

—Leo Tolstoy

(It's too easy to accuse a man when he's out of favor, and make him take the blame for everybody else's mistakes.)

Most of Noah's descendants, at least those descended[70] from Shem and Ham, moved southward from Ararat into Mesopotamia.[71] They were a pastoral people, constantly on the move. There were other peoples living in that valley, and some of them had been practicing agriculture for 2000 to 3000 years. To them the invaders were predators, and they began gathering into settled communities for self-defense.

Villages grew, culture developed, language was more extensively used and became more sophisticated. Tyrants arose, trying to grab more than their shares of the wealth, and trying to establish authority and prestige over others. The strength in numbers was no longer just for defense, it could be used for aggression.

All of these peoples had legendary oral histories of their ancestors. The earliest writing appeared about 3500 BC, and within a few centuries many of those legends were written down. Nearly all of them start with the story of Noah, and there are many similarities throughout, but no two of them are identical. Genesis includes the Hebrew version of the legend. The best history of the time can be produced by considering all of

[70] From *War and Peace*.

[71] A Greek name meaning "between the rivers". The Ancient Hebrews called it "Shinar", which is cognate with more modern "Sumeria".

all of these legends, together with archaeological evidence.

The first large city on earth was Eridu, near the then-mouth of the Euphrates River.[72] It was founded about 5400 BC. Like most of the ancient cities of Mesopotamia, it has been long abandoned and reduced to a huge pile of rubble (a "tell" to archaeologists). Tell Eridu is the oldest and largest ruin in Iraq. It also contains the largest amount of meaningful material from which the history of the city can be reconstructed.

Each of the ancient cities of the Valley had a ziggurat as its center. The ziggurat was a large building which served as a religious and governmental center, but whose main purpose was to glorify the ruler. From the amount of rubble we can determine the overall size of the structure, but not its profile. Those that we see in contemporary art are all quite high, probably too high to have been safely built of unreinforced brick.

[72] It is now nearly 150 miles upstream due to silting of the Tigris-Euphrates Delta.

Tell Eridu contains enough bricks to have erected a building several hundred feet high. But the engineering skill to support such a tower did not exist at that time.[73] If an attempt were made to build it, it would have collapsed long before completion. The ruler whose god-lust was thus thwarted would have needed a scapegoat. He had one.

Artifacts in the lowest layers of rubble at Eridu represent three different cultures. Each had its own way of life and, no doubt, its own history and language. It was the first time people speaking different languages had lived in the same community, and bigotry was to be expected. The ruling class would rather blame the disaster on ignorant workers, who couldn't understand their instructions or communicate with each other, than on a poor design. There are enough clues in the rubble at Eridu to confirm the Biblical story of the Tower of Babel.

[73] Later ziggurats had significant setback in their upper portions. It would be almost 2000 years before the Egyptians discovered the stability of the pyramid.

The ruling class in Eridu consisted basically farmers. Many of them were descendants of Ham. There were many Semites, mostly working in animal husbandry. Genesis gives the names of many of Shem's descendants who had migrated to this general area, but no specific dates or places are associated with any of those names. The third culture at early Eridu subsisted on resources of the river and the sea. They were descended from the colonists sent there from Dilmun, and were thus not descended from Noah, but from Cain.

Nimrod is an important character in the history of Sumeria. There are many accounts of him, and they do not all agree. They do agree that he was descended from Noah's son Ham, that he was a mighty hunter, and that he seized control of Eridu by violence. Some say he was the first ruler, but most put him later in the king list. The story that Nimrod and Abraham were contemporaries is apocryphal. Abraham was separated from Noah by four or five more generations than Nimrod.

There may be some substance to the tale of Abraham's arguing about whether Nimrod or Yahweh was God, though his opponent would have had to be one of Nimrod's descendants. There are several references later in the Old Testament to cities in Mesopotamia, or to the country itself, as "the Kingdom of Nimrod.

§

There are problems in making the story of Babel completely coherent. They are not going to be solved here. All the possible answers are controversial, and there is not enough evidence to prove any of them. They are mentioned as food for thought.

Nimrod was supposed to be a "servant of servants", but he was a mighty king who tried to become a god. If he was indeed the great grandson of Noah, where did all the people to form his "great kingdom" come from, only three generations later? If Cush was Nimrod's father and founder of an African nation, how did Nimrod get back to Mesopotamia. It was 3000 years from Noah to Abraham. This suggests that the cult of Nimrod lasted longer than has Christianity.

MONOTHEISM

ەللا الإ ةلآ ال كانەو

—The Inshada[75]

(Lā ilāhā ïllā-ilāhu) (There is no god but God)

The early Hebrews, like all their neighbors, believed in many gods. The interactions between God and individual humans described above were initiated by God, and the humans had only a limited understanding of what was happening. The idea of one supreme God who created and controls the world and everything in it originated in the mind of a rebellious teenager.[74]

Abraham, originally Abram, was born about 2050 BC in Ur. Ur is just a few miles north of Eridu. It became a city about 3810 BC, though a small settlement had already existed for several centuries. The early population was a mixture, probably much like that of Eridu. It came under Semitic control about 2350 BC.

We have three versions of the story of Abraham, one in Genesis, one in the Book of Acts, and one in the Quran.

Terah, Abram's father, was a maker and seller of idols. Abram did not believe they had any power, so he smashed them. Punished by being thrown into a fire, he came out unhurt, and attributed his survival to the protection of the one true God, in whom he believed. Later, he accompanied his father on a business trip to Harran, on the upper Euphrates. Unable to convince his father that there was only one God, he left for the

[74] Daily recital of the Inshada is one of the five pillars of Islam.

land in Palestine[75] that God had promised him, taking his wife Sarai, who was also his niece, and his nephew Lot.

Abram and his family were the first to adopt a monotheistic religion. Judaism, Islam, and Christianity all grew out of his religion.

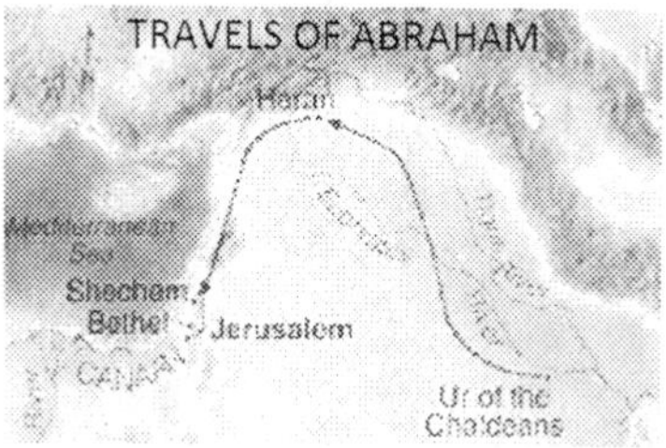

Abram was a colorful character. After escaping the prescribed punishment for his youthful vandalism, he abandoned his aging father (Why not? – he was an unbeliever), married his brother's daughter, then allowed other men access to her, and lied, apparently due to cowardice. His redeeming grace was his firm faith in, and unquestioning obedience to, God.

[75] The country was called Canaan at that time. It is almost certain that the inhabitants were descended from Canaan, the fourth son of Ham.

Hebrews (Jews) are descended from Abraham's son Isaac, Arabs are descended from his son Ishmael.

The severe drought of the mid-22nd Century BC[76] in the Near East was probably too early to have been associated with Joseph's dream interpretation, but it may have been what drove Abraham to Egypt. Pharaoh considered the disaster in his country to have been due to his taking Abraham's wife, and tried to mitigate the situation by making lavish gifts.

§

Archaeological information to correlate with the story of Sodom and Gomorrah is very hard to find. The area now suffers an oppressive environment, and is rife with noxious chemicals. Yet there is evidence that it was not always that way, and there is nothing to contradict the Biblical account.

[76] Bernhardt, Christopher, et. Al., *Nile Delta Response to Holocene Climatic Variability*, Geology, July 2012.

When Lot chose the valley to the east as his portion of the Promised Land, it was described as "well-watered". There are many wadis (dried-up river beds) that once carried water descending into the valley. The most outstanding archaeological feature is the large number of cemeteries, holding hundreds of thousands of human remains, most of them showing no signs of violence. This valley once supported a large, prosperous, and peaceful population.

The Dead Sea itself, and the land surrounding it, are full of salt, sulfur, asphalt (pitch) and ashes. Any artifacts or ruins that might have been there for four thousand years could well have been corroded beyond recognition. There are several formations that might be the remains of ancient cities, but positive identification is lacking. "Lot's Cave", overlooking the Dead Sea, may have been his family's refuge, but there is no way to prove it. Discovery of the Dead Sea Scrolls in a cave not far away shows that it was not unusual to use these caves for human habitation. A salt pillar known as "Lot's Wife" is a tourist attraction, and is only one of many spectacular salt formations in the area. If it is really her remains, she would have had to be 65 feet tall.

A major fault line, which is connected to, and is actually part of the East African Rift System, goes through the valley of the Dead Sea. It is capable of producing earthquakes and volcanoes, but there is sparse history of its having done so. A theory that the destruction at Sodom and Gomorrah was due to a shower of the debris from a shattered comet has been published, but there is no evidence to support it.

Abraham, Sarah, Isaac, Jacob, Leah, and Rebekah are all buried in the Cave of the Patriarchs near Hebron. It is still a well-maintained mausoleum, with individual tombs designated.

EGYPT

There's a tide in the affairs of men, which taken at the flood, leads on to fortune. Omitted, all the voyage of their life is bound in shallows and in miseries.[78]
—William Shakespeare

To get the whole story of the Israelites in Egypt, we must study Hebrew records (the Bible), Egyptian records (hieroglyphics), and archaeology. Chronology is difficult. Both Hebrew and Egyptian dates are educated guesses. Archaeological dates are based on margins of error. If a traditional date falls within the probable error of a scientific measurement, it can be accepted. Otherwise a reasonable compromise is necessary.[77]

Joseph, the Hebrew slave who became Grand Vizier of Egypt, was an important person, and his biography is a remarkable story. If such things actually happened, the Egyptians would surely have taken note, and left their own record.

According to Egyptian records Imhotep, Grand Vizier to Pharaoh Netjerikhet (Djoser), built the earliest grain silos in Egypt. Imhotep was a commoner who had interpreted the Pharaoh's dream as a warning of seven years of famine. He also designed the first pyramid, which was financed by the profits from sale of the stored grain.[78]

Jacob had accompanied his sons to Egypt, and had asked them to bury him in the tomb with his parents, back in Canaan. When Jacob died, Joseph was Grand

[77] From *Julius Ceasar*

[78] J Ashton & D Down, *Unwrapping the Pharaohs, how Egyptian archaeology confirms the Biblical timeline,*

Vizier. He asked Pharaoh's permission to comply with his father's wish, and was given a large entourage for a funeral procession.

And there went up with him both chariots and horsemen: and it was a very great company. *– Genesis 50:9.*

This is a problem, because there were no chariots in Egypt or the Near East until a century or two later. To resolve it, let's look at the translation.

About a dozen English versions of the Bible all use the work "chariots" in this verse. But translators of the Douai Version seem to have caught a subtlety in the original language. That version says:

He had also in his train chariots and horsemen, and it was a great company.

The word "train" at that time meant a line of people, animals, and/or vehicles carrying burdens. So these were not war chariots, they were freight wagons. The ancient Hebrew language simply did not have words to distinguish them.

Imhotep was declared a god after his death, and his body was supposed to have been treated the same as that of a pharaoh. But the body disappeared. The whereabouts of Imhotep's mummy and tomb has long been a subject of speculation in both science and popular culture. Two movies have been based on that speculation. The answer is in the Bible!

And Moses took the bones of Joseph with him: for he had straitly sworn the children of Israel, saying God will surely visit ye; and ye shall carry up my bones `away hence with ye.
— Exodus 13:19.

It is deduced that Imhotep was Joseph's Egyptian name, and that he was born about 1920 BC in Palestine. His brothers and their families came to join him in Egypt about 1876 BC. The grateful pharaoh gave them the "Land of Goshen", i.e. the eastern Nile Delta.

§

A new people appeared in the Near East during the Nineteenth Century BC. Its origin, organization, and ethnicity are uncertain. We have four different names for them from contemporary literature. (1) The Egyptians called them Hyksos, which means "foreign rulers". (2) The Hebrews at first called them Egyptians; the Pharaohs who enslaved them were of that group. (3) After the Exodus, the Israelites called them Philistines. (4) There are vague references, from several sources, to the "Sea People", who supposedly came from the Aegean area at that time.

Scientific studies support, at least partially, all these ideas, but cannot determine whether they were all from one source, or whether they were different groups joined under a common leadership.

They were based in southwestern Palestine and along the Mediterranean coast of the Sinai. They had achieved Iron Age technology while all their neighbors were still in the Bronze Age. They were almost surely of mixed ancestry, and we have two indications that much of that ancestry was Canaanite and/or Semitic. (1) The native Egyptian Pharaoh who ordered the murder of Hebrew babies had perceived enough similarities between the Hebrews and the Hyksos that he feared they might make common cause against him. (2) The Israelites struggled against the Philistines for centuries, but never had any language problems in communicating with them.

The spoked wheel chariot was invented about 2000 BC by Aryans in Central Asia. With this powerful new military device they quickly dominated their neighbors, and began campaigns into Persia, India, and Anatolia. A small band of roving charioteers somehow moved out several hundred miles in advance of their compatriots and settled in southwestern Canaan. They became the rulers of the Hyksos. Having no chariots, the Egyptians were unable to resist their incursions.

The Israelites were not the only foreigners who came into Egypt from Canaan. And not all the immigrants were welcomed in peace. The Hyksos came in force, and soon dominated all of Lower Egypt, including Goshen. They adopted Egyptian culture and titles. About 1730 BC[79] one of them established a capital at Avaris and proclaimed himself Pharaoh. The native Egyptian Pharaoh continued to rule Upper Egypt from his capital at Memphis.

Now there rose up a new king over Egypt, which did not know Joseph. — *Exodus 1:8.*

The Hebrews, in both parts of Egypt, were reduced to slavery.[80] They had become quite numerous, and were unhappy with their lot. The Pharaoh in Upper Egypt ordered the death of all male Hebrew babies.

[79] Traditional dates for these events do not agree, and neither do historians. Proof that the Hyksos ruled Lower Egypt before the Exodus is found in the facts that (1) Minoan artifacts are found in Hyksos ruins, and (2) the Hyksos had horses and chariots, the Egyptians did not.

[80] The Hyksos pharaoh needed slave labor to build his capital; the Egyptian pharaoh was afraid the Hebrews might support the invaders.

Jochabed, a Hebrew woman in Upper Egypt, hid her baby boy in a basket, and floated him on the river. He was found and adopted by Pharaoh's daughter Sobelkneferu. She named him Moses.

The story of Moses is told almost identically by the Bible and the Quran. There are also references to him in Egyptian records.

Neither Pharaoh Amenemhet III of Upper Egypt nor his daughter had a son. Moses was his adopted grandson and heir-apparent. The list of pharaohs includes Moses as Amenemhet IV, but states that, after co-ruling for a very short time, he disappeared without a trace before the death of his adoptive grand-father. His foster mother ruled in his place, but she was quickly overthrown by a usurper.

Moses, having killed a brutal slave overseer and fearing his true identity would be discovered, had fled to Midian (northwest Arabia). He married and moved in with his in-laws. After some years he encountered God in a flame from a bush which was itself not burning[81], and was told to go back to Egypt and lead his people out of slavery.

Moses' initial negotiations with Pharaoh got nowhere. But soon an Act of God, which had worldwide repercussions, concentrated so much damage on Lower Egypt that the Israelites were permitted to go.

[81] The chaparral, also known as greasewood or creosote bush, stores water in its branches. They will not burn until cut and dried. The surface is coated with a flammable, oily substance, which is now being exploited as a substitute for petroleum.

PLAGUES

An obstinate man does not hold an opinion, it holds him.
—Alexander Pope

The island of Thera,[82] in the Aegean Sea, exploded in 1628 BC. It was the largest volcanic eruption in recorded history.[83] In addition to a wealth of scientific data, we have three literary sources, two of them in the Bible, to which we can turn for information.

The Greek author Plato described the wealthy, populous, and technologically advanced Atlantis, which sank into the ocean.[84] Of course he ascribed the disaster to the Atlanteans having displeased the Greek gods.

The sufferings in Egypt from the Thera eruption are listed in the Book of Exodus. In this source they were brought on by Pharaoh's incurring the ire of Yahweh.

Saint John the Divine, author of the Book of Revelation, lived as a hermit, some 1500 years later, on the nearby island of Patmos. He heard legends passed down to the islanders from their ancestors, who had witnessed effects of Thera, and he dreamed that the horrors described in those legends would be repeated in the Last Days.

§

Patmos was about 60 miles upwind of Thera, close enough to have suffered the initial shock wave and heat, and some of the

[82] The atoll-like remnant of the island is now called Santorini.

[83] The much larger Toba eruption, described above, was prehistoric. All the information we have on it is from scientific investigations.

[84] In his works *Timaeus* and *Critias*.

earlier low-level fallout. But continuing fallout was directed toward Egypt.

And the fourth angel poured out his vial upon the sun; and power was given to him to scorch men with fire.
— Revelation 16:8.

Fourteen cubic miles of dense lava was spewed into the atmosphere. Most of the Island of Thera plummeted into the emptied magma chamber below, and was quickly covered by the inrushing sea. A giant tsunami spread through the eastern Mediterranean, damaging all coastal 90communities and wiping out the Minoan civilization on the island of Crete.

And the third angel poured out his vial on the rivers and the fountains of waters; and they became blood *— Revelation 8:4.*

Once airborne, the lava became dust and ashes. Heavier particles moved south-southeastward on the low level winds, and fell out on the sea and on Egypt. Lighter particles were carried by the high-level winds over the entire globe. Ten feet of red pumice was deposited on Santorini, and amounts ranging from a few inches to several feet on the other Aegean islands and nearby shores. Prevailing winds carried the ash cloud south-southeastward over central Egypt, raining down acidic and poisonous red dust for weeks to come. (Most of the Hebrews lived in the Land of Goshen in the northeastern extremity of Egypt, which was outside the main area of the plume.) The Nile River turned red, and all living creatures in it, that could not escape, perished.[85]

And the second angel poured out his vial upon the sea; and it became as the blood of a dead man: and every living soul died in the sea. *–Revelation 16:3.*

...behold, I will smite with the rod that is in mine hand upon the waters, which are in the river, and they shall be turned to blood. *–Exodus 7:17.*

[85] Scientists disagree on whether the pollution was the direct result of the fallout, or the result of a bloom of red algae which was nourished by the fallout. The result on riverine life would be the same in either case.

Frogs could escape from the poisoned water, and they overran the lands.

And Aaron stretched out his hand over the waters of Egypt; and the frogs came up and covered the land of Egypt. - *Exodus 8:6.*

Rotting fish caused a population explosion of many kinds of obnoxious insects.

Exodus 8:17-24 states that Egyp was overrun by lice and flies. Thus there were both crawling and flying insects.

Livestock, feeding on the poisoned vegetation, sickened, and many died.

...the hand of the Lord is upon thy cattle which is in the field, upon the horses, upon the asses, upon the camels, upon the oxen, and upon the sheep, there shall be a grievous murrain. — *Exodus 9:2.*

It took a little more time for human and animal skin to be penetrated by the acidic dust and become infected.

And they took the ashes...and sprinkled it up toward heaven; and it became a boil breaking forth with blains upon man and upon beast. — *Exodus 10:10.*

And the first went, and poured out his vial on the earth; and there fell a noisome and grievous sore upon the men which had the mark of the beast, and upon them which worshipped his image. *–Revelation 16:2.*

Thunderstorms are relatively rare in Egypt, but volcanic heat destabilized the air and dust provided a huge quantity of vaporized water and condensation nuclei. The rain and the hail were acidic, of course.

Pm Revelations 16:18 we read that people upwind from Tjera heard loud noises, saw the sky light up, and felt a great earthquake.

...and the Lord sent thunder and hail, and the fire ran along upon the ground...
— Exodus 10:24.

A severe attack by locusts comes once every ten to twenty years in Egypt.[86] They came as usual that year, but did not stay long. There was nothing they could eat, and they left earlier than they normally would have.

And the Lord said to Moses, stretch thine hand over the land of Egypt for the locusts that they may come upon the land of Egypt, and eat every herb of the land, all that the hail hath left.
– *Exodus 10:12.*

And the Lord turned a mighty west wind, which took away the locusts, and cast them into the Red Sea, there remained not one locust in all the land of Egypt.
– *Exodus 10:19.*

As the influx of ash continued into the high atmosphere, the cloud became more and more opaque until it completely blocked out the sunlight over the entire earth.

And Moses stretched forth his hand toward heaven; and there was a thick darkness in all the land of Egypt three days.
– *Exodus 10:22.*

And the fifth angel poured out his vial on the seat of the beast; and his kingdom was full of darkness;... — *Revelation 16:10.*

Humans, at the top of the food chain, eventually got poisoned fresh produce and meat. These high quality foods were mostly for the rich, especially their favored older sons. Poor people subsisted primarily on stored grains, which had not been poisoned. Most of the Hebrews lived in Goshen, which was outside the area of heaviest fallout.

§

The traditional date of the Thera eruption is 1540 BC, about a century before the traditional date of the Exodus. Neither of these dates is based on anything more than pure guesses, and there is even an indication of superstitious numerology in them. Fortunately several scientific clues, many of them giving remarkable precision,

[86] The desert locust (*Schistocerca gregaria*) is related to, but does not swarm with such strict periodicity as, the American 17-year locust.

are found in widely scattered locations.

In 2002 several intact, mostly unburned, olive branches were found buried under a thick lava flow on the island of Santorini. The tree rings were still readable, providing unusually precise dating for an event so many years ago. The tree had died in 1627 BC. Several pieces of charred wood in the same deposit were dated by radioactive carbon to 1613 ± 7BC.[87]

The bristlecone pines of California are the oldest living things on the planet. At least two of those trees now living were growing during the Thera event. Their rings indicate a volcanic winter in 1627 BC.[88] Similar studies on fossilized trees in Ireland and Sweden yielded dates of about 1628.[89]

The ten Plagues of Egypt occurred in 1628 BC, probably over a period of several months. The departure of the Hebrew people from Egypt was a huge undertaking, and it may well have taken a year or more to get it organized after the permission was granted.

§

The rich Minoan civilization, which was centered on the island of Crete, was wiped out by the Thera explosion. The Mycenaean Greeks took over the remains and started to build the Hellenic culture which would dominate the western world for the next millennium.

---

[87] Walter L Friedrich *et alia, Santorini Eruption Radiocarbon dated to 1627-1600 B, C.*, Science, 28 Apr 2006.

[88] M K Hughes, *Ice layer dating of the eruption of Santorini,* Nature, 335, 211-212, 1988.

[89] V C Lamarche & K K Herschboek, *Frost rings in trees as records of major volcanic eruptions,* Nature, 307, 121-126, 1984.

TIME TABLE (BC) OF HEBREWS IN EGYPT					
EVENT	PROBABLE DATE	SCIENTIFIC DATE	METHOD	HEBREW DATE	EGYPTIAN DATE
Abraham in Egypt	**c2150**	2150±25	Sediments	1876	
Joseph arrives in Egypt	**c2090**			1814	2620
Brothers arrive in Egypt	**c2055**			1713	
Hyksos Pharaoh in Lower Egypt	**c1730**			1600	1783
Birth of Moses	**c1691**			1525	
Moses becomes co-ruler	**c1669**			1494	1825
Moses flees to Midian	**c1660**			1485	1816
Plagues & Departure	**1628-27**	1628-27	Tree rings	1445	
Death of Moses	**c1583**			1405	
Battle of Jericho	**c1581**	1572±25	Carbon 14		

EXODUS

Freedom is never given voluntarily by the oppressor, it must be demanded by the oppressed.[84]
—Martin Luther King, Jr.,

Some scholars claim that the Exodus never happened.[90] No archaeological evidence of it has been found. But there is geological and other scientific evidence that some of the most spectacular events described in the Bible did actually happen. Scientifically determined dates are more precise than dates estimated from literary sources. As explained above, we find that the Exodus from Egypt began in the mid-1620s BC. That is almost two centuries before the traditional date.

Scholars have argued for centuries about the route of the Exodus. That argument is not going to be settled here. There is simply not enough information available. Based on the data we do have, most of the traditional route seems more likely than any of the proposed alternatives. One question we can explore – where did the "parting of the waters" take place? It was definitely not at the Red Sea.

The Hebrew host gathered where the largest number of them had been used as slave labor to build the city of Rameses. They were steered away from the direct route to Canaan, because it went through Philistine territory.[91] The Philistines were, at that time, loyal subjects of the Hyksos pharaoh, from whom the Israelites were fleeing, and they had the same superior weapons. The Hebrews

[90] From *Why we Can't Wait.*

[91] Exodus 13:17.

went farther south into a maze of waterways, natural and artificial.

The Torah (Hebrew Bible) says the Israelites crossed the) ים סוף yam suph) which means "Sea of Reeds". There is no way it can be properly translated "Red Sea". And there would have been no reason for the Israelites to have attempted a crossing of the Red Sea, with or without the presence of a pursuing army. It would have added hundreds of miles across a burning desert to their journey. The actual Red Sea is more than one hundred miles wide, several hundred feet deep, and has a volcanic fissure along its bottom.

Translators of the Septuagint, in the Third Century BC erroneously rendered it "Ερυθρά θάλασσα".[92] And Saint Jerome, in the Fourth Century AD, translated that as "Mare Rubrum", without bothering to check the original. Translators of the King James Version also failed to check the original, and translated that Latin phrase as "Red Sea". All modern English versions use the correct translation: "Sea of Reeds".

> This is one of the most unfortunate of the mistranslations in the Bible. Our society has built a huge repository of art and literature, and even movies, based on this falsehood. The tradition is so deeply ingrained in the culture that no amount of research and investigative reporting is likely to change beliefs. Folklore is so much more comfortable than truth.

§

So, where is the Sea of Reeds? It can't be found on any map, ancient or modern. We must search for it, using every clue available, giving primary emphasis to those clues found in the Book of Exodus.

There are many varieties of reeds and reed-like plants that grow in Egypt. All of them grow with their roots in shallow water, and they have a limited tolerance for salt. So the Sea of Reeds had to have a significant area of shallow water, and it had to be fresh water or have only a small amount of salt. That immediately rules out the Red Sea and the Bitter Lakes. But it also had to contain another

[92] Some ancient Greek authors called any body of water south of the Mediterranean, including the Indian Ocean and the Persian Gulf, the "Red Sea".

area of water too deep for wading or fording by chariots.

Between Great Bitter Lake and the Mediterranean there is low-lying land containing many depressions. In ancient times many of these depressions held small lakes. The source of the water in those lakes was the annual midsummer Nile flood, which in most years spilled over, bringing new supplies of fresh water and reducing the salinity. Many of the lakes dried up due to evaporation at other times of the year.[93] The topography and the shape and position of the lakes often changed due to shifting sands. Several pharaohs built canals through the area, both as defensive works and to allow small boats passage between the Nile and the Red Sea. Those canals were not well maintained, and there is no record of exactly where and when they existed.

Since the lakes are seasonal, we must try to determine at what time of year the Crossing took place. Tree-ring analyses show that the growth season of 1628 BC had ended before the Plagues.

The Israelites took an erratic route, generally eastward from Rameses in the Land of Goshen.

THE HEBREWS ESCAPE FROM EGYPT

And the Lord went before them by day in a pillar of cloud, to lead them, and by night in a pillar of fire to give them light; to go by day and night. – *Exodus 13:21.*[94]

The cloud that resembles a column is a cumulonimbus. That is not a common cloud type in Egypt. But in an air mass that has been warmed, moistened, and destabilized by recent volcanic activity they are likely to form. Then in, the absence of a cold front or a squall line,

[93] Construction of the Suez Canal in the 1860s connected all these lakes directly to the ocean. Opening of the Aswan Dam in 1971 stopped the overflow of fresh water from the Nile. There are now no reeds.

[94] This navigation by cloud is not unique. Both \ mountains and islands produce distinctive cloud forms. Travelers on both land and sea use them as beacons marking objects beyond the horizon. Crossing the Pacific Ocean, using sightings of distant atoll clouds, by the ancestors of the Polynesians is legendary.

such clouds remain isolated and relatively weak. But they still produce lightning and curtains of rain. They propagate, rather then actually move, along the prevailing wind. An individual cell lives only a few hours. But in its dying stage it triggers new cells along its periphery.

The Israelites followed such a cloud until it led them into a cul-de-sac. They were almost surrounded by bodies of water, some natural, some artificial. The most likely place for that cul-de-sac is the southeast end of Lake Pinsah, where it was joined by the Wadi Tumilat. Lake Pinsah was only a few miles long, oriented northwest to southeast. It was joined by the Wadi, which was usually dry, but in early July brought in fresh water from the Nile. Most of the Lake was only about three feet deep and filled with reeds, but the southeast end had up to ten feet of water and was reed-free. The two bodies of water joined at an acute angle pointing eastward. A sustained east wind would push water away from the junction. Water in the Wadi would simply back up with little change in elevation. But water in the Lake had nowhere to go – it would have piled up at the other end of the lake.

Passover, which is celebrated in late March or early April, commemorates the Tenth Plague. It probably took Pharaoh a little time to recover and decide to expel the Hebrews. Then, gathering and organizing that huge horde of armed men, families, hangers-on, and livestock did not happen instantly. They had wandered for an indefinite time, and made many camps, in the wilderness. It seems reasonable to suggest that the Crossing took place in July 1627 BC.

The Israelites' only apparent escape route was to the rear, right into the arms of the pursuing Egyptians.[95] But, then something happened!

...The Lord caused...a strong east wind that night... - *Exodus 14:21.*

[95] Actually, they were Hyksos, who ruled Lower Egypt including Goshen at that time. The Egyptians themselves ruled only Upper Egypt, and had neither horses nor chariots.

There is no scientific explanation for the sudden appearance of a strong east wind. But its consequences, both on the cloud and on a body of water, are known. The cloud would have been pushed westward until the force of the east wind came into balance with the force of the prevailing northwest wind. Then the converging winds would have caused the cloud to grow and become more active.

...and the pillar of cloud went from before their face, and stood behind them: And it came between the camp of the Egyptians and the camp of Israel; and it was a cloud and darkness to them, but it gave light by night to these... — *Exodus 14:19-20.*

A tall cumulonimbus cloud can cast a very large shadow. If the phase of the moon had been anywhere from approaching its first quarter to just after full moon (a period of about ten days each month), it would have beamed down its light on the Israelites, but would have left the Egyptians in darkness.

A strong wind that begins or ends suddenly can affect lake waters in two spectacular ways. A persistent wind pushes water toward the downwind end of the lake,[96] leaving the upwind end very shallow or even dry. If the wind suddenly ceases, the water surface will return to its normal level by an oscillatory motion known as a seiche. The height and period of a seiche wave depends on the shape and dimensions of the lake. The initial wave is the highest, as water rushes back to where it had been, and inertia carries it to even higher than it previous level. It then rebounds, and bounces back and forth in several waves gradually diminishing in height, until the lake becomes relatively calm again. [97] The wall of water that rushes across the lake comes first from one direction, than from the opposite direction.

§

[96] This phenomenon is called wind set-up, or storm surge.

[97] A notorious seiche occurs occasionally on Lake Michigan. It concentrates its fury in Chicago's North Avenue Pier. Persons caught on the pier may suffer the same fate as the Egyptian army.

The twelve sons of Abraham's grandson Jacob (Israel), led by Joseph, went into Egypt. Their descendants remained there for about 300 years, much of that time in slavery. While the population undoubtedly grew substantially, it could hardly have reached the size reported – 600,000 fighting men, or 2 million persons total. That would have required the population to more than triple in each generation. They would have outnumbered the Egyptians themselves. (That is exactly what Pharaoh was afraid might happen.) Their marching column would have been 150 miles long, and would have taken five days to march past a point.

The Bible says they crossed in one night. It is calculated that, with perfect organization and an all-out-effort, the maximum number that could cross in twelve hours is about forty thousand.

The return phase of the first wave of the seiche would have covered the tracks if the Hebrews, but left the shallow, reedy part of the lake dry. The Egyptians saw their opportunity.

And the Egyptians pursued, and went in after them to the midst of the sea, even Pharaoh's horses, chariots, and his horsemen. And it came to pass… that the Lord looked into the host of the Egyptians…And took off their chariot wheels, that they drave them heavily:…
—Exodus 14:24-25.

The first attack ended with the chariots tangled up in reeds. Then the second wave of the seiche cleared the reed-free end of the lake, so they tried again, just in time to be inundated by the return of the second wave.

And the waters returned and covered the chariots, and horsemen, and all the host of Pharaoh that came into the sea after them.
—Exodus 14:28.

§

Many alternative routes have been proposed for the Israelites' journey from Egypt to Palestine. None of them are supported physical evidence. But there are some practical considerations that suggest something approximating the traditional route is the most likely of those alternatives. They wanted to avoid the Egyptians and other potential enemies. And they had to have a supply of fresh water and food. A route down the west side of the Sinai Peninsula, then crossing the peninsula along a water course or wadi, and up the east side to the vicinity of the Dead Sea, would fill the bill. A date two centuries earlier than the traditional date would have allowed a more moist climate and the corresponding better supply of food and water. It is likely that they usually travelled in several smaller groups, coming together only on special occasions. Forty years seems like a long time, but they probably spent most of it searching for food and water.

"Manna from heaven" is problematical. There are detailed descriptions of it in both the Bible and the Quran.[98] It obviously fell with the dew, which is abundant in that area, and was highly perishable. The descriptions imply that it would have had relatively little nutritive value, and circumstances suggest it would have been a minor part of their diet. After 40 years of living in this manner they would have arrived "lean and mean".

Moses received the Ten Commandments on the summit of Mount Sinai. No mountain exists which has been consistently known by that name. There is a group of peaks at about the midpoint of their trek. The highest of them is Jebel Musa (Arabic for Mount Moses). There is a Moslem shrine and at least three Christian shrines on the various mountains in the group, each purporting to be the source of the Commandments.

[98] Sura 2,57.

Moses is said to have received the Ten Commandments inscribed on two stone tablets. The written Hebrew language did not exist until 500 years later. Later, in Exodus 24:4, 32:15-16, and 35:27 Moses was told to write something down. He could have done it, in Hieratic script, which he had undoubtedly learned while growing up in the Egyptian royal palace. No such written material has survived,[99] and it is a mystery how the Israelites preserved the large amount of received by Moses in Sinai for hundreds of years until it could be transcribed into the Torah. Paintings of the Commandments in Hebrew letters engraved in stone are certainly incorrect. Those letters did not yet exist when Moses went up Mount Sinai.

§

The Commandments include instructions for honoring God, for orderly family life, and for living peaceably among neighbors. That last group of four has sometimes been called the "Universal Commandments". They appear, in some form in the holy scriptures of every major religion. They are easy to identify among the Judeo-Christian Commandments, they are the ones that start with "Thou shalt not...".

Compare: Exodus 20:

13. Thou shalt not kill

14. Thou shalt not steal

15. Thou shalt not commit adultery

16. Thou shalt not bear false witness

The Quran

6,151. And do not kill anyone that Allah has prohibited ...

51,28. Let the thief's, hands be cut off ...

17,12. Do not even go near adultery.

25,12. Servants of God do not testify falsely.

The Hindu Yamas

[99] Some simple symbols scratched on stones have been found in ancient mines on the Sinai Peninsula, and also in Canaan. Archaeologist have named them Proto-Sinaitic script. They have not been deciphered, but appear to be grossly simplified hieroglyphic signs used as mnemonic marks rather than words.

Ahimsa. Do not injure, harm, or cause pain to any living creature

Asetya. Do not steal, covet, or borrow

Brahmacharya. Be continent and celibate when single, faithful when married

Satya. Word and thought must conform to the facts.

The Buddhist 10 Courses of Unwholesome Actions.

1. Take the lives of living things

2. Take what is not given

3. Engage in sexual misconduct

4. Speak falsely when questioned as a witness.

Both Buddhism and Hinduism are gentler than Judaism and Christianity. Islam is harsher.

§

A lot of verbiage in the Book of Exodus is devoted to detailed instructions for building the Ark[100] of the Covenant. The Ark was a container for the stone tablets on which were engraved the Ten Commandments. It was supposed to have received an honored place in Israel's Holy-of-Holies. Actually, it received rather shabby treatment, and eventually it disappeared.

The Ark was constructed while the Israelites were still camped by Mount Sinai. It led their marching column to Canaan, and across the Jordan River, and it played an important part in the Battle of Jericho.

After Joshua's death some of the tribes fought against each other as well as against the Canaanites. There was no central location where the Ark could be kept. It was at Bethel for a while, then at Shiloh. From there it was foolishly carried into battle against the Philistines, and was captured. The Philistines then suffered a series of disasters, which they blamed on the wrath of Yahweh. They took the Ark to a remote

[100] There is no relationship whatsoever between Noah's Ark and the Ark of the Covenant. The word "Ark" was used with two entirely different meanings.

place, where it could be found by the Israelites, and abandoned it. It was put in a "temporary" shelter at Kirjathjearim.

Years later King David retrieved the Ark and took it to his new capital at Jerusalem. It was David's son Solomon who built the first temple, and provided the resting place that the Ark should always have had – after some 600 years of wandering.

In 587 BC the Babylonian king Nebuchadnezzar burned Jerusalem, including the Temple. Most Biblical scholars assume that the Ark of the Covenant was lost. But there are many dissenters and many fascinating rumors.

The Apocryphal book 2 Maccabees[101] 4:10 says that Jeremiah removed the Ark and hid it in a cave on Mount Nebo. No such thing is mentioned in the Book of Jeremiah. Many searchers have failed to find anything on Mount Nebo.

An amateur digger, in 1983, claimed to have found the rotted remains of the Ark in Golgotha Hill under the site of the Crucifixion. The story got much attention by the media, but nearly all Biblical scholars and archaeologists have ignored it.

The Ethiopian Orthodox Church claims to have the Ark of the Covenant securely and reverently installed in the Church of Our Lady Mary of Zion in Axum, Ethiopia. The story they tell of how it supposedly got there is logical, but unverifiable. No outsider has ever been allowed to set eyes on the actual Ark.

There are several other churches, at widely scattered locations, which have claimed to have either the Ark or information about its present whereabouts. These claims have been given little attention.

Members of the Seventh Day Adventist Church have been very active in searching for the Ark of the Covenant, and in checking out all claims related to it. They have concentrated efforts on Mount Nebo, but haven't found

[101] 1 and 2 Maccabees, and several other Apocryphal books, are included in Catholic and Orthodox Bibles, but not in most Protestant Bibles.

a clue worth following. They rushed to the Golgotha dig site, only to be disappointed.

Most Adventists believe that their founder Ellen G White (1837-1915) had the gift of prophesy.[102] She predicted the Second Coming of Christ during her lifetime, and stated that Jesus would open the Ark so that God could use its contents toward an "investigative judgment". Many of her followers want to find the Ark so that the prophecy can come true.

Most Americans have no idea what the Ark of the Covenant really was. They have heard of it only through the blockbuster movie *Raiders of the Lost Ark.* That movie was based on the preposterous idea that the Nazis believed the Ark had magical powers, and that possession of it would make them invincible. The movie was so popular that subsequent Indiana Jones films continued to make reference to the Lost Ark.

The Ark is still missing, and may remain so forever. But its contents, the Ten Commandments, are ever with us.

[102] There are numerous dissenters from this belief. Attacks on her prophesies, from both inside and outside the Church, sometimes become vitriolic.

GENOCIDE

"Joshua fit the battle of Jericho,
And the walls come a-tumblin' down."
—African-American spiritual

The walls certainly did come tumbling down. The rubble is still there for anyone to see. And within that huge pile of rubble is a vast amount of material that is grist for the archaeologist's mill. Charcoal is scattered throughout, ideal for carbon-14 dating. Much of it came from Joshua's burning of the city. But fire had been used to heat and cook for centuries. And wandering tribesmen set fires in the area for years to come.

Five randomly chosen charcoal samples yielded dates (BC) of 1590±110, 1527±110, 1660±40; 1347±85, and 1597±91. The three of these with overlapping error ranges are assumed to be from the fire following the Battle, the others from earlier of later events. Combining those three, we find that the most probable date for the Battle of Jericho is 1572±25 BC. Thus the Biblically reported forty years in the wilderness is well within the range of the scientifically measured dates of the Plagues of Egypt and the Battle of Jericho.

It is easier to find the date of the Battle of Jericho than it is to find than a moral justification for what followed.

And they utterly destroyed all that was in the city, both man and woman, young and old, and ox, and sheep, and ass, by the edge of the sword.[103]

It happened over and over again, each time another city in the Promised Land was taken. Was it necessary? Was it justified?

[103] Joshua 6:21.

'Several centuries after the battle the Book of Deuteronomy was written. It gives the then-current explanation for Joshua's action.

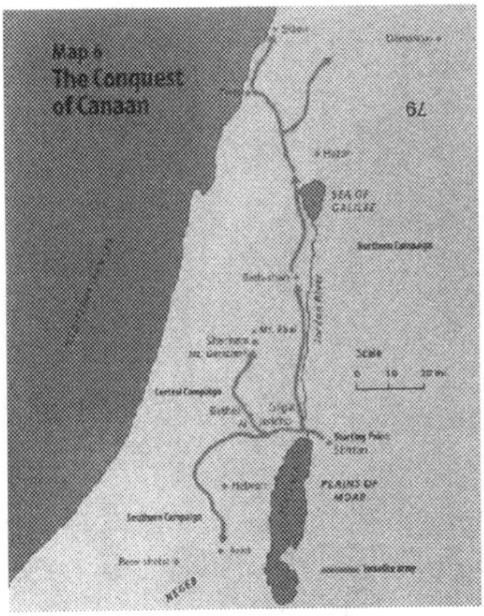

But of the cities of these people, which the Lord thy God doth give thee for an inheritance, thou shalt save alive nothing that breatheth.[104]

This is the word of God?
Compare:

When I send the flower of German youth into ... war, ... should I not have the right to – eliminate millions of an inferior race that multiplies like vermin? - - *Adolf Hitler*[105]

[104] Deuteronomy 20:16.

[105] Joachim Fest, *Hitler, 1975,* 690-691.

We – with God's help – call on every Muslim who believes in God and wishes to be rewarded to comply with God's order to kill Americans and plunder their money whenever and wherever they find it. – *Osama bin Laden*[106]

Christians have always been embarrassed by the Biblical account of Joshua's atrocities. They have ignored it, denied it, excused it, explained it, and tried to mitigate its horror. In a long lifetime of regular church attendance, the writer has never heard a clergyman read this portion of the Scripture aloud from the pulpit. But it won't go away. The most innocuous explanation is that Christ's teachings did away with the command to commit such acts, and that His sacrifice absorbed the guilt associated with the past. But not everyone accepts that explanation.

The idea of exterminating enemies was not exclusively Joshua's. It permeated the entire culture. King Saul's dynasty was terminated because he had allowed a few of his defeated enemies to live.[107]

[106] Broadcast in February 1998

[107] 1 Samuel 15:3.

The harshness of these supposedly divine commands has been a turn-off for many highly moral people, especially since the Enlightenment of the Eighteenth Century. The loving God, whose existence and kindness has been confirmed by science, would hardly permit, much less command, such atrocities.

We have no right to mercy from the Jihadists while we maintain that the Word of God tells us that mass murder had His approval.

The human soul, which was created by God, and partakes of His essence, yearns for a simple, yet all-encompassing, definition of His loving kindness, and is sick-and-tired of exhortations to war and killing.

PAX VOBISCUM!

§

Problems with the Jericho story do not end with the claimed divine right to commit genocide. An admittedly lesser problem carries right on into the New Testament. According to the King James Version. Saint Paul[108] said:

By faith the harlot Rahab perished not with them that believed not, when she received the spies with peace.[109]

He was making the point that God forgives repentant sinners, and this was the example he offered. What was Rahab's sin? What was her faith? What was her penance? And what was her reward?

The word "harlot" existed in spoken English for only about a century. It was borrowed from Norman French, meaning "low class and disgusting", with or without sexual connotations. It was chosen by the puritanical translators of the King James Bible, rather than any of the other less intolerant words available, to translate the word "πόρνη" ("porne"). It meant prostitute, but prostitutes in ancient Greece often had just a few rich customers and, high social status.

[108] Only the King James Version of the Bible lists Paul as the author of this letter. Other versions, and virtually all scholars, say the author is unknown.

[109] Hebrews 11:31.

The word was taken directly from the Septuagint, where it had been used to translate "הנזן". That word has two pronunciations with different meanings: 'zonah" ("prostitute") or "zanah" ("innkeeper"). There is another word in ancient Hebrew: "שזקז" ("qadesh") which means only "prostitute". That word was not applied to Rahab. In translating homonyms, it is a good idea to look at the context in which the word is used to determine which meaning is intended. The spies "lodged" at Rahab's house. To find lodging, would you go to an innkeeper or to a prostitute?

What was Rahab's faith? Did she believe in Yahweh? She would have had to be converted during the time it took for the king's agents to reach her house. She believed that the Hebrews would win the upcoming battle and that the losers would be slaughtered, and she acted on that belief. She committed treason. And her salvation? She was permitted to participate in mass murder rather than being a victim of it.

The point about the forgiveness' of sin is a good one, and should be taken seriously. But can't we find a better example to illustrate the point?

§

The problems of Rahab do not end there. Whatever her profession, she had a husband, Salmon, and a son, Boaz. All three of them are listed in Saint Matthew's genealogy of Jesus Christ.[110] Christian theologians have struggled with that, trying to find some way to avoid admitting that our Savior was descended from a prostitute. Some scholars, now a small minority, claim there were two women named Rahab in the Bible. Translators of the King James Version even spelled her name two different ways, making her appear to be two persons. Other versions, including the New Revised Standard, remain true to the original text. Circumstances of the event, and chronology of the genealogical tables both support that view.

§

On another occasion during the conquest of Palestine, Joshua

[110] [b] Matthew 1:5.

commanded the sun to stand still. How ironic! Three millennia later Copernicus proved that God had already made it stand still at the center of the Solar System, and his follower Galileo was punished by the Church for proclaiming the truth. The apparent motion of the sun is due to the Earth's rotation. Had the Earth stopped rotating, the resulting earthquake would have caused more than just tumbling walls. The entire Near East would have been ripped from the planet and flung out into space. After all, has any soldier involved in an all-day battle thought that day would ever end? (The story of Joshua's making the sun stand still is also in Islamic literature.)

The Israelites must have been quite proud of their conquest of Canaan. It is written up in the books of Joshua, Numbers, Deuteronomy, and Judges. The versions differ wildly, and most of them contain serious internal inconsistencies. Archaeologists have found the sites of some of the reported battles, but the dates they have been able to determine for them are completely out of line with the sequences of events listed in any of the Biblical accounts. It is not possible to write an accurate detailed history of the campaign. But the general outline of what happened is discernible, and the motivations and tactics are painfully obvious.

Soon after the conquest began, leaders of the tribes met to determine the division of the lands they planned to seize among them. Each tribe was given the responsibility of exterminating the inhabitants of the land allotted to it. They set about their tasks with varying degrees of dedication and determination. They could, and some did, call on the other tribes for military support when needed. About half the tribes succeeded in a thorough "ethnic cleansing" of their assigned territories. Those in the extreme south could not defeat the locals, who had earlier been neighbors, and possibly kinfolk, of the Hyksos, and shared with them the technology of horse-drawn chariots. Others could not prevail in more conventional battles, and some simply did not have the stomach for human slaughter. The frame of mind of their leaders is illustrated by some semantic equivalents:

Chosen People = Master Race

Promised Land = Lebensraum.

All ancient writers, and some modern scholars, branded as "failures" those tribes who allowed some of the Canaanites to survive.

Moses had appointed judges to govern the Israelites after his death. Such a government could not enforce a consistent policy, either domestically or internationally. The people demanded a king who would give them more prestige among the nations.

King David, universally admired by Jews and Christians, ascended to the throne of Israel by completing a genocidal act his soft-hearted predecessor had refused to commit.

§

The Geneva Convention of 1949 is the current international law concerning the treatment of enemies in wartime. It has been ratified by the United States, all Christian nations, and many other countries. It is enforceable by the United Nations. Article 3 of that document reads (in part):

The following actions remain prohibited at any time and in any place whatsoever, with respect to ... persons taking no active part in hostilities ... Violence to life and person, particularly murder of all kinds, mutilation, cruel treatment, and torture.

Scientists, some of whose work had been condemned by the Church, developed their own moral code. Their dedication to Truth is well-known, as is the punishment meted out to scientists who depart from the truth. Many of them conscientiously refuse to do weapons research. Some of them are now putting a major effort into developing a moral code that is completely independent of religion. A recently published statement of part of that evolving code states:

The highest moral purpose is served by actions which improve the survival and flourishing of every individual sentient being.[111]

Our political leaders and our scientists have put acceptance of genocide behind them. When, Oh When, will the Word of God join them?

[111] Michael Shermer, *The moral arc*, Henry Holt, 2015.

LAWS?

Cuex qui peuvent vous faire croire une absurdité, peuvent vous faire commettre une atrocité.[104] *—Voltaire*
(Those who can make you believe an absurdity, can make you commit an atrocity.)

If a man also lie with mankind, as with a woman,[112]***both of them have committed an abomination: they shall surely be put to death; their blood shall surely be upon them.***[113]

That is undeniably a death sentence for homosexuals. And in this case the King James Version is relatively mild. Some others say "***must be put to death***". The Douai Version (Catholic) says "***let them be put to death***".

This is the "Word of God"?

§

Legal protection under the civil rights laws was extended to homosexuals in 2009. During the next two years 57 homosexuals died violently in the United States as a result of hate crimes. Most of the murderers confessed, and many proudly explained that they were doing their "Christian duty". None of their attorneys had the effrontery to claim that as a defense. And none of the juries were swayed by the idea. In convicting and punishing these criminals, the jurors and judges violated a direct Biblical command. Did they sin?

One judge did listen. Texas Judge Jack Hampton handed down a very light sentence to the killer of two homosexuals, saying, "I put prostitutes and gays at about the same level, and I'd be hard put

[112] *Questions sur les Miracles.*
[113] Leviticus: 20:13

to give somebody life for killing a prostitute." He was censured by the Judicial Review Board, and defeated in the next election.

How did such bigotry and cruelty become part of the "Word of God"? Many otherwise kind and tolerant people are ashamed of their loving dispositions, and put aside their natural feelings to hate those whom "God wants them to hate". And those who are inclined to hatred have a ready-made justification for atrocities. Few of those now serving prison terms for these crimes have the slightest remorse. They are Christian martyrs, being persecuted for their faith by a sinful society.

§

The Book of Leviticus purports to be the compilation of three speeches Moses made to the Israelites after coming down from Mount Sinai, about 1600 BC. They are presented as advice from Moses, not necessarily commands from God. The earliest Hebrew writing occurred about 1100 BC, so the words were handed down orally for at least 400 years. Writing of the Book began about 710 BC, and was not completed until 500 BC.

This book was written by the Levites. The Levites alone, of the tribes of Israel, did not receive an allotment of land. They were dependent on temple offerings for their sustenance. They had a vested interest in how those offerings and sacrifices were made. The Levites are the same persons who told us that God ordered Joshua to exterminate the previous inhabitants of the Promised Land. Leviticus gives detailed instructions, many of them just for priests, on maintaining the tabernacle, sacrifices, cleanliness, and sin and punishment. It specifies the death penalty for:

1. Using profanity,

2. Fortune telling,

3. Adultery,

4. Cursing your parent,

5. Incest,

6. Prostitution (only for priest's daughters), and

7. Murder.

Lesser punishments are specified for:

1. Eating pork, shellfish, fat, or blood,

2. Cutting your beard or the hair on your temples,

3. A handicapped man, or a woman who has given birth to a boy within 33 days or to a girl within 66 days, entering the tabernacle,

4. Cross-breeding animals or plants, 5. Wearing a garment made of more than one material,

6. Harvesting a crop all the way to the edge of the field,

7. Sex with someone else's slave (your own slave is OK), and

8. Being tattooed.

Doves, bulls, goats, and lambs are to be killed to atone for human sins. Slavery is approved, as is polygamy, wife-beating, child abuse, and prostitution (except for priest's daughters), and patronizing prostitutes.

The actual detailed text of Leviticus would be comical today if it didn't lead to such horrific results. Would we wring the neck of a pigeon, or slit the throat of a bull or a lamb? Where would we get the animal? Who is so unfeeling as to do such a thing? What aboult animal cruelty laws? And to burn them? There are air pollution regulations. The Bible commands us to do all those things.

§

Every civilized nation has outlawed some of the actions that Leviticus tells us God has commanded. Hasn't anybody paid attention to the Word of God?

Yes! Nazi Germany amended Section 176 of its Criminal Code in 1935 in order to eliminate homosexuals from the pure Aryan society. All known or suspected homosexuals were required to wear a pink triangle on their outer clothing. 100,000 homosexuals were imprisoned, and 15,000 were executed. A companion program, *Lebensborn*, adopted at the same time, paid single girls and women to have illegitimate babies by certified Aryan Nazis, and authorized the kidnapping and germanization of blonde blue-eyed children from occupied countries. The obvious intent of these measures was to increase the supply of soldiers for future wars.

Most Nazi discriminatory laws were immediately nullified by the victorious Allies. But the prohibition against homosexuals was not repealed until 1970.

Nazi Badge of Shame 1942

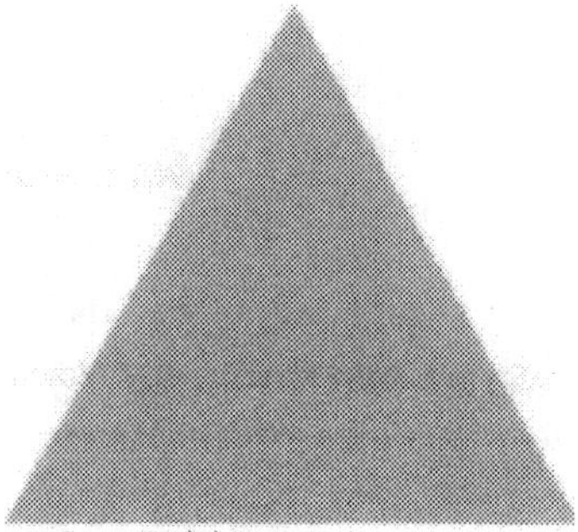

Gay Pride Symbol 1985

(Hitler had suspended the law briefly during the 1936 Olympics, to avoid an international boycott.)

Soviet Russia had a similar, though less draconian, law which is still in effect. President Vladimir Putin was severely criticized for refusing to suspend that law during the 2014 Sochi Olympics. Some foreign athletes openly defied it, and were not molested.

§

Homosexuality was common in all the societies surrounding ancient Israel, and was usually associated with the worship of idols. In Greece it had been honed to a fine art. Militaristic Sparta demanded that its soldiers sire children for future armies. Women were disguised as men on their wedding nights, so that their husbands would not be embarrassed by heterosexual intercourse.

Ancient Rome had laws regulating relations between homosexual partners. This changed suddenly when Christianity became the Empire's official religion. The practice of persecution of homosexuals, which then began, continues today.

> In bothe the Democratic and Republican Presidential Nominating Conventions of 2016, the nominees drew applause by promising to respect the rights of homosexuals.

It is ironic that modern Christian countries ignore Leviticus, and often adopt laws that contradict it, while dictatorships still enforce many of its provisions.

§

When a clergyman, or a lay helper, reads a selection from these words in church, he adds, "This is the Word of God", and the congregation responds, "Thanks be to God". Just how sincere are we at that moment? And do we unconsciously transfer that level of sincerity to our other religious beliefs?

§

Christianity tells us that Jesus' death on the Cross ended animal sacrifices once and for all. Two thousand years later, we still tell people that these gruesome lines are the "Word of God". Is there a clergyman or Sunday school; teacher who would dare read Leviticus word-by-word to small children?

The words of Leviticus, taken out of context, give encouragement, moral support, and solace to some of the most sadistic thugs in our society, and bring guilt, loneliness, and depression to some of God's most harmless and loving children.

ISRAEL

Ours is a country built more on people than on territory.
—David Ben Gurion

While under Joshua's leadership the Israelites defeated thirty-one kings, destroyed their cities, and slaughtered the inhabitants. The Gibeonites voluntarily surrendered, having never been attacked, and were enslaved. Before Joshua's death, the land was divided among the tribes. Some of it had not been completely conquered. Each tribe was given responsibility of completing the extermination of other people remaining on their assigned land.

Although Joshua had reported complete victory over the Canaanites, there were many cities near the coast still to be taken. Some of the tribes assigned lands succeeded, some didn't. Most of the remaining Canaanites were eventually forced into servitude, but there were some exceptions.

The Philistine cities of Gaza, Ashkelon, and Ekron, in the southwestern extremity of the Promised Land, were impregnable. That area had been assigned to the large tribe of Judah. The Philistines were not ethnic Canaanites; their ancestry is uncertain. They were allied with, and probably related to, the Hyksos, from whom the Israelites had fled in Egypt. The Israelites had been warned not to take the direct route, which went through Philistine territory. And now attacks on that territory from the opposite direction could not succeed. The Bible excuses Judah's failure, saying those cities were defended by "iron chariots". Centuries later, King David was still fighting the Philistines.

Joshua reported capturing and burning Jerusalem, and killing all its Jebusite inhabitants. Perhaps so, but eventually David had to do it all over again.

In the northwestern extremity of the Promised Land lived a group of Canaanites who had developed a high `civilization, and lived in peace with their neighbors. They called themselves Phoenicians, and were especially adept at the arts of navigation[114] and writing.[115] The tribe of Asher not only did not take Sidon nor several other Phoenician cities, they lived peaceably alongside the Phoenicians and learned much from them.

Moses had tried to establish a quasi-democratic government for the Israelites by appointing judges to rule them. But there was no procedure for replacing deceased judges, and they had no enforcement powers. Most of the actual power soon gravitated to the Levites, who had a vested interest in assuring that prescribed sacrifices to Yahweh were properly made, and that all non-Yahweh-worshipping people were eliminated.

Conditions deteriorated. Israelites intermarried with the surrounding peoples that they were supposed to have exterminated. Some of them adopted both the material culture and the gods of those peoples. The tribes began accusing each other of backsliding, and fought among themselves, even to the extent of trying to annihilate one of their own tribes. Of course, each claimed to be doing the "will of Yahweh".

Prophets arise among them, warning them to return to the laws of Moses. They did, intermittently, but always soon fell back into bad habits. A stronger prophet, Samuel, created a more stable government, when he anointed Saul king.

[114] The Phoenicians established colonies throughout the Mediterranean. There were Phoenician colonies on Malta and Sicily, at Nice, France, and Cadiz, Spain. The mighty Carthaginian Empire, which was centered in present-day Tunisia and almost destroyed the Roman Empire, began as a Phoenician colony.

[115] Phoenicians invented alphabetic writing. Nearly \ all alphabets in use today were derived from the Phoenician alphabet.

Saul was an effective military leader, fighting off several invading armies. But he did not follow his supposed instructions to kill every last one of the defeated Amekelites, and his sons were disinherited. He was succeeded by his son-in-law David.

David ruled at first only in the territories of the tribes of Judah and Benjamin. One of Saul's sons held all the other territories until his death. Then the two kingdoms of Judah and Israel were united under David. But eventually they would again separate.

By this time a few of the Hebrews were able to write in their own language, using the alphabet they had received from the Phoenicians, and important events were written down as they occurred. They still did not have a calendar whose dates can be translated accurately into the Gregorian calendar used today. But the sequence and duration of events they recorded can be accepted, and sometimes a precise calibration is available from an outside source.

David was born in 1040 BC at Bethlehem, became. King of Judah in 1010 BC, King of Judah and Israel in 1002 BC, and died in 971 BC. He settled the Ark of the Covenant, which had been moved several times since its creation at Mount Sinai, in Jerusalem, and established his capital there. David had at least eight wives and at least eighteen children. He is notorious for his extra-marital affair with Bathsheba, the Hittite,[116] whose son Solomon was his successor.

King Solomon, who was known for his wealth and his wisdom, died in 831 BC. He built the temple at Jerusalem. Through the next several centuries the Kingdom gradually weakened due to wars and internal disputes. The nation was separated into two kingdoms in 913 BC. The northern kingdom (Israel) was conquered by Assyria, and its people taken away as slaves, in 732 BC. Assyrian records show that some Hebrews rose to positions of prominence and authority during the next century.

[116] The Hittites are now known to have been descended from Noah's son Japheth,

But in 612 BC Assyria itself was conquered by Babylonia.

The Babylonians continued their conquests, taking the southern kingdom (Judah) in 597 BC. In 586 they destroyed the temple, burned Jerusalem, and took the rest of the Israelite people into slavery.

The Captivity ended in 516 BC when King Cyrus of Persia took Babylonia and sent all foreign slaves back to their former homes.

The recorded dates within this period are questionable. The official calendar used had only 336 days per year. It no doubt had to be adjusted every few years to get back into synchronization with the natural seasons, and there is no documentation of when this was done.

From the hardships of their captivity the people acquired a great respect for their prophets, who had given them fair warning. Even though the Israelites were united under one king after their return from the Exile, that king had less authority over them than the many new prophets who now appeared. The prophet Daniel had been with them in Babylon, but his predictions were not generally known until they had returned to Jerusalem.

… and will I return to fight with the prince of Persia, and when I am gone forth, lo, the prince of Greece shall come. *–Daniel 10:20*

Alexander the Great led his army up to the gates of Jerusalem in 332 BC. The city fathers told him of Daniel's prophecy, and Israel was peaceably integrated into Alexander's empire and the Hellenic world. It kept its own self-government, but the Kings of Israel were henceforth subjects of foreign rulers. Greek dynasties controlled Israel until 141 BC, when it rebelled and reestablished its independence. The Romans conquered it in 63 BC, ruling sometimes with, sometimes without, a Jewish king.

WRITING

If it's not documented, it didn't happen
—Alleged Medicare Rule[103]

The[117]first mention of written language in the Bible is the engraving of the Ten Commandments on stone tablets. And on several occasions not long afterward Moses was instructed to write something down. Casual readers of the Bible assume that those writings were in the classical Hebrew language. There are works of art that portray it as such. Certainly Rembrandt's painting showing one of those tablets is incorrect. The alphabet shown didn't exist until several hundred years after the event.

At the time of the Exodus, nearly all the Hebrews were illiterate. Moses was an obvious exception. He had grown up in the Egyptian royal palace, probably spoke Egyptian as well as, or better than, Hebrew, and was certainly familiar with Egyptian writing.

The Egyptians had two forms of writing: Hieroglyphics, which were engraved in stone and many of which survive to this day, and Hieratic, written on fragile, perishable papyrus. Very few examples of Hieratic have survived. Scholars were unable to read either of them until the Rosetta[118] Stone had been deciphered in the Mid-Nineteenth Century.

[117] Other government departments and insurance companies have also been accused of following the same rule, but Medicare auditors have caused the most grief and suffering.

[118] "Rosette" is the French spelling of the Arabic place name "Rashid".

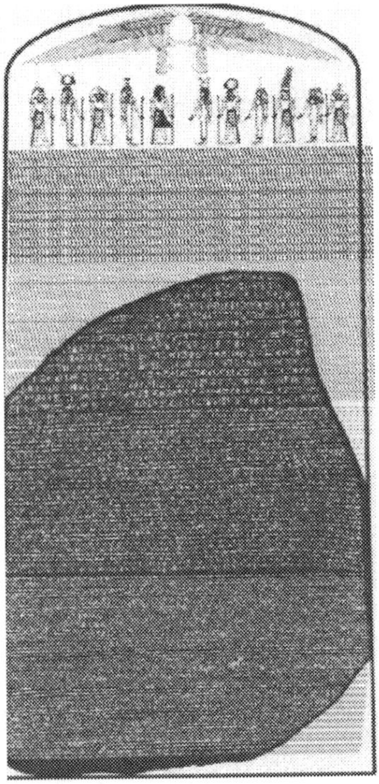

The Rosetta Stone was found by French soldiers invading Egypt in 1809. It contains a royal proclamation written in each of the three languages in use during the Second Century BC: Greek, Hieroglyphic, and Demotic (a late form of Hieratic). It took several decades of study before scholars were able to use it in translating ancient Egyptian texts. Then a treasure trove of ancient documents, some of them referring to Biblical events, was available.

But the attention they received was controversial. Biblical scholars had decided long ago how to interpret ambiguities in the Bible. Their speculative ideas were thoroughly congealed, and were not about to be altered by facts. Some theologians' heads are harder than the Rosetta Stone.

§

The first attempts at writing were simply sketches (pictographs) of objects for nouns and symbols suggesting gestures for verbs. This was first done in Egypt about 3400 BC, and in China much later. There is evidence that the same thing was done in several other locations, but none of those others developed into complete writing systems.

The Sumerians began using cuneiform tally marks about the same time, and, a few hundred years later, were able to write narratives in that form.

Alphabetic writing was invented be the Phoenicians, a Canaanite tribe, about 1500 BC.[119] Many of their neighbors soon adopted the Phoenician alphabet for writing their own languages. By about 1100 BC the Israelites had written down some of their legends in Hebrew using the Phoenician alphabet. Very few of those documents survive today, and none survive written in whatever form they may have used earlier.

Many of the old Hebrew legends were no doubt written down in this early form of writing between the years 1100 and 710 BC. None f these manuscripts have survived,. and it is almost certain that none of them were organized as the books of the Bible eventually would be.

OLD TESTAMENT ALPHABETS			
Phoenician	**Hebrew**	**Greek**	**English**
𐤀	א	Α,α	A,a
𐤁	ב	Β,β	B,b
𐤂	ג	Γ,γ	G,g
𐤃	ד	Δ,δ	D,d
𐤄	ה	Ε,ε	E,e
𐤅	ו		Y,y
𐤆	ז	Ζ,ζ	Z,z
𐤇	ח	Η,η	H,h
𐤈	ט	Θ,θ	Th,th
𐤉	י	Ι,ι	I,i
𐤊	כ	Κ,κ	K,k
𐤋	ל	Λ,λ	L,l
𐤌	ם	Μ,μ	M,m
𐤍	מ	Ν,ν	N,n
𐤎	ס	Ξ,ξ	X,x
𐤏	ע	Ο,ο	Ŏ,ŏ
𐤐	פ	Π,π	P,p
𐤑	צ		Ts,ts
𐤒	ק		Q,q
𐤓	ר	Ρ,ρ	R,r
𐤔	ש	Σ,σ	S,s
𐤕	ת	Τ,τ	T.t
		Υ,υ	U,u
		Φ,φ	Ph,ph
		Χ,χ	Kh,kh
		Ψ,ψ	Ps,ps
		Ω, ω	Ō,ō

Probably the first sections of the Bible to be written down in any form that might be recognizable today was a selection of some of the earliest Psalms. These were needed for use in the Temple. Any that actually were so used have disappeared long ago. Traditionally, authorship of the Psalms has been ascribed to David. There is no doubt of his

[119] Several other writing systems have been developed, especially in the Far East. Some of them are in use today. But none have been used in any of the languages through which the Bible has been transmitted to us.

skill as a poet and a musician. And it is likely that he did write a few of the Psalms himself.

Some written Psalms were taken by the Hebrews when they went into Babylonian Exile, many more were written during the Exile, but the majority first appeared after the Exile. The earliest extant collection of Psalms is divided into five books, the first two of which were, at that time, ascribed to David. The first version in Greek added several more, and gave David the credit for an additional fifteen. The complete Book of Psalms, in approximately its present format, appeared about 150 BC. Listing David as author of the entire book is a relatively modern phenomena.

The first complete books to appear in written form were the prophesies of Amos and Hosea, both about 750 BC. Amos protested exploitation of the poor by the rich, and Hosea protested the worship of foreign gods and the prevalence of improper religious practices. Both predicted the destruction of the Kingdom. Those predictions came true in 731 BC, when the northern kingdom was conquered by Assyria, and its people carried into captivity.

Cts the About 730 BC Micah wrote a very similar prophecy concerning the southern kingdom.

§

The Bible, as a significant work of literature, began with the Book of Isaiah. The Book was slowly assembled over a long period of time from about 740 to about 400 BC. At least four different authors had contributed by the time it was finished. Isaiah himself wrote the first thirty-nine chapters. He criticizes the same sinful practices and predicts the same consequences as had the earlier prophets. But he wrote from a different viewpoint. Amos, Hosea, and Micah had been poor rural people. Isaiah was a member of Jerusalem's elite, and he had the ear of the King. He was very concerned about the continuance of David's dynasty.

Isaiah died about 711 BC. His writings were very popular, though his warnings were little heeded, and many copies were made. His final prediction, the destruction of Assyria, which was verified before the Jews were taken into exile, gave confidence in the power of prophecy.

By the time the people of Judea were taken into Babylonian captivity, in 586 BC, all of Isaiah's major prophecies had been fulfilled. They were ready to follow his advice in order to avoid further calamities, and hopefully to regain their freedom in the Promised Land.

Chapters 40 through 55 of Isaiah were written during the Captivity by an unknown author. They were added to the manuscripts by scribes, who produced many copies of this popular work. Prophesies of the return to Jerusalem and the glorious future of the Hebrew nation are found here. Chapters 56 through 67 consist of many short segments, each written by a different author after the return from captivity.

The most famous, and most controversial, part of the Book of Isaiah is the prophecy of the Messiah to come. Verses purporting to be part of that prophesy are found in two widely separated chapters. Written hundreds of years apart and by two different authors

:תקא–םכל ,אויה ינזא ןתי ןכל
,ןב תלין הדה ,המלעה הנה
לא ונמע ,ומש תאדקן

The Lord himself shall give you a sign; behold, a virgin shall conceive and shall bear a son, and shall call his name Immanuel. – *Isaiah 7:14*

The King James reading of this verse appears to be a clear prediction of a virgin birth. But it can be applied to Jesus only if it is taken completely out of context. Isaiah was speaking directly to King Ahaz, assuring him that the enemies of whom he was so afraid would soon be brought down. The King demanded a sign that this was true. Isaiah promised the young woman's child as a miracle, saying that the enemies would be destroyed before the child grew up. This child was to be seen by Ahaz, so it couldn't have been a reference to Jesus. The Hebrew word "almah" (העלמה) does not mean "virgin", it means "young woman". The Greek word for either of these terms is "παρθενα", and that Greek word was translated into the King James Bible as "virgin". More recent English versions are translated "young woman" from the original Hebrew.

Chapter 53 of the Book of Isaiah speaks of a "suffering servant", who will give his life to save Israel and will bring her untold glory and authority. It is very detailed, and accurately describes the life of the Savior. This is no doubt the text to which Jesus was referring when He said, "I came to fulfill the Scripture". Of course, it was not written by Isaiah himself, but it does seem to be a true prophecy.

§

The Books of Zephaniah and Nahum were written about the same time as the early chapters of Isaiah. They also bewailed the falling away from proper religious practices and the dangerous political situation, and they predicted the downfall of Assyria.

The name Deuteronomy is a misnomer. It is a Greek word meaning "second telling". Actually, Deuteronomy was written before those other books, and even eventually served as an outline for their construction. It was composed by priests about 620 BC from various old writings found in the Temple. It was meant to be a handbook of the Jewish nation, presenting their history, their customs, and their religion. It was taken with them during the Exile, and was instrumental in preserving their national identity. After it had been used as a resource in preparing the other books for the Torah, its original text was simply appended to them, and it was given a new name.

Habbakuk was the last prophet to finish his writing before the Exile. Assyria had already fallen, and he warned of the growing power of Babylonia.

Jeremiah was a worthy successor to Isaiah in the importance of his warning and the quality of his writing. He was still at it when Jerusalem fell, but he escaped and went to Egypt. His work was taken to Babylonia, where it was extensively copied and much appreciated.

Ezekiel was a priest who was carried into captivity in Babylon. He preserved the literature that had already been created, and wrote further prophecies of his own. He reminded the Jews that theirs was a highly developed culture, and promised that they would survive the Captivity and go on the greater glory.

The Books of Samuel, Kings, and Judges were history books, written during the Exile from memories, legends, and fragmentary records, to preserve to story of an independent Israel.

The Books of Haggai, Zechariah, and Joel celebrate Israel's release from captivity, and ascribe their salvation to their faithfulness to Yahweh. They are promised a brilliant future if they will continue in their faith.

The Book of Ruth is a romantic novel, possibly with fictional elements. Written about 381 BC, it marks the beginning of the civil rights movement. Since the time of Joshua prophets had warned against contact with foreigners, which might contaminate their religion. Marriage to foreigners was especially ostracized, though it was not uncommon. Ruth was a Moabite woman who remained faithful to her Jewish husband through very trying circumstances. The main purpose of the Book was to remind proud Jews that a foreign woman became the great-grandmother of their beloved King David.

The Book of Job begins to move away from the concept of God as the protector of His chosen people. The relationship between Yahweh and Job is intensely personal. It is a relationship that could exist between God and any person, regardless of race or ethnicity. This book might be considered the beginning of modern philosophy. It is a deep exploration of the meaning of suffering. It has nothing to do with history, theology, or science. It is just food for thought.

TORAH

History will be kind to me, because I intend to write it.
—Winston Churchill

Cyrus the Great, King of Persia and Medea, conquered the Babylonian Empire in 539 BC. The following year he ordered that all captives be released, and that their holy places which had been destroyed should be rebuilt.

Not all the Jews returned to the Promised Land. Many of them had prospered in Babylonia, and now that they were free they stayed to enjoy the good life. The lands of Palestine had become less productive, and some of the Jews went on to establish colonies in such places as Egypt and Anatolia.

Israel was now ruled by her priests. They received financial aid from Persia to rebuild their infrastructure. Nehemiah was actually an agent of the Persian King, sent to Jerusalem to oversee the rebuilding of the Temple.

Israel's strength was no longer military or economic. It now lay in her rich store of literature. That literature, which had been accumulating since before the Exile, became richer during the Exile, and was on the verge of an even greater expansion. Jews living at widespread locations shared their writings, both the classical books and the new productions.

The ruling priests planned a comprehensive work, which would lay out the history of the Jews, their legends about pre-history, their religious beliefs and practices, and their laws and customs. It took more than two centuries to complete this work, and obviously many writers were involved. After the first phase of partial completion, it was organized into four books, which we now call Genesis, Exodus, Leviticus, and Numbers. An important source of material for these books was the already-written Book of Deuteronomy, which was then appended to produce the Pentateuch, also known as the Books of Moses. Moses didn't write them of course, though some of the words he had written may have been used as source material.

The Book of Joshua was soon added, producing the Hexateuch. The prophecies of Nehemiah and Ezra were produced during this time. They called for more attention to quickly restoring the Temple and the ancient ways of worship.

The Book of Jonah is fiction, but it carries a significant religious message. There is no claim of primacy in God's favor for any ethnic group. Jonah could have been of any nationally, and he had a close, though sometimes fragile, relationship with God. There is an implied message that God's power and His love are available to anyone, anywhere.

Authorship of the Book of Proverbs is traditionally assigned to Solomon, just as that of Psalms is assigned to David. They may have originated a small part of the material included, but each book is a compilation of wisdom accumulated through the ages. Every society has such an accumulation. A colonial American equivalent is Poor Richard's Almanack.

Most of the Jewish literature was written in classical Hebrew, though, by the end of the Exile, few Jews could speak that language. They had adopted Aramaic, the language of the Assyrians and Babylonians, as their vernacular. Many of them could still understand much of the Hebrew used in their religious liturgy and literature.

A few forward-looking authors began to write in Aramaic. Some of Ezra's work, and much of the Book of Daniel were so written.

Daniel lived and wrote in Babylonia. He served, and was

favored by, the Babylonian kings, though he had his differences with them. After the fall of Babylonia he stayed on and served the Kings of Persia, never to return to Israel. He is particularly noted for his accurate predictions of the conquests of Babylonia by the Persians and off Persia by the Greeks. Although his book was written in captivity, it was not published (i.e. copied by hand) until long after the Return. The leaders of the Jewish state were cognizant of Daniel's work by the time Alexander the Great reached Jerusalem in 333 BC.

The Book of Ecclesiastes and the final portion of Psalms were among the last portions of the Old Testament to be completed. They were produced by a collaboration of many authors.

The Book of Esther is romantic fiction. It was apparently based on one historical fact, but it was written long after and far away from that fact. Other more accurate stories of the same event are readily available. In a way it tells the other side of the story of Ruth. A Jewish woman married to a foreign king risks everything to save her people. A nice, even an inspiring, story, but not entirely true.

§

The Torah was originally supposed to have consisted of only the first four books. But, as time went on, most of the other literature mentioned here was added to it. There is no universal agreement as to what is and what is not properly included. The questioned books are called the Apocrypha. Even Christian denominations disagree on which of these books are acceptable. Some modern Jews even speak of the "written Torah" and the "oral Torah".

The apocryphal Books of Maccabees are worth mention. They represent a brief period of independence for Israel. The nation was under Persian rule from 538 to 333 BC, then under Greek rule until the Maccabean revolt in 141 BC. The Romans took over in 63 BC.

By the time the Torah was in substantially finished form, few Jews could read it. The common people spoke Aramaic. Educated people and businessmen spoke Greek, the *lingua franca* of the eastern Mediterranean. King Ptolemy II at Alexandria ordered the Torah translated into Greek about 250 BC. The work was done by a team of seventy scholars, and was named the Septuagint.

The Septuagint was the most popular version of the Scriptures mentioned often by Jesus, though the Hebrew Torah was used in the Temple.

WORSHIP

In real worship we do not just do rituals; we try to imbibe the qualities of the One we worship.
—The Rig Veda

All the early species of the Genus *Homo*, were brought forth by the Earth at God's command, just like all the other species of animals. Many of the first *Homo sapiens sapiens* probably were too,

God selected only two of those human animals to be remade into His image, i.e. to be given souls. This section explores the relationship that developed between God and His living images.

God initiated all His contacts with Adam and Eve. Their only action was to try, unsuccessfully, to obey Him. When they failed, He punished them appropriately. Cain and Abel made sacrifices[120] to God. Why? He hadn't asked it. Perhaps they were trying to regain the preferred status that their parents had lost. The point of the story is that Cain was jealous of his brother's better performance, and that jealousy led to murder. Cain was banished from his parents' home, but he found other company. He and his descendants faired rather well. The "mark of Cain" was not a punishment; it was given to protect him.

The only relationship with God mentioned for the patriarchs from Seth to Enoch is that "the people

[120] The story was written in the 6th Century BC, and the sacrifices described are typical of those made at that time. Certainly, neither agriculture nor domesticated animals existed at the time of Cain and Abel.

called on the name of the Lord", Enoch "walked with God". See the chapter on EXTINCTION, above, for a discussion of what that may mean.

Noah was very trusting to undertake the major construction project that God had designed. God had become so disappointed in his creatures that he was ready to destroy them, apparently the animals as well as the people. Noah was considered righteous, though he had no specific instructions from God as to what constituted righteousness. After the Flood, Noah built an altar and sacrificed "clean" animals, although there were still no instructions as to which were clean and which were not clean.[121]

God was neither invoked nor involved in the unfortunate post-flood affair among Noah and his sons, and none of the consequences of that affair should influence our thoughts or actions today. Whatever, if any, sin was committed has been erased long ago.

The list of patriarchs from Noah down to Terah again does not mention any relationship with God. Terah himself and, no doubt, most of his contemporaries were idol worshippers. It was Terah's young son Abram who conceived the idea of one God. The conflict at that time shows that the purveyors of commercial religion were disposed to take drastic action against those whose ideas of spirituality threatened their profits.

Although Abram did not immediately begin to worship that one God, he seems to have been protected by Him. In Abram's first recorded conversation with God, he was told to leave his father in Harran and go to the "Promised Land" to which God would lead him, Arriving there, he built an altar near Bethel[122], which became the first fixed location for worship of the one true God.

[121] Some English versions of the Bible begin to use the personal name Yahweh, or Jehovah, at this point, indicating that God was considered the protector of a special group, rather than the ruler of the Universe.

[122] The name in Hebrew means "house of God".

They could not remain there because of the drought, so they continued to Egypt. As the intensifying droughf affected even the flow of the Nile, Pharaoh sent them away, fearing he had offended their God.[123]

Abraham had good reason to thank God after his sojourn in Egypt; he had arrived starving and departed wealthy. He felt it appropriate to do so only when he had returned to the altar he had built earlier. God was still to be sought in one particular place.

Abraham's obedience to God is shown by his willingness to sacrifice his son. Genesis says it was Isaac to be sacrificed. The Báhá'i faith says it was Ishmael. The Quran says only "Abraham's son", but most Moslems believe it was Ishmael.

The Quran says that Hagar and Ishmael went to Mecca when Abraham sent them away. Abraham visited them several times, and eventually Abraham and Ishmael worked together to build the Kaaba.[124]

Abraham's worship consisted of obedience and an occasional sacrifice. He believed that he must keep his family aloof from defilement by non-believers. Those he dealt with respected "Abraham's God", but did not renounce other gods.

Much the same attitude prevailed among the three generations of Abraham's descendants who lived in Canaan, and among those who lived in Egypt. Wherever they settled for a while they built an altar on which to offer their sacrifices. Their only expectation of God was that he would help them prevail over their enemies. Their only obligations were to obey Him and not to worship false gods. They believed that God ignored thievery, deceit, and bigamy.

§

Moses changed everything. He had grown up in the royal household of the most tightly organized government on Earth.

[123] Each tribe was believed to have its own god, who might punish outsiders who hurt them. When the tribe moved, their god would go with them.

[124] Quran, 2, 125-127.

He was thoroughly familiar with crime and punishment. He had been exposed to, but did not believe in, a very complex polytheistic religion, with an influential and affluent priesthood. In Midian he became part of a simple unassuming family, living off the land by their own labor. He saw what cooperation and humility can accomplish.

In the burning bush he encountered God, remembered the land promised to his ancestors, and became convinced that he could, and should, lead his people to that land.

The Israelites at the beginning of the Exodus called on God to force the Egyptians to let them go. The phenomena that led to the Plagues and to the parting of the Sea of Reeds were certainly Acts of God.

The Passover was instituted as a commemoration of the final Plague, which convinced Pharaoh that he must let the children of Israel go. The strict rules of its observance presaged the religious discipline that Moses would bring down from Mount Sinai.

The Ten Commandments were just the beginning. When Moses came back down the mountain, he found the people engaged in pagan idolatry. After venting his anger, he went back up. When he returned the second time, he laid down the law, at great length and in intricate detail. The Levites (members of Moses' own tribe) somehow recorded his speeches, took it upon themselves to enforce his commands, and eventually got it all written into the Holy Scriptures.

One of the first of those instructions was to build a vessel, called the Ark of the Covenant, to protect and transport the slabs on which the Ten Commandments were inscribed. Although no contemporary pictures of the Ark were made, its written specifications were so precise that many more recent artist's renditions appear to be almost identical. Once completed, the Ark immediately became the center of Hebrew worship. Prayers and sacrifices were offered before it. It was carried before them when they went into battle. Whenever they camped, a special tent, called the tabernacle, held the Ark.

Both the Israelites and their enemies believed the Ark had supernatural powers. When a porter accidentally touched the Ark itself, rather than one of its carrying handles, he dropped dead. The Philistines once captured it in battle, but soon returned it voluntarily because they thought that their holding it was responsible for a series of misfortunes. Some Hebrews believed that God actually lived inside the Ark.

As the conquest of Canaan neared completion, the Tabernacle settled down in a semi-permanent position near Shiloh. Many persons made pilgrimages to worship before the Ark.

When King David finally completed the conquest of Jerusalem, he established his capital there, and brought the Ark to the city. But it was still kept in a movable tent. It was Solomon who built the Temple. The Ark was placed in a small room in the Temple, called the Holy of Holies. As the Kingdom broke up, the Temple remained a center of worship for Jews in both Israel and Judah.

§

Beginning in 587 BC, Jerusalem was conquered, the Temple was destroyed, the Ark disappeared, and the upper classes of the Judean people were taken into Babylonian Captivity. That catastrophe would seem to have ended the Jewish ethnic experience – but far from it! They had already amassed a rich and growing store of literature. The prophets were exploring newer and gentler ideas. Absolute obedience to God was still required, but foreigners were no longer looked on as implacable enemies who must be destroyed. They had already lost several battles, and had survived. There were even hints that Yahweh might rule over, and care for, more than just one nation.

The Babylonians treated their captives well, recognizing their high culture and their abilities. Many of them were appointed to positions of great responsibility. They produced some of their best literature during the Captivity. They found that they could continue the worship of their God, although the Temple and the Ark were gone. The idea of the ubiquity of God was strengthened, and tolerance of other peoples, even as rulers, followed. They absolutely refused to worship any foreign gods, and their feelings in this respect were generally honored.

Fall of both the Babylonian Empire and the Persian Empire were successfully predicted during the Captivity. When the Persians took over, in 539 BC, the Jews were allowed to return to Judea, but not all of them did. Judea 0nce again had its own king, though he was a vassal of the Persian king. Jews, and their religion, were found in various parts of the Empire. Aramaic was the *lingua franca*, making the movement of people and the exchange of ideas easier than ever before. Most of the work of producing the Torah was done during this period.

Many of the ideas expressed in the Torah were obsolescent before they were ever written down. Actual religious beliefs and practices had become much less prejudiced, much less vengeful, and even less sacrificial. The Levites, who wrote the Torah, had a vested interest in maintaining as much of the ancient requirement as possible.

The Persian king had authorized rebuilding of the Temple, but the Hebrews seemed to be in no hurry to get it done. They were now able to practice their religion without either the Temple or the Ark.

The Jews accepted Alexander's conquest of the Persian Empire peacefully, and hurried to take advantage of the benefits it offered. Alexandria, Egypt soon became the world's largest city, and Jews flocked to it for the urban environment and economic opportunities. Soon there were more Jews in Alexandria than there were in Jerusalem. Wherever they were, they all spoke Greek, and they had their Holy Scriptures in that language.

Not all Hebrews were happy with these innovations. A group called the Maccabees wanted to return to the pride and austerity of their ancestors. As Greek power weakened before the rising Roman Empire, they rebelled, and set up an independent Israel.

Religious diversity developed within Judaism. The Pharisees, Sadducees, Essenes, and Zealots each had a slightly different way of worshipping God. All honored the Torah, which was i available to them in both Hebrew and Greek, but none followed all of its strict rules.

The Romans conquered Judea in 63 BC, and established a puppet king to rule their new province. Herod the Great was distinguished primarily for his extensive building activity, including a massive enlargement of the Temple. Otherwise he was a poor monarch. His paranoid fear of losing his throne to a usurper caused him to murder his own son, and to attempt to eliminate the Messiah who was born during his reign.

NATIVITY

Christmas waves a magic wand over this world, and behold, everything is softer and more beautiful.
— *Norman Vincent Peale*

The Gospels of Matthew and Luke each present a genealogy of Jesus. They disagree with one another, and with the snippets of genealogy in the Old Testament. These disagreements have been used by some critics to discredit the Bible and even the Christian religion. Let's take a close look at them, not to find fault, but to seek the truth.

Matthew states that his listing is "the generation of Joseph, the husband of Mary, of whom was born Jesus". He thus implicitly recognizes the virgin birth, and states that he is tracing the ancestors of Joseph. His book omitted four generations. Matthew seemed to harbor the superstition of numerology. Apparently he was trying to prove that a great leader comes along in every fourteenth generation. But to make the numbers come out right a little manipulation was needed,

Luke's genealogy is less organized than Matthew's. He began it with "Jesus, being (as was supposed), the son of Joseph, which was the son of Heli". He also hints at the virgin birth. The list of ancestors is quite different from that given by Matthew, and most of it cannot be found in the Old Testament. The word "son" in the Bible can mean "son-in-law", "stepson", "grandson", or even "descendant". It is the opinion of most scholars that it sometimes means "stepson" in Matthew and "son-in-law" in Luke. What we find in Luke's genealogy is a list of Mary's ancestors.

Heli (Eli), listed as Jesus' grandfather, is not an individual, but an entire lineage. The actual names of Mary's parents, Joachim and Anna, are found only in the forbidden Gospel of James[125]. It is ironical that they are both listed among the saints, though they are not mentioned in the canonical gospels.

Both Mary and Joseph were descended from David. This should be neither surprising nor denigrating. Computer analyses of modern family trees show that almost every married couple share a common ancestor less than ten to fifteen generations back.

Another problem is the appearance of Zerubbabel and his father Shealtiel on the lists for both Joseph and Mary about halfway back to David. It could be, but it requires a little thought. Jerubbabel could have had two sons. But did Shealtiel have two fathers? Only if one of them was actually a father-in-law. Since Luke did this one other place in his genealogy, it is assumed that he did it again here. Now the family tree is completely in order.

The purpose of all this genealogy was to prove that Jesus had a right to the throne of David. His disciples thought that was his purpose in being here,

<u>JESUS' ANCESTRY</u>

David	
Nathan	Solomon
Mattatha	Rehoboam
Menan	Abijam
Meles	Asa
Eliakem	Jehosaphat
Joanan	Jehoram
	Joseph
Judah	Uzziah
Simeon	Ahaziah
Levi	Jehoash
Matthat	Azariah
Jorim	Jotham
Elieer	Ahaz
Jose	
Er	Hezekiah
Emodan	Manasseh
Cosam	Amon
Addi	Josiah
Melchi	Jejoiakim

125 The son of Joseph by a previous marriage. He was sometimes called Jesus' brother, though there was no blood relationship. His Gospel gives many details of Jesus' childhood and His family.

Neri (in-law?)	Jeconiah
Shealtiel	
Zerubbabel	
Abrud	Rhesa
Eliakem	Joanna
	Judah
Azor	Joseph
Zadok	Semer
	Mathaas
Achim	Maath
	Nagge
liud	Naum
	Amos
Eleazar	Mattathias
	Joseph
Maathan	Melchi
	Levi
Jacob	Maathat
(Heli)	Joahim
Joseph	Mary

§

Jesus' virgin birth is one of the mainstays of the Christian religion. How is that possible? Science suggests three ways: 1. Artificial insemination, 2. Parthenogenesis, and 3. Cloning.

Artificial insemination is a modern medical procedure. Some people consider it objectionable, mainly for religious reasons. But is has allowed many married couples to have cherished children they could not have conceived in any other way.

Cloning is an even more modern procedure, which involves the manipulation of genetic material. It has worked with a variety of animals being raised for commercial purposes. But there are serious ethical problems which prevent the application of such methods to humans.

Parthenogenesis is now a scientific term for birth from an unfertilized egg. Like many scientific words, it is derived from Greek. But unlike most of them, παρθενογένεσης is exactly the same word that is used in the original version of the New Testament. Natural parthenogenesis has been observed among arthropods, fish, and reptiles, and is suspected among amphibians and birds. It has been induced artificially in laboratory mice. The offspring are always female.

Most religions, and many ethnic groups, claim that their gods and/

or heroes were born to virgins. They include Krishna, Kama, the Buddha Gautama, Mary, Kabir, Mithras, Horus, Ra, Perseus, Hercules, Pan, Ion, Romulus & Remus, Helen of Troy, and Quetzalcoatl.

A study of interviewees' candor[126] found that 0.08% of young American women who have just given birth claim to be virgins. Those who made such a claim were twice as likely to have made a chastity vow as those who did not, and only half as likely to have been told the facts of life. The study was made to assess the credibility of data bases containing highly personal information. But it unintentionally proved that pressure to avoid sex, and withholding of information, about it increase not only the likelihood of precocious sex, but also the likelihood of lying about it.

Just a few women have publicly claimed to have given virgin birth. Not one of them permitted the simple DNA test that could have proven or disproven it.

§

The Bible does not say Jesus was born on December 25. And it does not say He was born in the Year One. Either of those statements would have been false. But it does give several hints as to his birthdate, from which we might draw some useful conclusions.

The shepherds were watching their flocks by night. They don't do that in the winter, so that eliminates the months from November through March. They congregate to watch as closely as possible during the lambing season. So the most likely time of year for Jesus' birth is late April or early May.

Matthew and Luke both give details of Jesus' birth. Matthew was found to be the more dependable for genealogy, and appears to be also for timing. Luke says that Joseph and Mary travelled to Bethlehem to be enrolled in a census when Quirinius was Governor of Syria. Both say that Herod was king when Jesus was born. Quirinius became governor in 6 AD, and Herod is traditionally said to have

[126] British Medical Journal, Christmas Edition 2013.

died in 4 BC, but new historical studies suggest it was more likely 1 or 2 BC. There is agreement from several sources that Herod was alive when Jesus was born, but died not more than a year or so afterward.

The historian Josephus tells us that Herod learned of his son's treachery during a lunar declipse, and ordered him killed. Herod himself died five days after the murder, in the 37th year of his reign. (The Battle of Actium, 31 BC, took place in the seventh year of Herod's reign.) Jewish records say Herod died on Shebat 2, which is 72 days before Passover The date of Passover varies, but it is always within a couple of weeks after the spring equinox. So Herod died during the early part of the year. There was a lunar eclipse on January 10, 1 BC. So Jesus was born before Herod died on January 26, 1 BC.[127]

Astronomy can further refine the date by considering the Star of Bethlehem. A temporary bright object in the sky can be a comet, a nova, or a conjunction.

[127] Murrrell Selden, *The Date of Herod's Death.*

Ancient peoples considered comets omens of disaster, and would hardly have accepted one as heralding the birth of the Messiah. Comets follow regular orbits, and the times of their appearances, in either the past or the future can be calculated. Halley's Comet appeared in 12 BC, too early to qualify.

Novas appear at random times, and are not predictable. Chinese astronomers have been recording novas for thousands of years. They reported a relatively small nova in 5 BC. It would have been too inconspicuous to have impressed the Magi.

A conjunction is the appearance of two planets, or a planet and a star, along the same line of sight so close together that they seem to be a single body.

Several conjunctions occurred during Herod's reign. By far the most spectacular was the triple conjunction of the two brightest planets, Venus and Jupiter, with the bright star Regulus (he King Star of the Greek astrologers) in 3 BC and 2 BC. The brightness of Venus varies, because it goes through the same sequence of phases as the Moon. During this conjunction its full face was reflecting sunlight toward Earth, and it alone was bright enough to be visible during the day.

During the last half of 3 BC Jupiter and Regulus were very close together for several months, moving westward across the eastern sky before sunrise. Then Jupiter went into retrograde motion (one of Aristotle's infamous epicycles), separated from Regulus, and appeared to earthly observers to stand still for a while. Then it was lost in the solar glare for a few months. When it emerged on the other side of the sun, it was in close conjunction with Venus in the evening sky. They moved westward together, becoming ever closer until on June 17, 2 BC they were at maximum brilliance, one of the brightest objects ever seen in the sky.

The Bible says only that the Magi came from the East. They seem to have come a long way, probably from Mesopotamia or Persia. Their actions show that they were unfamiliar with Hebrew culture, but they understood Greek astrology. Conjunction of Regulus, the 'King Star" with Jupiter, the "God Star" could mean only that a king with godlike qualities had appeared, They travelled to Jerusalem, capital of the province over which the "star" had stopped its apparent motion. From there, its celestial elevation was to the south (toward Bethlehem).

The Magi began preparing for their trip after the Star appeared, witnessed its standing still enroute, and spent some time with Herod before heading again toward the Star. It was brighter than before, and still increasing in brilliance when they reached Bethlehem.

Jesus was probably born in May, 2 BC, while shepherds in the surrounding hills were at their busiest with the newborn lambs. The Magi arrived a month or so later, and the Holy Family left for Egypt a few months after that. Herod and his son died the following January, and the Romans abolished the Kingdom of Judah, replacing it with a provincial governmen

MINISTRY

I like Christ. I do not like Christians. They are so unlike Christ.
— Mohandas K Ghandi

Jesus grew up at Nazareth in Galilee. He chose to begin his ministry in that remote province, far from the seats of power. His disciples were poor people, with little education and no connections to famous or wealthy persons,

Jesus went first to Bethabara, on the Jordan River, where he was baptized by John the Baptist. Three of John's followers, Andrew, Philip, and Nathanael,[128] followed him back to Galilee. Andrew and Philip were from Bethsaida, Nathanael was from Cana.

They went first to Nazareth – Jesus' mother Mary was with them when they arrived at Cana, where Jesus performed his first miracles. Jesus then continued to Capernaum, on the northwest shore of the Sea of Galilee, where He would reside during much of His ministry.

Why did He choose Capernaum? Not much thought has been given to that question. But recent archaeological excavations have shown that it was very fertile ground in which the Gospel could take root.

§

Two of the original three disciples had been from Bethsaida, as were all of the next three (Simon, James, and John). Five out of twelve, that's a pretty good percentage. What was special about that village that made

[128] Most scholars consider Nathanael and Bartholomew to be two different names for the same person,

it such a prolific producer of disciples?

Jesus is, enigmatically, quoted as saying, "Woe is Bethsaida". Some have interpreted this as a curse, but cursing a village would have been out of character for the Savior.

References to Bethsaida in the Bible and in other contemporary literature are ambiguous as to it location. Some scholars have concluded that there must have been two Bethsaidas. The ruins of one have been found, only quite recently, by archaeologists.[129] Most references that will not fit that location suggest a site on the east shore of the Sea, but nothing at all has been found there.

When Herod died, he had already murdered his own eldest son and heir-apparent. Each of the younger sons schemed to grab as much as he could. The Romans restored order by converting Judea into a province with an appointed governor. Each of Herod's sons was given a tiny kingdom known as a tetrarchy. Herod Antipas was named Tetrarch of Galilee, but his authority extended only from Bethsaida northward.

Archaeologist Rami Arav unearthed the remains of a Roman-style pagan temple in the midst of the ruins of Bethsaida. Its construction was dated to the First Century AD. The centerpiece was a statue of the Roman goddess Livia, who was the recently deified mother of the Emperor Tiberius. Obviously, it had been built by Herod Antipas to curry favor with the Romans in order to wheedle more concessions from them. His Jewish subjects, who were forced to worship there, must have been very unhappy. Some of them heard the distant call of John the Baptist, and decided to investigate whether he had a solution to their problem. John introduced them to Jesus, and they heard of even greater possibilities.

[129] Arav, Rami & Richard A Freud, *Bethsaida, a City by the North Shore of the Sea of Galilee.* 2 Volumes, 1995 & 1999.

Andrew quickly recruited his brother Simon (later known as Peter), and their neighbors James and John. The four men were waiting in their boats when Jesus called them from the shore, and they responded instantly. Now there were seven disciples. And the word was spreading like wildfire through the downtrodden masses of Bethsaida, and its satellite village Chorazin, that redemption was not far away.

The second village known as Bethsaida was possibly just a temporary camp for refugees fleeing from the tyrant. It may also have been the place where Jesus restored sight to the blind man. He would have been more needed, and more welcome there than in the royal city.

Bethsaida was just a few miles north of Capernaum. About the same distance to the south was another town very important in early Christian history. Its location had also been long unknown to archaeologists.

§

During the construction of a tourist hotel, in 2009, at Migdal Beach, on the west shore of the Sea of Galilee, remains of an ancient stone structure were uncovered. It was found to have been a synagogue, built in the First Century AD in the ancient town of Magdala. It contained seating for 200 worshippers, a beautiful mosaic tile floor, and a remarkable scale model of Herod's Temple in Jerusalem.[130]

Very few synagogues existed that early. Religious life was still centered red in `the Temple. There had been much anguish over the destruction of Solomon's Temple, and again over the delay in the construction of its replacement. That had finally been accomplished. But somehow it wasn't the same, Nobody fretted much anymore over the continuing absence of the Ark of the Covenant. The idea that Yahweh lived in the Temple had faded away. But the Levites continued to insist that prayers and sacrifices be offered at the Temple.

---

[130] Israel Ministry of Tourism, *Unique Ancient Synagogue exposed at the Sea of Galilee*, Sep 14, 2009.

The Bible says that Jesus taught in synagogues all over Galilee. But, with one known exception, those were not real synagogues as we know them today. They were simply places set aside in private homes or elsewhere for communal worship. The only fully authorized synagogue was in Jerusalem.

It took a lot of chutzpah for the people of Magdala to build their own synagogue. It took a lot of devotion to their God for them to have constructed it so lavishly. And, above all, it took some very rare expertise to have reproduced so meticulously the details of Herod's Temple. The designer of that model must have seen, with his own eyes, every part of the actual Temple, including the innermost Holy of Holies. Access to that area was restricted to the senior priests. One of them must have violated tradition and allowed his secret knowledge to be used in the building of this unauthorized synagogue.

Miniature Temple - Magdala Synagogue

The people of Magdala were fervently religious Jews, but at the same time they were free thinkers. They poured out their resources and their efforts for the glory of God, though they ignored tradition and authority. People who would do such things would have been predisposed to listen to the message that Jesus was bringing.

These recently discovered ruins may well be the remains of the first *de facto* Christian church. Jesus Himself sometimes led the worship of God here.

§

It is no wonder that Jesus attracted huge crowds to His outdoor meetings. Bethsaida, where Jews were suffering the imposition of pagan gods, and Magdala, where other Jews were experimenting with a new and more accessible, though unapproved, style of their own religion, were both within walking distance. Both groups needed assurance that their lifestyles would survive, and both were aware of the ancient Messianic prophecy.

Such crowds do not go unnoticed by the authorities. They imply that a novel cause is gaining public support, and might eventually threaten the Establishment. The high priests in Jerusalem were well aware of the anomalous situation in the two Galilean towns. They could do nothing about Bethsaida – Herod Antipas was a puppet of the Romans. They could not take direct action against Magdala; one of their own members was involved. Like the elites of most rigid social orders, they equated innovation with immorality. And their weapons against it were rumor and innuendo.

The common people noticed it, too. Word spread throughout the land of the star power of a new charismatic teacher. When Jesus rode humbly into Jerusalem, He was surrounded by an adoring and a raucous mob. Those in the seats of power felt themselves under siege.

§

Rumors of immoral goings-on at Magdala long outlasted their originators. They were passed along even by the disciples, and then magnified by the early church. The Magdala Temple fell into ruins, and the indiscretion of its builders was forgotten. The entire weight of the opprobrium and prurience heaped on Magdala fell upon the one Magdalene whom history remembered – Mary.

Mary of Magdala is mentioned in the canonical gospels more times than any other disciple. And she was mentioned even more often in the apocryphal gospels. All these sources agree that she was a person of good character and great wisdom. But she was a feminist; that was a no-no. And everyone "knew" that nothing good could come from Magdala.

The persistence of Mary Magdalene as a whipping-girl is well illustrated by two late Twentieth Century productions: the rock opera *Jesus Christ Superstar* and the novel *The Da Vinci Code*. Both authors treat Mary kindly, but they repeat ancient lies that are flatly contradicted by the Scriptures.

The entourage of Jesus and his disciples included a retinue of women. At least three, and possibly five or six of them were named Mary. Jesus' mother was with them, at least during the early part of His ministry. There was also Mary, the mother of James and John. In several places a Mary is mentioned with no indication of what, if any, relationship she has to anyone else. Whenever a partial list of the women is given, Mary Magdalene is always named first.

The forbidden gospels give us a more complete story of Mary Magdalene's life than do the canonical gospels. That, of course, is one of the reasons they are forbidden. The Gospel of Mary is most illuminating. Not all of it has survived, but all the known fragments have been assembled, and published along with a knowing commentary.[131]

Excepts from the prohibited gospels of Mary, Philip, and Thomas are given below, without comment. The Council of Nicaea expunged these scriptures from the Bible, and ordered all copies destroyed; they expressed concepts incompatible with Roman ideology.

The Gospel of Thomas

Simon Peter said to them, Let Mary go forth from among us, for a woman is not worthy of the life. Jesus said, Behold, I shall lead her that I may make her male, in order that she may also become a living spirit like you males. For every woman who makes herself male shall enter into the kingdom of heaven.

[131] King, Karen L, *Mary of Magdala: Jesus and the First Woman Apostle.*

The Gospel of Philip

There were three women who always walked with the Lord: Mary, His mother, and her sister, and Magdalene, who was called His companion (κοινονωος). His sister, His mother, and His companion were each a Mary.

The companion of the Savior was Mary Magdalene. Christ loved her more than all the disciples, and used to kiss her often. The rest of them were offended by it and expressed disapproval. They said to Him, Why do you love her more than us? The Savior answered and said, Why do I not love you like her?

The Gospel of Mary

Peter said to Mary, Sister, the Savior loves you more than the rest of women. Tell us the words of the Savior which you remember which you know that we do not nor have we heard them. Mary tells of Jesus appearing to her in a vision [the following text remains lost] *Andrew and Peter do not take for granted what she says, because she is a woman. Did He then speak secretly to a woman, in preference to us? Are we to turn back and listen to her? Did He prefer her to us? Then Mary grieved and said to Peter, My brother, what* [the rest is missing] *Levi said, Who are you to reject her? The Savior knew her very well. For this reason he loved her more than us.*

MIRACLES

Love is the magician that pulls man out of his own hat.
— Ben Hecht

A miracle is an event whose explanation is beyond the understanding of the observer. Educated observers see fewer miracles than their ignorant counterparts.

The ancient world was full of miracles. The causes of natural phenomena were unknown. Supernatural agents were given credit for the results, whether beneficial or disastrous. Clever or unscrupulous men claimed to have influence over such agents, to enhance their own wealth and power.

There were also human miracles: birth and death, sickness and health, sanity and madness, courage and cowardice, ambition and sloth. Medical and psychological phenomena were as poorly understood as physical phenomena.

Every society ascribed miraculous powers to its gods and religious leaders. Rulers employed prophets and magicians. They sometimes made lucky guesses, and saw to it that those successes were well publicized. More often, they promoted confidence among the timid, and encouraged the carrying out of projects that were inherently likely to succeed, if only someone had the drive to get started. By keen. observation they learned much about psychology and natural phenomena, but they kept that knowledge secret, and used it for their personal profit. At the very least, they were good entertainers. The common people loved them, and put unwarranted trust in their supposed supernatural powers.

Hesitant rulers sometimes demanded "signs" before they would undertake a seemingly risky action. The magicians offered all sorts of slight-of-hand tricks and false promises Their profession is still flourishing today. Nearly all of them now are honest enough to call themselves "illusionists".

§

Jesus wanted nothing to do with this kind of action. He wasn't here to entertain people, He was here to save them. And He certainly wasn't going to deceive anyone. Of course, He could perform miracles, either real or apparent, but he consistently chose not to do so unless it would relieve suffering. He never spoke of his miracles, and He never claimed supernatural powers. He repeatedly warned the disciples not to speak of miracles, either those that He had performed or those that He assured them they could perform.

Perhaps the Savior's attitude toward miracles is best illustrated by the story of His temptations. This story is especially worthy of our attention because it had to have been told first by Jesus Himself – no one else was present at the event.

Two of the three temptations involved Jesus' refusal to perform a miracle. Each time He stated His reason, and gave us food for thought. To the suggestion that he change stones to bread, He responded with the old adage, "Man does not live by bread alone". He would not do an unnecessary act just to prove he could. So we should not waste time or resources on projects that serve only to boost our egos.

When told that God would save Him from harm if He jumped from the top of the Temple, He answered, "Thou shalt not tempt thy God". It is wrong to ask God to protect us from our own stupidly dangerous actions. In a way, such a request would be 'taking the name of the Lord in vain".

(The final temptation did not involve miracles. It showed that a person confronted by a choice between right and wrong should always choose the right, even though it may be to his apparent disadvantage.)

Jesus entered his active ministry having stated clearly that miracles were not to be used to draw attention to Him or His message, or to impress the gullible. He wanted people to worship the Loving God, not a sly sorcerer. The only emotion that Jesus showed in connection with His miracles was love for the person whose suffering was being alleviated.

§

Then certain of the scribes and of the pharisees, answered saying, We would see a sign from thee. But He answered and said unto them, An evil and adulterous generation seeketh a sign, and there shall be no sign given to it, bu the sign of the prophet Jonas.[132] *— Matthew 12;38-40.*

The Pharisees and also the Saducees came, and tempting, desired Him that He should shew a sign from heaven. He answered and said unto them, When it is evening, ye say, It will be fair for the sky is red. And in the morning it will be foul weather to day, for the sky is red and lowering[133]***. O ye hypocrites, ye can discern the face of the sky, but can ye not discern the sign of the times?*** *— Matthew 16: 1-3*

And the Pharisees came forth and began to question Him, seeking of Him a sign from heaven, to tempt Him. And He sighed deeply for His spirit, and saith, Verily I say unto you, There shall no sign be given.
— Mark 8: 11-12

And when the people were gathered thick togerher, He began to say, This is an evil generation: they seek a sign,

[132] Apparently a reference to Jonah's three days in the belly of a great fish, as a premonition of Jesus' three days in the tomb. He wanted people to remember no other miracle.

[133] Red sky in the morning – sailor take warning, Red sky at night - sailor's delight. This folklore has a scientific basis. Red light is reflected from the bottom of a cloud low on one horizon when the sun is low on the opposite horizon. A cloud in the west is approaching. A cloud in the east is moving away.

and there shall be no sign given. *– Luke 11:29*

The Gospel of John was written almost a century later by an author who never met Jesus. It is replete with second-hand tales of miracles. Since the synoptic gospels agree unanimously that Jesus refused to perform unnecessary miracles, such tales must be considered hearsay.

§

Now, when Jesus was risen early on the first day of the week, He appeared first to Mary Magdalene, out of whom He had cast out seven devils. *– Mark 16;9*

This is one of the most spectacular, and yet one of the most enigmatic of Jesus' miracles.

Mary Magdalene suffered psychogenic non-epileptic seizures.[134] Jesus had a perfect understanding of psychiatry, and the ability to read brain waves without equipment. Successful treatment of the disease involves repeated (perhaps seven times) counseling, with great patience and loving sensitivity to the sufferer's concerns. A cure effected in this way may be permanent.[135] Such a complete cure of this terrible disease by a modern psychiatrist may still be called a miracle.

It is not unusual for s\a young woman who has been cured of a debilitating disease by extended treatment to fall in love with her doctor, The exact relationship between Jesus and Mary Magdalene is unknown, and rightly so. Whatever that relationship might have been, it cannot change the fact that Jesus Christ was the Savior of all humanity, nor that Mary Magdalene, his devoted disciple, was a good and decent woman.

§

The disciples were thoroughly impressed by Jesus' miracles,

[134] Pre-treatment diagnosis of this ailment requires electroencephalogram analysis. This post-treatment diagnosis is based on symptoms, length and nature of treatment, and nature of recovery.

[135] Benbadis S R, Heriaut L, *Psychogenic Non'Epileptic Seisures, A Handbook for Families and Patients.*

but only partially understood their purpose. They understood that, with enough faith and love, they could perform many of the same acts. (Anyone can – and knowledge of the scientific principles involved helps.)

Their exuberant reports, in the Book of Acts, of the crowds that gathered to witness the miracles appear a little overblown. It sounds more like an audience than a congregation.

§

The miracle of Jesus' calming the sea is worth examining. It is reported in all three of the synoptic gospels. They agree that (1) Jesus was asleep, (2) the waves came up suddenly and almost swamped the boat, (3) the disciples were frantic, and (4) Jesus first criticized them for their lack of faith and then told the waves to cease.

Translations of these verses vary, and commentaries on them fly into wild speculation. Let's look at the original words.

Matthew 8-24

Και ιδου σεισμος μεγαζ εγεντο εν θαλασοη τήν.
Mark 4:37

Και γινετοι λαϊλαψ μεγάλη άνέμου...
Luke 8:23

Πλεόντων δέ αυτών αφρύπνωσεν. Και καιέβη λαϊλαψ ανέμουα είς, τήν λίμνην, και σηυνεπληροϋντο και έκινδύνευον.

Both Mark and Luke use the word "lailaps", which is best translated "squall", to describe the disturbance. Nowhere are the words for "storm" or "tempest" used, though those words are found in many translations. Matthew is more direct – he calls it "seismos". Anyone who lives in California knows that "seismos" means "earthquake".

The Dead Sea Transform Fault runs near the east shore of the Sea of Galilee. The Golan Heights area is moving northward, with respect to the Sea, at about one inch per five years. It is not a steady movement. The strain builds up over many decades before it is finally released, sending tremors through nearby land and water. The disturbance in the water begins suddenly, continues for a few minutes, and then dies down.

Jesus knew what was going on, and His faith told him when and how it would end. He expressed his disappointment that His disciples did not share that faith.

Magic and supernatural powers do not make miracles. Knowledge and faith make miracles.

§

Greeks and Romans both loved to tell and hear amazing stories. Their mythology abounded with tales of miracles performed by a myriad of gods. Those stories had to be matched if they were going to give up their colorful religions for a new faith.

The Gospel of John put more emphasis on miracles than had the synoptic gospels. Its writer was less familiar with Jesus' admonition to not make a big deal of miracles. The disciples went a little farther in rejoicing at the huge crowds that gathered to witness their "signs".

The Greek version of the Torah, the Septuagint, included several questionable translations that made Old Testament events seem more miraculous than the original Hebrew had implied.

The concept of sainthood was first applied only to Christian martyrs. After Christianity became the established religion, and martyrs were scarce, other persons believed to have lived exemplary lives were granted the title of "Saint". When some bishops became too generous in canonizing questionable candidates, during the Middle Ages, that power was restricted solely to the Pope. The rules have changed from time to time, but always require proof of miracles performed directly by, or following a prayer in the name of, the candidate.

In modern times 99% of the approved miracles have been medical in nature. When John Paul II made the latest update to the procedure for canonization, he remarked that, as medical science advances, acceptable miracles become scarcer.

CHRISTIANITY

Conformity is the jailer of freedom and the enemy of growth.
— John Fitzgerald Kennedy

It is said that Jesus spoke Aramaic. Presumably His disciples did too, and also the people to whom h\ He spoke,

Aramaic was the Semitic language of the Assyrian and Babylonian Empires. The Jews adopted it during the Captivity, between 710 and 500 BC, keeping their own language only for religious use. Much of the Books of Daniel and Ezra, and a few fragments of other Old Testament books, were written in Aramaic.

But all three of Jesus' disciples who wrote gospels wrote them in Greek. The epistles of Saint Paul and others, even those to the Hebrews and to the Romans, were written in Greek. There is virtually no Christian literature in Aramaic. Greek was the language of nearly all early Christians, until the faith had spread to areas beyond Roman control.

Alexander the Great impressed Greek government, culture, and language firmly on all the countries he conquered between 335 and 323 BC. He established seventeen cities, all named Alexandria. The largest of them, on the Mediterranean shore of Egypt, was meant to be the capital of his worldwide empire. Though the empire fell apart with his death, Alexandria was the world's largest city until two centuries later, when Rome succeeded to that distinction.

By about 200 BC Greek had become the vernacular of Syria and Egypt, and the language of the upper classes, businessmen, and government officials in Judea. Those who still spoke Aramaic were mostly illiterate. There were more Jews in Alexandria than there were in Jerusalem, and they all spoke Greek.

Ptolemy II, King (not Pharaoh) of Egypt and son of one of Alexander's generals, ordered the Hebrew Torah translated into Greek for the benefit of his Jewish subjects. The resulting Septuagint served as the first edition of the Christian Old Testament.

Rome conquered the Greek city-states and the remains of the western part of Alexander's empire in a series of wars between 146 BC and 63 BC. The Romans excelled in military power, engineering, and political organization. But they recognized that the Greeks were far ahead of them in philosophy, science, and art. They took advantage of the resources that had come under their control, and fostered continued flowering and expansion of Greek culture.

The Emperor Constantine was such an admirer of the Greeks that he moved his capital from Rome to the Greek city of Byzantium in 324 AD. Its name was later changed to Constantinople.

Constantine had already decreed an end to the persecution of religious minorities. He wanted law and order within the Empire, and that meant doing away with religious strife. He noticed that, when left alone, Christians were orderly, and even docile. They accepted the vicissitudes of earthly life in anticipation of a heavenly reward. They disagreed, both as individuals and as congregations, on theology and morals. Constantine's mother, Saint Helena, was a Christian and had made a pilgrimage to the Holy Land.

The earliest Christians enjoyed considerable freedom of conscience. They developed a great diversity in their beliefs and ceremonies, and a vast trove of literature was scattered among their many churches. The message of Christ was being effectively spread, but in a manner that was too messy for Roman tastes.

Constantine called leaders of churches from all over the Empire (nearly all were in the Greek-speaking eastern part) to a council in Nicaea in 325. The Council ironed out some theological disputes, wrote the Nicene Creed, and assembled the Bible. They then had a clear statement of what Jesus was and what He was not, of what Christians must and must not believe, and what they may or may not read. That was the Roman way of doing things, and Constantine was now ready to promote missionary efforts which eventually made Christianity the official religion of the Roman Empire.

Not all Christians were eager to accept Constantine's largesse. Some felt that Roman pomposity, prudery, pageantry, and authoritarianism were inconsistent with Jesus' teachings. But the power of imperial sponsorship was just too much to refuse.

The few delegates who refused to endorse the Council's decisions were expelled from the Church. The Nicene Creed became part of the liturgy, and its acceptance was required by all Christians.

BIBLE

Censorship ends in logical completeness when nobody is allowed to read any books except the books that nobody reads.
— George Bernard Shaw

Bible" is the English form of the Greek word "Βίβλα". The Septuagint, with some minor rearrangement, became the Old Testament. Many Christian writings were available from which to construct the New Testament. But those accepted had to agree with Roman ideals. The authority of the Emperor was to be unchallenged. Male supremacy was honored. But a feminine deity, subordinate to male deities was required. Sex was treated as basically dirty. (A legacy from Rome's infamous Rape of the Sabine Women.)

The final result was declared the "Infallible Word of God". Christians were forbidden to continue reading the rejected scriptures, and all copies were ordered destroyed. A few churches far from Nicaea, some of them outside the borders of Rome, did not comply. Archaeologists have found many of those distant document caches, and made them available to modern scholars. But some irreplaceable material disappeared forever. The most grievous loss was the burning of the great Library of Alexandria in 391[136] by Bishop Theophilus, who interpreted his instructions to mean that all literature except the approved Bible was to be destroyed. No one will ever know how much ancient history and wisdom was lost for all time by this barbaric act of vandalism.

At least twenty-two gospels were in use. Only four were retained.

[136] Earlier accidental fires may have destroyed parts of it, but this one was intentional, and finished it off.

Matthew, Mark, and Luke were all written by individuals who had known Jesus, and were writing from their memories within a few decades after the events. The Gospel of John is a compilation of stories from various second-hand sources, written down a century later.

The rejected Gospel of James could have been important. It is ironic that this Gospel was expunged from the Bible. The Catholic Church has proclaimed as dogma several ideas that were documented only by James. It states that Mary's mother was a virgin. It gives the information needed to settle the bitter, ongoing argument over Mary's lifelong virginity. Like the accepted gospels, it names several individuals as Jesus' brothers, but it alone explains their exact relationship. According to James, the Jewish elders selected the aged widower Joseph as a suitable husband to protect the purity of the 12-year-old virgin in their care. Joseph had several children, the oldest of whom was James. (James the Just, James the Greater, James the "brother" of Jesus, James the Bishop of Jerusalem). James believed that Christians should also be Jews, and it was probably Paul's opposition to that point of view that kept his gospel out of the Bible.

Only fragments of the Gospel of Mary have survived. They probably constitute about half the original work. This gospel shows that Mary Magdalene was with the disciples much of the time after the Resurrection, and that she played an active part in their discussions. Some of them resented both her closeness to Jesus and her assumption of equal status with men. But they did ask her advice in interpreting some of Jesus' sayings. This gospel could obviously not be in the Bible, because of its feminism and the faint suggestion that the Savior might have had a romantic interest.

The Gospel of Thomas consists largely of a list of sayings attributed to Jesus. Most of them are duplicated in other gospels, either canonical or non-canonical. The extant copy is written in Egyptian Coptic, but was probably translated from a

Greek original. Little would have been gained by including this gospel in the Bible.

The Gospel of Philip is religious dynamite! It should not be even mentioned without a thorough examination of its source. The surviving copy was bound in the same leather codex as the Gospel of Thomas and several other works. It was one of thirteen such codices packed together in an earthenware container and buried in the desert of Upper Egypt near Nag Hammadi. The texts were all written in Coptic, but most of them showed signs of having been translated from Greek.

The cache was unearthed accidentally in 1945 by Arab peasants. They hid them, hoping to profit from a sale. Their superstitious mother burned several, fearing they contained evil spirits. Unscrupulous antiquity dealers traded and retraded them. It was more than three decades before they were retrieved and made available for scholarly study.

Scholars dated the pottery and the leather binding to the Fourth Century. The text had been written in the Third and Fourth centuries, but some sections appeared to have been translated from Second Century writings. The Gospels of Thomas and Philip, and several other documents were written by the same person. The Christian monastery at Nag Hammadi was ordered, in 368, to destroy all non-canonical literature. It had one of the finest collections of such literature in existence. They circumvented the order and used the best technology they had to preserve their library, and then put it where it remained hidden for sixteen centuries.

The Gospel of Philip called Mary Magdalene the "partner" ("κοινονως") of Jesus. That word has, in some cases, been translated as "wife". The Gospel states unequivocally that Jesus and Mary Magdalene frequently shared physical affection.[137] It also quotes Jesus as saying Mary Magdalene was a full-fledged disciple. That text is considered

[137] Dan Brown's novel *The Da Vinci Code* was inspired by the publication of the Gospel of Philip. The novel itself is fiction.

by most scholars to be a strong endorsement of women in the priesthood.

This radical concept is an anathema to Roman religious tradition, but not to early Christians. Roman temples were cared for by the vestal virgins. The Cybilene Cult, a rapidly spreading part of the Roman religious establishment required priests to be castrated.

Most early Christian priests, including the early popes, were married and had children. A few women had already served as priests. Most of the delegates at the Council of Nicaea were married men, and a proposal to require clerical celibacy was rejected.

The only early Christian texts to specifically criticize sex were Saint Paul's letters to the Corinthians. Paul himself was a Roman, though his mother was Jewish. It would have been unusual for a Roman to have been unmarried, but after his conversion (age about 30) he had no wife. Corinth was the "Las Vegas of the ancient world" with flourishing gambling and prostitution.

During the 1600 years that the Gospel of Philip was suppressed and hidden, some of the pagan practices it criticized became Christian dogma.

Fourteen other gospels are known, some of them only as fragments. For the most part they parallel or duplicate the gospels already discussed. There is nothing else worthy of detailed scrutiny. There are also a couple of dozen possible supplements to the Book of Acts, which are of uncertain origin and questionable value.

Most of the epistles included in the Bible are attributed to Paul, altho1ugh it is known that at least one of them was not written by him. Many other such letters must exist, but they are not accessible. The Bible had to end with an apocalyptic book. There were about a dozen available in learly Christian literature. The choice might as well have been random. All are equally macabre, unintelligible, and unlikely.

The final result of the Council's work was a stripped-down heavily Romanized version of the Hebrew and early Christian scriptures. Constantine approved it for use in the Greek-speaking part of the Empire, and ordered it translated into the contemporary degraded Latin then spoken in the western portions. St. Jerome spent the rest of the century creating the Vulgate Bible. The Vulgate remains the official Bible of the Roman Catholic Church to this day, though in the last century or so some translations have been approved. Within 200 years of its appearance, Vulgate Latin was no longer comprehenslible to the average person, but the Mass continued to be said in Latin. A few wealthy persons had fragments translated for their personal use, and some missionaries translated portions into languages that had not been written before. But the Bible became inaccessible, and almost unknown, to nearly all Christians. From about the time of the Crusades to the end of the Medieval Ages translations were forbidden and, in some cases, burned.

The first English Bible, translated by John Wycliffe in the late Fourteenth Century, was widely distributed, despite the Church's official ban on it. Wycliffe was declared a heretic, and after his death his body was dug up and desecrated,

One of the principal aims of the Protestant Reformers in the Sixteenth Century was to make available to every Christian a Bible in the language he could understand. They had a new tool, the printing press, which made that objective more attainable. Printed Bibles in every major European language soon appeared. Replacing earlier, poorer translations, the King James Version of the English Bible appeared in 1611. It was an eloquent and very readable example of Sixteenth Century English. But 400 years later it makes about as much sense as did the Vulgate at the same age.

The Catholic Church responded by producing the Douai English Bible, in several sections, the final one in 1635. A second edition a century later had better integrated text and smoother flowing language. Catholics were allowed, though not encouraged to read this Bible, but it could not be used in the Mass until 1968.

BIBLESE

When you talk to a man in a language he understands, you speak to his head;
when you talk to him in his own language, you speak to his heart.
Nelson Mandela

"Biblese" is the dialect of English spoken in England and the Colonies during the Sixteenth and Seventeenth Centuries. Both the Douai and the King James Versions of the Bible are written in this dialect.

Much of the misunderstanding of the Bible comes from the widespread use of Versions written in a language which nobody normally speaks.

Queen Elizabeth I (ruled 1558-1603) ordered a new translation of the Bible to be used in English churches. Most of the work was done during her reign, but finishing touches were added after her death, and her successor King James ordered it published.

To fully understand the Bible, one must read it in his own native language that he speaks every day. If he prefers not to do that, he must study the language in which his Bible is written as thoroughly as he would study the language of a foreign country to which he is planning to move.

This chapter explains the principal differences in grammar, pronunciation, and vocabulary between Sixteenth Century English and early Twenty-first Century English.§

The most noticeable change in the English language over the last 400 years has been loss of the distinction between formal and familiar speech. This affects the forms of personal pronouns and verbs.

Personal Pronouns (obsolete forms are in red.)

Person	Singular				Plural			
	Nom.	Obj.	Pos. A.	Pos. P.	Nom.	Obj.	Pos. A.	Pos. P.
1st	**I**	**me**	**my, mine***	**mine**	**we**	**us**	**our**	**ours**
2nd Fam.	**thou**	**thee**	**thy, thine**	**thine**	**ye**	**you**	**your**	**yours**
2nd Form.	**ye**	**you**	**your**	**yours**	**you**	**you**	**your**	**yours**
3rd	**he** **she** **it**	**him** **her** **it**	**his** **her** **his***	**his** **hers** **his**	**they**	**them**	**their**	**theirs**

*The forms "mine", "thine", and "an" were used before words beginning with a vowel or with an "h" (always silent). The word "its" did not yet exist.

Verb Conjugations

Present Tense								
I	**walk**	**give**	**do**	**am**	**have**	**see**	**speak**	**help**
hethou	**walkest**	**givest**	**dost**	**art**	**havest**	**seest**	**speakest**	**helpest**
ye	**walk**	**give**	**do**	**are**	**have**	**see**	**speak**	**help**
he	**walketh**	**giveth**	**doth**	**is**	**haveth**	**seeth**	**speaketh**	**H\helpeth**
(plural)	**walk**	**give**	**do**	**are**	**has**	**see**	**speak**	**help**
Past Tense								
I	**walked**	**gave**	**did**	**was**	**had**	**saw**	**spake**	**holp**
thou	**walkedst**	**gavest**	**didst**	**wert**	**hadst**	**sawest**	**spakest**	**holpest**
(others)	**walked**	**gave**	**did**	**were**	**had**	**saw**	**spake**	**holp**

The future was formed just as it is now, with the auxiliary verbs **will** and **shall**, both of which were conjugated as modal verbs. (See below) Much closer attention was paid to the reversed ut usw of these auxiliaries to show emphasis.

Pwefect tenses were formed by auxiliary verbs followed by the past participle. The auxiliary was usually a form of **to have**, but with reflexive verbs and verbs of motion **to be** was used instead. Thus **he is gone** is best translated into modern language as **he has gone.**

There were more modal verbs then than there are now. Modal verbs have only partial conjugation, and are usually used as auxiliaries. Some of the commonest modal verbs were:

Present Tense						
Usual form	will	shall	can	may	must	dare
thou form	wilt	shalt	canst	mayest	must	darest
Other tenses						
Usual form	would	should	could	might	must	durst
thou for	wouldst	shouldst	couldst	mightest	must	durst

The progressive verb form, now very common, was rarely used. It consists of a form of **to be** plus the present participle. The sam meaning was then expressed by the basix text. Thus, instead of **he goeth**, we would say **he is going**.

In negative sentences the word **not** followed the verb or the first word of s compound word. Forms of **don't** were not used. The phrase **look not** is, in modern speech, **don't look.**

Most of the many changes in pronunciation are unimportant to readers. Initial **h** was always silent, requiring a preceding **mine**, **thine**, or **an**. The ending **–ed** was always a separate syllable, changing the cadence of poetry. (The **e** is now silent except after **d** or **t**)

GLOSSARY

Words that have fallen into disuse or assumed different meanings since the publication of the King James Bible, with translations into modern English.

King James Word	Modern Word	King James Word	Modern Word	King James Word	Modern Word
abide	reside	bowels	interior	coulter	plowshare
abode	home	bravery	splendor	cousin	relative
admire	be amazed at	brethren	brothers	covert	shelter
adventure	hazard	brigadine	armor	cracknel	biscuit
affinity	relationship	broid	braid	crib	manger
	by marriage	bruit	rumor	crisping pin	hairpin
afore	before	buckler	small shield	crookbackt	hunchbacked
agone	ago	bunches	swelling	cruse	carafe
amaze	terrify	by and by	right now	cubit	19 inches
ambassage	delegation	cab	2/3 gallon	cuckow	gull
amerce	penalize	carbuncle	gem	cumber	burden
anathema	curse	carefulness	anxiety	dandy	fondle
ancient	elder	carriage	cargo	dash	hit
angle	fishing gear	caul	fat	daysman	mediator
apple	(any fruit)	causeway	paved road	descry	discover
aright	correctly	celled	paneled	despite	scorn
armhole	armpit	champaign	prairie	diet	allowance
assay	try	chapter	head of line	digged	dug
astonied	astonished	chapt	cracked	disannul	abolish
attent	attentive	charger	platter	discomfit	defeat
avouched	affirmed	cherub(im)	small angel(s)	dissemble	pretend
away with	endure	chide	argue	dissimulate	pretend

King James Word	Modern Word	King James Word	Modern Word	King James Word	Modern Word
bakenmeats	baked food	chode	argued	distil	drip
bason	bowl	churl	bum	doctor	teacher
bath	8 gallons	clave	split (past)	drave	drove
beeves	oxen	cleave	split (pres)	dure	endure
begat	sired	clove	split (past)	emerod	hemorrhoid
beget	sire	cloven	split (p part)	emulate	rival
besom	broom	clift	hollow	endamage	damage
bestead	distressed	clouts	patch	endue	introduce
bethink	remember	cockatrice	snake	enlarge	set free
betimes	soon	cockle	weed	ensample	sample
bewitch	fascinate	collops	flesh	environ	surround
bewray	reveal	comely	suitable	ephah	8 gallons
blains	sores	company	accompany	ephod	priest's cape
blaze	announce	coney	rabbit	espoused	engaged
blueness	bruise	confection	mixture	euroclydon	gale
boisterous	strong	contemn	despise	fain	gladly
boiled	swollen	converse	cohabitate	farthing	½ cent
bolster	cushion	corn	(any grain)	fats	Vat
botch	ulcer	cote	shed	felloes	Rim
firkins	cask	lapwing	plover	omer	½ pint
fitches	spice	latchet	thong	ossifrage	vulture
flag	reed	laver	washbasin	ouch	gem setting
flagon	pitcher	lease	deceive	outdoings	boundaries
flesh	meat	leathern	made of leather	peradventure	perhaps
flesnnook	fishhook	lees	dregs	phylactery	book cover
flowers	menstruation	let	hinder	pilled	peeled
flux	diarrhea	libertine	freed slave	platted	woven
forbear	endure	lieen	lain (or laid)	pommel	knob
foreship	bow of boat	liking	condition	pottage	stew
forswear	renounce	lively	alive	prate	boast
forum	market	lowering	gloomy	presently	now

King James Word	Modern Word	King James Word	Modern Word	King James Word	Modern Word
fourscore	eighty	lusty	robust	press	crowd
forward	stubborn	magnifical	glorious	prevent	precede
fray	scare	malignity	malice	prey	loot
furlong	220 yards	mallow	inedible	prick	goad
furniture	equipment	mammon	wealth	privy	in on
gainsay	contradict	mandrake	aphrodisiac	provender	fodder
Gay	happy	marish	marsh	psaltery	harp
gender	generate	matrix	womb	publican	tax collector
gerah	1/20 shekel	maul	hammer	pulse	beans
Gin	snare	,aw	stomach	purtenance	intestines
greave	leg armor	meat	food	pygand	antelope
halbergeon	vest armor	meet	properf	quaternion	set of four
haft	handle	mess	food portion	quick	ali e
hale	pull	meteyard	allotment	quit	release
halt	lame	minish	diminish	rank	full grown
hard	near	mite	small coin	rase	raze
heady	headstrong	mixt	mixed	raven	plunder
helve	handle	mock	deceive	ravin	plunder
hence	from here	morrow	tomorrow	redound	exceed
high-minded	arrogant	mortify	destroy	rehearse	report
Hin	6 quarts	mote	speck	reins	heart
hoar	aged	munition	fortification	rend	tear
holden	held	murrain	animal	requite	retaliate
homer	81 gallons		disease	rereward	rear guard
hosen	stockings	napkin	handkerchief	rifle	rob
howbeit	nevertheless	naught	nothing	ringstrake	stripe
hyssop	a small plant	nave	hub	rising	swelling
implead	sue	necromancer	fortune teller	rue	herb
infold	contain	neese	sneeze	sackbut	trumpet
inkhorn	inkwell	nephew	male	saith	says
instant	urgent		descendant	seethe	boil
Jot	tiny bit	noisome	offensive	sod	boiled

King James Word	Modern Word	King James Word	Modern Word	King James Word	Modern Word
kine	cows	oblation	offering	sodden	Boiled
knop	knob	offend	lead astray	shew	show
shittim	acacia	thyme	thyra wood	verily	surely
seraph(im)	angel(s)	timbrel	tambourine	viol	violin
slay	kill	tittle	scribble	visage	face
slew	killed	tow	flax fiber	waymark	guidepost
slewn	killed	train	proceession	wen	lump
slain	killed	translate	transport	wench	girl servant
spake	spoke	travail	work	whale	sea monster
strait	straight	trow	trust	whence	from where
strait	sincere	turtle	dove	whilst	while
sware	swore	twain	two	whit	know
Tale	linden	twine	twist	wimple	headdress
Tell	quota	unction	anointing	wise	manner
Tell	tally	vagabond	fugitive	wist	knew
tempt	attempt	vail	curtain	wit	know
teraph(im)	idol(s)	valour	importance	wot	know
thence	from there	variance	disagreement	wreathen	woven
hither	to there	vaunt	boast	wroth	angry
threescore	sixty	venture	event	ye	you (pl)

CHURCH

For where two or three are gathered together in my name there am I in the midst of them.
— Matthew 18:20

This statement by the Savior shows that a church need not be large, or organized. On another occasion He said "Render unto Caesar that which is. Caesar's, and unto God that which is God's". That one shows that the Church is meant to be independent of the State. In the forbidden Gospel of Philip[138] Jesus stated that Mary Magdalene was a full-fledged disciple, indicating that men and women are equals in church affairs. How have we done in following our Lord's instructions?

The first church consisted of the eleven remaining disciples. It rapidly expanded to seventy members, all called apostles. Then they dispersed to found new churches.

These early Christians considered themselves Jews who accepted Jesus as the long-promised Messiah. They began their missionary efforts on that basis. Each of the surviving disciples carried the gospel to some other country.

Peter went to Rome. He is considered the first pope, though that office did not then exist.

James, son of Zebedee, went to Spain.

John, James' brother, went to Ephesus, capital of the Roman province of Asia. He took Mary, mother of Jesus, with him, and cared for her the rest of her life.

[138] All copies were ordered destroyed by the Council of Nicaea. It has never been removed from the Catholic Church's list of prohibited books.

Philip went to Syria and Greece, and then to Hierapolis in Roman Asia.

Bartholomew (AKA Nathanael) is said to have gone to India, and then returned to Armenia.

Thomas established the Christian community at Goa, India.

Matthew worked first on Cyprus, and then established many churches in Upper Egypt.

James, son of Alphaeus, is said to have preached in Syria and Lower Egypt.[139]

Thaddeus (AKA Jude) went to Syria and Armenia.

Simon is said to have been in Syria, Persia, and Armenia, but the evidence is ambiguous.

Leader of the Jerusalem Christians was James, the step-brother of Jesus. He bore the title "bishop", though there was no official ordination. He was the author of the Gospel of James. He strongly advocated the position that a person must be, or become, a Jew before he could be baptized into the Christian Church. In this he was strongly opposed by the Apostle Paul.

Paul was a Roman. He was thoroughly versed in the culture and religion of Rome. He knew the wants and needs of the Roman people, and he knew how to package the Christian message to be attractive to them. That package definitely did not include circumcision, which was repulsive to Romans and even more so to Greeks.

Christians were persecuted almost everywhere. The way to stop that was to get government approval. But in most cases the monarch's approval is just a step away from his sponsorship. The religious organization must then adapt to the monarch's philosophy.

Most potential converts would quickly accept the religion of their ruler. Doing so not only protects them against persecution, it enhances their career prospects.

[139] There were three James's among the early Christians. Some source materials do not clearly distinguish them from each other,

In 301 AD Armenia, an independent kingdom under Roman protection, adopted Christianity as its official religion. The Armenian Apostolic Church still maintains its identity, in Armenia and among Armenian expatriates throughout the world. It has avoided subjection to any other religious authority.

The Roman Empire itself was the major target for conversion. Persecution of Christians in Rome had begun under Nero, and continued unabated for two centuries. Constantine became Emperor in 306, and granted religious freedom to all. He called Christian leaders together at the Council of Nicaea in 325, to organize the Church along Roman administrative lines, and to state its beliefs in terms compatible with Roman ideals. The resultant Roman Catholic Church had a hierarchy centered in Rome and a formal Creed to which all Christians were required to subscribe. The Council decided which literature would be included in the Bible, and which would be destroyed. All churches within the bounds of the Empire complied with the Council's orders. Individuals who refused were simply declared heretics.

Saint Paul was the person who had the most influence on the makeup of the New Testament, even though he was not present at the Council. He wrote more than half the books included, and was given credit for some he hadn't written. Most of the material excluded was put on the forbidden list. The Gospel of James was excluded, but not forbidden. The only apparent reason for its exclusion was the disagreement between James and Paul.

Outside the Empire it was different. The Armenian Church remained separate.

Egypt was in a state of turmoil. Rome had only recently replaced Alexandria as the largest city in the world. Christians (and Jews) in Alexandria far outnumbered those in Rome. Since the Diaspora of 71 AD there had been more Jews in Alexandria than in Jerusalem. Although Greek was the official language of Lower Egypt, most of the common people spoke Coptic, as did everyone in Upper Egypt. An extensive monastic system had translated all the Scriptures, canonical and otherwise, into Coptic. The Bishop of Alexandria was being called Pope almost as soon as was the Bishop of Rome.

A series of councils following Nicaea tried to iron out the differences. The arguments, on both sides, sound ridiculous today, although there are still a few theologians who can get upset about such things. By 451 AD the differences were irreconcilable. The Coptic Orthodox Church was separated from the Roman Catholic Church. (The Armenian Church also formalized its separation at this time.)

There were many Coptic churches in Upper Egypt, and even in Ethiopia, both of which were outside the area of Roman control. Coptic monks not only preserved the forbidden Scriptures, they translated the entire Bible, canonical and non-canonical, into the Coptic language.

The Muslim conquest of Egypt during the Seventh Century started the decline of the Coptic Church. Conversion of the population went rather slowly, and it was the Twelfth Century before Moslems outnumbered Christians in Egypt. The Copts remain a significant minority in Egypt even today and there are expatriot Coptic churches in many countries.

As the Coptic Church weakened, the Ethiopian Church moved out on its own, incorporating much of the culture of its people. The emperors of Ethiopia claimed descent from Solomon and the Queen of Sheba. It is also claimed that the Ark of the Covenant, which disappeared from Jerusalem in 707 BC, is in Ethiopia

The church founded in India by Saint Thomas existed in isolation until 1510, when the area was conquered by Portugal. It then became part of the Roman Catholic Church,

§

While the Church in the East was coming apart, in the West it was growing rapidly, in both membership and authority. Romans were accustomed to a strong central government. But their Emperor was now enjoying the good life in far off Constantinople.

For a while there were two emperors. The western emperor was never very strong. He could neither command the loyalty of the people, nor resist the incursions of the barbarians. Those barbarians who accepted Christianity were allowed to live in the Empire, and enjoy its material benefits. By such means the Church was increasing its power and spreading its influence even as the Empire was disintegrating.

When the last western emperor resigned in 477, the Pope became the effective ruler of the western world.

Pepin the Short unified, and seized control of all Frankish lands, both inside and outside the Empire. When Pope Stephen II recognized him as "King of the Franks" in 764, Pepin conquered, and donated to the Pope, for his personal support, all of central Italy, thereafter known as the "Patrimony of Saint Peter".[140].[141]

Pepin's son Charlemagne conquered most of western Europe, and was crowned Emperor in 810 by Pope Leo III. This new empire soon split into the Kingdom of France and the Holy Roman Empire (not Roman, but German; not an empire, but an agglomeration of warring states, and certainly not holy).

The power of the medieval popes is illustrated by an event in 1078. Holy Roman Emperor Henry IV stood three days in the snow begging for an audience to perform obeisance before Pope Gregory VII.

Increasing dissention between the Greek- and Latin-speaking parts of the Church resulted, in 1054,

---

[140] The independent state of Vatican City is the modern remnant of that donation.

[141] Pepin's refusal to return any of the conquered lands to the eastern Emperor marked the effective end of a unified empire. The West broke up into national kingdoms, and the East became the Byzantine Empire.

in the Pope and the Patriarch (Archbishop) of Constantinople excommunicating one another. Thus was born the Byzantine Orthodox Church. The eastern church abandoned some of the stricter rules of the Catholic Church. Clerical celibacy was no longer required. While Greek was the preferred language, translations of the Bible into, and celebrating the mass in, vernacular languages was permitted.

§

Papal authority became absolute during the late Middle Ages. In the feudal system the Pope was God's representative on earth. The Emperor and all kings were his vassals. The line of command reached down through dukes, counts, barons, etc. The clergy were exempt from all laws, including the commandments. Huge sums of money were raised by the sale of indulgences (permission to commit sins). In 1309 the Papal Court moved to Avignon, France, a resort noted for its atmosphere of dissolute wealth and immorality. In response to bitter criticism, the papacy was reestablished in Rome in 1377, but there were two competing popes until 1517.

There had been several attempts at reform, such as John Wycliffe in England and John Huss in Bohemia. All were brutally suppressed.

Martin Luther, in 1517, severely criticized the Church. He was excommunicated, of course, but many of the German princes and all the Scandinavian rulers followed him in breaking away from Rome. A few years later John Calvin did the same thing in Switzerland, and attracted a large following in that country, and in France, the Netherlands, and Scotland.

The Thirty Years War (1618-1648) killed eight million people, most of them non-combatants. Such carnage was necessary for the glory of God. Instigators of the War were doing their Christian duty. They had to draw a boundary between Protestantism and Catholicism on the map of Europe.

Today there are 1.000,000,000 Catholics in the world, 710,000,000 Protestants, 240.000,000 Orthodox Christians, and another 60,000,000 Christians who cannot be classified in any of these groups.

The Roman Catholic and the Eastern Orthodox Churches each claim to be the one and only true church, and consider all others heretics, though they no longer persecute heretics as they once did. Most Protestants will share the communion with other Protestants, though there are some exceptions. The Quakers, alone, consider Christians of all other denominations to be their Brothers in Christ.

SCHISM

Si vous avez deux religions dans votre pays, ils couperont la gorge des uns et des autres, mais si vous avez trente religions, ils vivront en la paix.
'— Voltaire

(If you have two religions in your land, they will cut each others' throats, but if you have thirty religions, they will live in peace.)

The Christian Church is fragmented, and perhaps should be. Jesus did not specify any type of church organization. He said that the smallest, most isolated group of worshippers wase a legitimate part of His Church. He resisted efforts of one disciple to obtain authority over the others.

§

The **Armenian Apostolic Church** is the oldest of Christian denominations. In 301 AD King Tiridates IV proclaimed Christianity the Armenian state religion. It still is! The size and extent of the Armenian Church has varied with the political fortunes of the Armenian State.

The Armenian Church was represented at the Council of Nicaea, and accepted most of the Council's recommendations, but refused to subject itself to the Roman Church.

There was no written Armenian language. Priests translated the Greek Scriptures verse-by-verse into spoken Armeniian. An Armenian alphabet had been invented, and the entire Bible written in Armenian by 436 AD. That version is still the only Bible recognized by the Armenian Church.

Armenia reached its greatest extent at about that time. Its territory extended from the Caspian Sea to the Mediterranean. Then surrounding empires began taking away its borderlands. often persecuting or expelling ethnic Armenians. It was usually ruled by foreigners, but it continued to support its own Church. In the early Twentieth Century, Armenia was eivided between the Russian and the Ottoman Empires. At the end of World War I things went from bad to worse. Two million Armenians living in the new Turkish Republic were massacred. There is still bitter hatred between Armenians and Turks.[142] In Russian Armenia communists sshot priests and anyone else who publicly rejected the official state atheism.

In 1991 Armenia successfully declared its independence from the Soviet Union, and its churches reopened immediately. In 2015 all those who died in the Turkish genocide were canonized. Thus the Armenian Church recognizes more saints than all other churches combined.

The Armenian Church has an authoritarian hierarchy. The leader, called the Catholicos, is at Etchmiadzin. A secondary Catholicos, at Antelias, Lebanon, administers churches outside Armenia, of which there are many. Priests are allowed to be married, but women are not accepted in the priesthood.

[142] When Congresswoman Nancy Pelosi, who has many Armenian constituents, proposed a memorial to the slaughtered Armenians, the security of U.S military bases in Turkey was jeopardized.

From a very early date the Albanian Apostolic Church and the Georgian Apostolic Church were closely associated with, and very similar to the Armenian Apostolic Church. When the nation of Albania[143] disappeared, the remnant of its church was absorbed, about 830, into the Armenian Church. Georgia was conquered by Russia in 1811, and its church gradually converted to Russian Orrthodoxy.[144]

§

The **Roman Catholic Church** was created in 325 AD on order of the Emperor Constantine, and eventually became the official church of the Roman Empire. Its claim to be the only true Christian church has never been fully realized, but throughout its history it has been the largest Christian community in the world.

The Council of Nicaea wrote the Nicene Creed, which is still accepted, with little or no modification, by nearly all churches. The Council also decided which books would be included in the Bible. The Catholic Church has never departed from that listing – many of the smaller churches which have broken away have either added a few more books or rejected a few of those selected by the Council. Those books that are not universally accepted are called the Apocrypha.

The Church adopted Roman ideas of strictly enforced order and conformity. Authority emanated from above. Although the vast majority of Christians were in the Greek-speaking East, the Bishop of Rome[145] assumed power, and was designated Pope.[146]

The Romans were used to many gods. The one God of the Hebrews evolved into the Holy Trinity. The Romans had goddesses. The Virgin Mary was raised to a semi-divine status.

---

143 This ancient nation, in the Caucasus, was entirely separate from, and not related to, the modern nation of Albania.

144 Young Josef Stalin studied for the Georgian Orthodox priesthood.

145 The Apostle Peter was leader of the Christians in Rome. His apparent mandate directly from Jesus, plus his strong personality, reinforced the advantage of his location in the capital.

146 A few of the early Bishops of Alexandria were also called Pope, But the Romans soon put a stop to that.

The Romans enjoyed some sexual practices forbidden to the Hebrews, but they were squeamish on the subject of sex itself. The Church kept all the Hebrew restrictions, and added the Roman proscription of sexual pleasure. Many Biblical writers criticized sexual abuse or sexual deviance, but only Paul, a Roman, criticized sex itself. The Church remains staunchly opposed to contraception, and to any form of sexual expression that does not have procreation as its prime objective.

The first generation of Roman children was a product of the infamous Rape of the Sabine Women. The mothers of those children had good reason to teach them that sex was violent and evil.

Greek was the original language of the Church. One of the earliest major projects was translation of the Bible into the vulgar Latin of that time. The Vulgate remains the official Bible of the Roman Catholic Church to this day, although since the mid-Twentieth Century approved translations into vernacular languages have been permitted in the Mass.

Catholicism spread rapidly through the western Roman Empire. After the fall of Rome, the Church survived in the successor states, and was further spread, especially by the Franks into northern Europe. In the Age of Colonialism, European countries, notably Spain and Portugal, and to a lesser extent France, established the Catholic Church in their overseas territories.

A few small oriental churches left the Catholic Communion very early. The entire Greek portion of the Church separated in the Great Schism of 1054. Much of northern Europe fell away during the Protestant Reformation of the Sixteenth Century.

A rule of clerical celibacy had been proposed at Nicaea, but it was voted down. After the

Schism, Rome completely dominated the Church, and the celibacy rule was adopted in 1123.

Women have never been accepted into the Roman Catholic priesthood.

> Splinter groups broke away from most of the eastern churches after the Schism, and reaffirmed their allegiance to Rome. These groups continue the practices of their former churches, but recognize the Pope as head of their Church. Three of them are worthy of note here.
>
> The **Uniate Church**, centered in the western Ukraine, follows all the traditions of the Russian Orthodox Church, with its Mass in the ancient Slavonic language. Ruthenia has never been an independent nation, and the Uniate Church symbolizes Ruthenian ethnicity.
>
> The **Maronite Church**, centered in Lebanon, is the religious home of most Christian Arabs. The **Chaldean Catholic Church**, centered in northern Iraq, also serves an Arabic membership. These two churches are prime targets for jihadist terrorists.

§

The **Coptic Church** takes its name from the Coptic language, spoken by the common people in Egypt at the time of Christ and for several centuries afterward. The Egyptians were the largest Christian community represented at Nicaea. They were reluctant to follow the lead of outsiders. They were especially jealous of all the power being concentrated at far-off Rome.

Orders of the Council were gently circumvented. Coptic monks preserved copies of forbidden books and other early Christian literature. All this material had been translated into Coptic and much of it into the Ge'ez language spoken in the Nile headwaters region, by the time the Vulgate was completed.

At the Council of Chalcedon, in 451, a disagreement on minor points of theology could not be resolved. The Copts left the Catholic communion and named their own Pope at Alexandria.

Islam conquered Egypt during the Seventh Century. Despite intensive missionary effort, it was 500 years before Moslems outnumbered Christians in Egypt. There are still significant

Coptic minorities in both Egypt and the Sudan.

The Coptic Pope moved from Alexandria to Cairo, Egypt's new capital, in 1047.

The **Ethiopian Orthodox Church** was originally part of the Coptic Church. It had the Bible and other literature in its own language, Ge'ez. Its separation from the Coptic Church was gradual. It is now larger than the Coptic Church. The Emperors of Ethiopia claimed descent from King Solomon and the Queen of Sheba.

The **Eritrean Orthodox Church** broke away from the Ethiopian Church in 1993, when Eritrea became independent.

§

The **Greek Orthodox Church** came into existence in 1054, when the Pope and the Patriarch of Constantinople each excommunicated the other. The western Roman Empire had disintegrated into a number of national states, in all of which the Catholic Church was established. The eastern Roman Empire had become the Byzantine Empire, which now had an established Orthodox Church.

Orthodox Cathedral – 537-1204
Catholic Church – 1204-1261
Orthodox Cathedral – 1261-1453
Mosque –1453-1931
Museum – Since 1931

The Orthodox Church ordains married men as priests, but bishops and higher officials must be celibate. Women are not ordained.

Islam had already taken political control of much of the territory served by the Greek Orthodox Church. This control was gradually gathered into the Ottoman Empire, which governed the entire Near East, and even Greece itself. The Moslem Ottomans were tolerant of Christianity, and the Church continued to flourish.

The Crusades, instigated by the Roman Catholic Church in 1095, were ostensibly to open the Moslem-held Holy Land to Christian pilgrim. But the route to the Holy Land lay across the territory of the Orthodox Church. The Crusaders did more damage to the Orthodox Christians and their churches than they did to the Moslems. They plundered Constantinople and operated its great cathedral as a Catholic Church during most of the Thirteenth Century. They even established Catholic kingdoms in the East, where other forms of worship were prohibited.

World War I destroyed the Ottoman Empire. The new Turkish Republic tried to exterminate Christians within its borders. War between Turkey and Greece resulted in a massive exchange of populations. Greece could not hold all the refugees, and a massive diaspora spread Greeks and their church to many other countries, especially to North America.

The most effective missionary of the Greek Orthodox Church was Saint Cyril, who invented the Cyrillic Alphabet and translated the Bible into Slavonic, the ancestor of all the modern Slavic languages, during the Ninth Century.

The **Russian Orthodox Church** has always been in communion with the Greek Orthodox Church. The differences between them are linguistic and cultural, not theological nor liturgical. Other Orthodox Slavic nations, including former Soviet republics, use the Slavonic Bible. Refugees from both tsarist and soviet tyranny have established Russian Orthodox communities throughout the world.

The "Third Rome Theory", espoused by both the tsars and the soviets, held that (1) Rome was the capital of the ancient world, (2) when Rome fell to the Barbarians, the capital moved to Constantinople, and (3) when Constantinople fell to the Turks, the capital moved to Moscow.

he Soviet government was officially atheistic. Christians were persecuted, and priests were shot. After seventy years of brutal suppression, there were still more Christians than communists in Russia when the Soviet Union disintegrated.

§

The Bohemian Jan Hus proposed clerical poverty, the equality of all believers, and universal education in 1414. He was invited to present his views to a church council the following year, and then murdered when he arrived. His followers continued his work in Bohemia, and achieved many reforms. In 1609 The Holy Roman Emperor (not the Pope) granted Bohemia religious freedom. The Pope then ordered a crusade against the Bohemian" heretics". The resulting Battle of White Mountain destroyed the Bohemian army and the Hussite movement.

Survivors fled, and founded the **Moravian Church**. They moved frequently around central Europe to escape persecution. Even so, they were very active in sending out overseas missions. They were especially effective in converting native Americans.

§

\\In 1520 Martin Luther, a German priest, publicly proclaimed that salvation could not be purchased from the Church and that divine revelation could be found only in the Bible. He was excommunicated, of course. Many of his followers voluntarily left the Catholic Church with him, and formed the **Lutheran Church**. Rulers of most of the small states in northern Germany, some in southern Germany, and all the Scandinavian kings made Lutheranism their official state religion.

Lutherans abolished clerical celibacy – Martin Luther himself married a former nun. There is little hierarchy in the Lutheran Church. Each congregation is ruled by elected elders, and questions of broader concern are ironed out in conferences.

It took the vicious Thirty Years War to firmly establish the Lutheran Church in Europe. Lutherans are not pacifists, they will take up arms for their faith.

§

The group of churches in the **Anglican Communion** originated in 1534 when the Pope excommunicated Henry VIII. Henry retaliated by seizing all the Church's property he could get his hands on, and declaring himself head of the **Church of England**. Most of the people of England, including the clergy, accepted the *fait accompli*.

These churches still consider the British monarch their titular head, though the Archbishop of Canterbury is actually in charge.

Dissidents, who had been trying to establish an English Protestant church, initially applauded Henry's action, but later went their separate way, calling themselves Puritans. Enough of the English remained loyal to Rome to maintain a somewhat smaller Roman Catholic presence.

Elizabeth I tried, with limited success, to modify the Church of England, so that it would be acceptable to all elements of the population.

In structure, liturgy, and practice, the Church of England is almost identical to the Catholic Church. The Mass and the Bible are in English. There is no clerical celibacy. Priests may marry. Some women have been ordained into the priesthood, but the practice is still controversial.

British imperialism spread the Church of England around the world. At the time of American independence, it was the largest church in the United States. Americans liked the Church, but not its name. A large number of congregations joined the newly-formed **Methodist Episcopal Church**, which had the same structure and practices, but was not affiliated with the Church of England. Those who chose to remain in communion with the Anglicans renamed their church the **Protestant Episcopal Church**.

§

Jehan Cauvin[147] (John Calvin). a French priest, fled from growing violence between Catholics and Protestants to Geneva. In 1536 he published his doctrine that the Church had no divine power, God was all powerful and rather severe.

Three Protestant denominations follow Calvin's theology. The **Reformed Church** arose in Switzerland, France, and the Netherlands. In France it was called the **Huguenot Church**. In 1595 it was officially recognized by the King, and given certain

[147] Anglicized spelling – John Calvin

rights. These rights were revoked in 1685, and Huguenots forced to either convert to Catholicism or emigrate.

Other followers of Calvin formed the **Congregational Church**, which recognizes no authority above the individual congregation. Congregationalists in England and its colonies called themselves **Puritans**, insisting that the Church of England was not purely Protestant.

§

John Knox, a follower of Calvin, established the **Kirk of Scotland** in 1559. After each of several wars against the English, defeated Scots fled to Ireland. They made common cause with, and intermarried with, the rebellious Irish. The church they had brought from Scotland was now called **The Presbyterian Church.** Emigration of Scots-Irish became very heavy after the English conquest of Ireland and during the Potato Famine. The structure of the Presbyterian Church is similar to that of the Lutheran Church, but it follows Calvinist doctrine.

§

In the early Seventeenth Century some Reformed Churches, both in Britain and on the Continent, adopted the practice of baptism by immersion. At first they were considered part of the Puritan community, and many settled in the Puritan colonies. They disagreed with the harshness of Puritan theology and social controls, and were forced to flee. Under the leadership on Roger Williams and Ann Hutchinson, the founded the Colony of Rhode Island and **The Baptist Church**.

The Baptist Church has no organizational structure. Each congregation is free to adopt its own interpretation of the Bible, and its own moral and social standards. It can select anyone it wants as its pastor.

Baptists are not enthusiastic about higher education. They often mistrust scientists, considering them inherently anti-religious. Many of them have been slow to adopt modern technology and the ideals of the Civil Rights Movement.[148]

Baptist churches do not have to, and many do not, include the word "Baptist" in their names. The **Church of Christ**, the **Church of God**, the **Free Will Church, the Full Gospel Church**, and many others are actually Baptist churches.

Despite their lack of organization, Baptists are effective missionaries. They have been very successful in converting communists to Christianity. The Baptist Church is the largest Protestant denomination in the former Soviet Union.

§

In the mid 1600s a group of people in England, having become disgusted with the upheaval and cruelty of the religious wars, formed the **Society of Friends**, commonly known as the **Quakers**. They rejected all church authority and all theology except that which an individual could get from his personal reading of the Bible. They refused to enter military service, to swear an oath to any government, or to participate in the persecution of any person for his religious belief. Though severely persecuted themselves, by both Protestants and Catholics, they would not retaliate.

Quakers do not have churches, they have meeting houses. They do not have clergymen, though some of them are trained in preaching. No preaching is required at their meetings; they may sit in silence until someone, man or woman, is moved to speak. They reject styles and fads. And sometimes technology.

Freed from their religious and feudal inhibitions, the Quakers became skillful business people. One of them, William Penn, maneuvered the King into giving him a large tract of land in America. Not only Quakers, but downtrodden minorities from all over Britain, Europe, and even the other colonies flocked to Pennsylvania, the land of tolerance and peace. The Quakers even dealt fairly with the

[148] However, note that many of the leaders of that Movement, including Martin Luther King, Jr, have been Baptists.

Native Americans, and enjoyed a peaceful frontier.

Both the dour New Englanders and the frivolous southerners hated the liberal ideas of the Quakers, but they admired and envied the rapid growth and wealth of Pennsylvania. It was to get some of that for themselves that they supported the religious freedom clause of the U. S. Constitution.

The **Anabaptists** are' in many ways similar to the Quakers, with the added features that they will not baptize a child too young to understand the meaning of the sacrament, and that they reject all modern technology. They came from central Europe, where they had fled persecution from one place to another until they heard about the tolerance in Pennsylvania. Their principal sects are the **Mennonites** and the **Amish**.

§

John Wesley, an Anglican priest in the Georgia Colony, was disappointed by his limited success in converting Native Americans. He noted better results obtained by Moravian missionaries. Back in England, he formed a group to study Moravian ideas and methods within the Church of England. These "Methodists" eventually separated from the Church of England in disputes over theology. There were many small independent churches calling themselves Methodists.

At the end of the American Revolution, some Methodists in America formed the **Methodist Episcopal Church**. It departed radically from Wesley's ideas, and was almost an imitation of the Church of England itself. But it had no connection to the English religious hierarchy or the English royalty. It Americanized clerical titles and the names of observances and practices. Many Anglican congregations in the newly-independent United States found it attractive, and joined it *en masse*. It grew rapidly as settlements spread westward, and soon it was the largest Protestant denomination in America. Several small Methodist groups remained unaffiliated.

In 1968, nearly as the disparate churches bearing the Methodist name joined together as the **United Methodist Church**. It retained the episcopal form of church government, but adopted some new ideas from the smaller churches and from the social mores of the time.

§

In the early 1830's, Joseph Smith, with divine help, translated the text he had found engraved on golden plates in upstate New York. The literature he produced included the Book of Mormon, and many other previously unknown works.[149] The **Church of Jesus Christ of Latter Day Saints**, which he founded, accepts these translations as Holy Scripture.

Mormon Temple - Salt Lake City

Hounded out of New York and across several other states, they finally settled in the Great Basin, which was then outside the United States. They prospered and created a theocratic state called Deseret, with its capital at Salt Lake City. After the Mexican War their land was annexed to the United States. It took another small war to replace the Mormon state with a territorial government. As surrounding area were admitted to statehood, Utah remained a territory.

[149] Some of those works were later found to be identical to ancient writings found elsewhere.

On two occasions, angels have appeared to Mormon leaders to announce changes in moral standards. In 1890, as Congress was debating Utah statehood, polygamy was forbidden. In 1968, after the passage of Civil Rights legislation, the prohibition against African-Americans in the priesthood was removed. In each case a small splinter group broke off and continues their former practice.

Mormons believe that unrepentant long-dead ancestors can still be saved by prayers of their descendants. They even have a procedure for baptizing persons who died long ago. The person praying for an ancestor must have proof of his relationship to that person. To facilitate finding that proof, the LDS Church maintains one of the finest genealogical libraries in the world. It is available to the general public as well as to members. Mormon Churches everywhere cooperate with local genealogical societies.

HEALING

Every human being is the author of his own health or disease.
— Guatama Siddharta[130]

Primitive man considered demons to be the cause of disease. Those demons were either gods or agents of the gods. Seeking a cure involved propitiating the appropriate god with prayers and/or sacrifices. In some faith healing religions health was seen as a constant struggle between good and evil spirits.[150]

Then, as now, a considerable part of the healing process must have depended on the attitude of the sick person. Faith healing was as effective then as it is now. A person with a strong faith in something will heal faster, with or without medical treatment.

The "unclean" rules in the Book of Leviticus indicate that, by the time of the Exodus, people were aware that physical causes of illness existed. Their procedures for minimizing their exposure to those causes were far from modern sanitation practices, but they were a start in the right direction.

Greek scientists of the Third and Fourth Centuries BC studied the causes of disease. They had a poor understanding of diseases because their respect for the beauty of the human body did not permit experimenting with it. They had two theories, which were not entirely mutually exclusive. The word μιασμα (miasma) has been translated into English as "pollution", "corruption", "defilement", and "filth". The Miasmic Theory was the prevailing theory of disease well into the Nineteenth Century, and was supported by the Church against alternative theories.

150 AKA The Buddha.

The persistence of the fear of miasmatic diseases is well illustrated by the name of the Spanish colonial city Buenos Aires (good air). The name was chosen to convince prospective colonists that they could enjoy a disease-free environment.

The other Greek theory of disease was contagion. That principle was already widely understood, as can be seen from the treatment of lepers in ancient Israel.

The contagion theory of disease got a great boost from the work of Louis Pasteur in the Nineteenth Century. Modern medical practice makes good use of both theories, with a great deal of attention to the control of infecting organisms.

§

Hippocrates created the first formal physical practice of medicine about 400 BC. From the beginning faith healers opposed his methods, and many of them are still doing so today. But Hippocrates and his followers were praised by the other Greek scientists. Respect for Greek culture was so great among the early Christians that physicians were allowed to develop and practice their skills, though faith healers were also tolerated;

The Church generally did not take part in the disagreements between these two schools of healing. After Christianity became fragmented, smaller churches adopted radically different attitudes toward sickness and health, and some of them became insistent in their support of one viewpoint or another.

The Bible mentions several occasions on which Jesus seemed to cast out a demon. Exactly what happened on these occasions is uncertain, either what happened to the demon or to the patient. Those scriptural passages are being used, even today, to support the practice by the Catholic Church[151] and by several American fundamentalist churches.

Exorcism rites do often have a therapeutic effect on mental patients, at least temporarily. There are commercial as well as religious exorcists. Their extravagant advertisements can be found on the Internet and elsewhere. There is no scientific data to prove the efficacy of exorcism, whatever its motive.

§

[151] Pope Francis formally recognized it in October 2014.

The gospels list forty supposed miracles performed by Jesus. Twenty-eight of them involved healing. The apostles also performed many miracles, some of them involving healing. Reports of miracles were exactly what people wanted to hear. There is no doubt that early missionaries emphasized, and probably exaggerated them.

Belief in miracle cures has not subsided one bit in all the centuries of the modern era. And it should not be looked down on. People do sometimes enjoy recovery from a serious disease which cannot be explained scientifically. And even sophisticated medical procedures may occasionally get much better results than expected.

Faith in medical miracles is not evil *per se*. That faith itself may improve a believer's health has been well demonstrated. But there are two caveats that must be borne in mind. Naïvity can be, and often has been, exploited by charlatans. And unwarranted faith in a hoped-for miracle that is not forthcoming can lead to omission of an available and needed treatment.

The Catholic Church has cautiously recognized medical miracles, but has not actively promoted them. It requires miracles for canonization, but carefully examines all purported miracles before approving them. Prayers to the saints, especially the Virgin Mary, are sometimes followed by acceptable miracles. Miraculous appearances of the Virgin may establish locations to which pilgrims can go to pray for cures.

By far the best known site for miraculous healing is Lourdes in southern France. Millions of pilgrims visit the site every year. In the century and a half since the Virgin's apparition[152] 7100 of these pilgrims have publically claimed to have been miraculously cured. The Vatican has certified 68 (one percent) of these as genuine miracles. Of those, eleven were to priests or nuns. Whatever the spiritual or medicinal blessings of Lourdes, it is unquestionably the basis for a thriving business. The small town of Lourdes has

271 hotels, nearly one for every fifty inhabitants. Bottles of Lourdes water, real or phony, can be purchased almost anywhere in the United States.

Two other shrines devoted to the Holy Mother are visited by large numbers of pilgrims, and are occasionally credited with miraculous cures, through that is not the main thrust of their influence. The Shrine of Our Lady of Fatima in Portugal celebrates several successful predictions announced at that location. It has a strong anti-communist orientation which sometimes almost borders on pro-fascism. The Virgin of Guadelupe is a symbol of Mexican nationalism. Pronouncements of the Virgin here were the first significant steps in racial equality for native Americans.

§

Another type of faith healing is found among a small group

[152] The movie *Song of Bernadette* describes the apparitions, and the Church's efforts to avoid sensationalism and commercialization.

of Pentacostal churches in the southern Appalachians. Worshippers expose themselves to bites by venomous snakes. There are tales of miraculous cures from snakebites in the Bible, but no case of intentional exposure. This is considered a test of faith – faith that the snake won't bite and/or faith that God will neutralize the poison. These churches, which also practice "speaking in tongues" are not affiliated with any major denomination,

At least 72 persons have died of snakebites received during these religious practices. The death toll is particularly high among ministers and their wives and children. Most of the victims are categorized as "persons of little faith".

State laws have attempted to prevent these deaths, but neither their enforcement nor their constitutionality can be assured. The results of these laws has varied greatly. In 1995 a Tennessee minister was convicted of attempted murder. At the other extreme, West Virginia law prohibits interference in any purported religious activity by law enforcement authorities.

One matter totally ignored in the arguments over snake handling is the welfare of the snakes. They are also God's creatures, and should not be mistreated for religious purposes. Snakes maintained for handling in church live an average of three to four months. The same species in their natural habitat live ten to twenty years.

§

The Christian Science movement, founded by Mary Baker Eddy in the late Nineteenth Century, is devoted almost entirely to faith healing. Its principal tenet is that sickness was an illusion and that, with correct thinking, supported by prayer, the sickness would disappear. Medical treatment is not necessary.

Actually Christian Science is almost as effective as the primitive medical technology of that time in alleviating suffering. And the public was becoming polarized between rapidly advancing science and stubbornly traditional religion. Christian Science leaders remained above the bickering, avoiding all words and actions that might be found offensive by the public. The *Christian Science Monitor* has set new standards in journalistic excellence, with no attempt at proselytizing. Refusal of the medical community, supported by Big Pharma, to consider such alternative treatments as chiropractic, acupuncture, and natural herbal medicines has steered many toward faith healing.

The Christian Scientists maintain clinics where intensive or extended counseling are available. There are also thousands of trained and certified Christian Science practitioners who provide service for a nominal fee. Christian Scientists are not prohibited from obtaining traditional medical care, but they are told that prayer is preferred.

There has been much argument; and even litigation, about the legal status of Christian Science treatment. Fees paid for counseling are generally considered deductible by the IRS. Medicare will pay for stays in faith healing clinics, but will not pay Christian Science practitioners' fees. Short periods of sick leave, for conditions treated by faith healing, are usually granted, but longer periods may require a documented diagnosis. Most practitioners feel that they have neither the expertise now the legal authority to provide a written diagnosis.

Most states have laws exempting from prosecution parents whose children die because of refused medical treatment. Most such children are members of Christian Science families,[153] but authorities are powerless to do anything about it. Statistics show that Christian Scientists, of all age groups, have a slightly higher death rate than the general public.

The Christian Science movement reached its zenith during and after World War II, when it included a galaxy of movie stars and other glamorous persons, Since then it has lost more than half its membership, and the

[153] Asser, Seth M & Rita Swan, *Child Fatalities from Religion-motivated Medical Neglect.*

ranks of practitioners has been decimated.

§

Jehovah's Witnesses do not practice faith healing, and they sometimes criticize those who do. Still they get involved in disputes over accepting medical treatment because of their staunch refusal to take blood transfusions. They base that practice on the prohibition against eating blood found in the Book of Leviticus,

Mortality rates for Jehovah's Witnesses are strongly elevated among newborn infants and their mothers.

§

In 1998 Andrew Wakefield published, in the British medical journal *Lancet,* a purported study stating that the vaccination for measles, mumps, and rubella (MMR) was associated with autism. Vaccination rates in the United Kingdom plummeted. Measles, a potentially deadly childhood disease which had been nearly eliminated, came roaring back. Many children were sickened, and a few died. Alarmed public health officials pled for confirmation, and researchers throughout the world tried and failed to duplicate the reported results. Measles approached epidemic levels in many areas.

An investigation in 2004 found that Wakefield had been paid for this 'study' by a lawyer representing parents of an autistic child, who were suing the vaccine manufacturer. *Lancet* withdrew and denounced the article. Wakefield was stripped of his right to practice medicine.

But the cat was out of the bag. The media were having a circus, and politicians were taking advantage. The discredited statement continued to be published, and its author's punishment was rarely mentioned. The names of politicians appeared in these articles far more often than the names of doctors and scientists. The gullible believed – and their children suffered.

By 2011 the number of measles cases in the United States had tripled. 87% of the victims were unvaccinated school children. Most of the others were infants who had caught the disease from older children. Every state now requires vaccination for school attendance, but nearly all of them allow exceptions for religious and/or philosophical reasons. Ten percent of parents were finding reasons to selectively omit vaccinations.[154] Whether the excuse is religion, politics, perversity, or just plain apathy, the result is the same – children die!

[154] Liz Szabo, in USA Today, 11/14/2011'

EVOLUTION

Maybe your grandaddy was a monkey, but mine wasn't.
— Heckler at the Scopes Trial[135]

And God said, Let the earth bring forth grass, the herb yielding seed, and the fruit tree yielding fruit after its kind, whose seed is in itself, upon the earth, and it was so. *– Genesis 1:11*[155]

(On the following day God did not order the bringing forth of more living things.)

And God said, Let the waters bring forth abundantly the moving creature that hath life and fowl that may fly above the earth in the firmament of heaven.
- Genesis 1:20

And God said, Let the earth bring forth the living creature after his kind, cattle and creeping thing and beast of the earth, and it was so. *– Genesis 1;24*

So God created man in his own image, In the image of God created He him, male and female created He them. *– Genesis 1:27*

§

And that is exactly how it happened! Any tale that disagrees with the Biblical account of the creation of living things is to be looked at with suspicion. But we cannot defend the Bible unless we know exactly what it says. We cannot defend what we think the Bible should have said, when it doesn't actually say it.

What does it say? Does it say that all living things were created at the same time? No, it says that there were three groups of living things separately ordered by

155 From the movie *Inherit the Wind.*

God to be brought forth. Most of the thousands of species with which we are familiar are not mentioned at all. But all those creatures must be represented; God created the heavens and the earth, presumably including everything in the heavens and the earth. Grass, herbs, and fruit trees, mentioned on the third day, are all plants. No plants are mentioned on any of the other days. So that first command must have resulted in creation of the entire plant kingdom.

On the fifth day God ordered the creation of sea creatures and birds. What do they have in common? They all lay eggs. And no egg-layers are mentioned on the other days. So this command resulted in a wide variety of invertebrates, fish, amphibians, reptiles, and birds. There had been a delay between the third and the fifth days, as God prepared the earth to receive and support these complex creatures.

On the sixth day God ordered the bringing forth of cattle, creeping things, beasts, and man. All are mammals, and they represent all the thousands of mammalian species. At the very end of the sixth day God took direct action to mold one of those mammals into his own image.

§

Does the Bible say that God created living things by His own action? No, God said "Let the earth (or the waters) bring forth…". He was using agents, agents He had already created. On the first, second, and fourth days He created not only those agents but also the raw materials, tools, and procedures they would need to carry out his commands, and the environments to support their creations. When God created something on His own He used the command, "Let there be…".

The command given on the fifth day held one of Nature's long-hidden secrets. God commanded the waters to "bring forth fowl". Humans, scientists and laymen alike, ignored that subtle hint for millennia. They knew intuitively that birds couldn't come out of the waters. But the Bible says they did! A few maverick biologists stated, as early as 1810, that, based on skeletal morphology, dinosaurs must be related to birds. They were ignored. Biologists and preachers carried on their rancorous argument about the origin of birds, neither paying any attention to the Biblical verse which could have steered them toward the true answer.

In 1996 the unusually well-preserved remains of a Tyrannosaurus Rex were found in northern China. They contained enough soft tissue that the DNA could be sequenced. It was found that a chicken is more closely related to that fearsome dinosaur than is an alligator.[156] The Bible is right! Birds are descended from dinosaurs, which had long been known to have been descended from sea creatures.

Mankind was brought forth on the sixth day, right along with all the other mammals. Thus the Bible recognizes the position that humans occupy among God's creatures in the family of living beings. It tells us that, though we are made of the same stuff as the other animals, and by the same process, we still have a special relationship to the Creator-Spirit.

§

Virtually all of our domesticated animal and plant species have been produced by genetic engineering, selective breeding and/or by taking advantage of favorable mutations. Sheep, goats, and what we now commonly call cattle were developed from wild animals several thousand years before Noah, in the general area where he lived. Modern cattle are descended from wild aurochs. They were the cattle referred to in Genesis. The chicken was created in Southeast Asia from the red jungle hen, which could fly, but provided little meat and laid few eggs. Nature did not bring forth dogs. Man himself created them from wolves.

The early people of Meso-America made grass grow large nutritious ears, and the corn plant appeared. Separate groups of people, working with the same wild mustard plant have produced cabbage, cauliflower, broccoli, kale, and kohlrabi. The seedless

156 Feduccia, A., 1999, *The origin and evolution of birds.* Yale University Press

orange is a good example of a mutation. The earth brought forth just one tree, which could not reproduce. But men found a way to manipulate it. And most of our oranges are now seedless.

If lowly man has produced such miracles of evolution, who will deny that God can do, or has done, it even better? The Bible says he did.

§

The AIDS epidemic, which began about 1981, brought new, and unwanted, attention to the process and result of evolution. The etiologic agent was hard to find, but obviously something new had appeared, something which hadn't existed before the mid Twentieth Century. What was it, and where did it come from?

Some of the earliest, well-publicized, victims were known homosexuals. Televangelists, such as Jerry Falwell and Oral Roberts thundered about God's wrath upon these sinners. But it soon became known that homosexuals were only a minority of the sufferers, many were new-born babies. God was wrathful toward them?

Then the human immune-virus (HIV) was discovered; a living thing which had existed for no more than a few decades. It resisted treatment because it could quickly develop new varieties which survive newly created drugs. Here was evolution taking place right before our eyes, affecting people whose names we knew.

The chain of contagion was traced back to West Africa. But what had given birth to the first HIV? DNA analysis showed that it was descended from simian immuno-virus (SIV), with which monkeys in the area had been infected for thousands of years. It caused them only mild symptoms. Economic conditions associated with independence of the former colonies had caused many people to start eating monkeys. (Bush meat they called it.) Ingested in this manner, SIV quickly evolved into HIV, with lethal consequences for its human hosts.

Eating monkeys is not exactly cannibalism, but it's a little too close for nonchalance. What was that about the wrath of God? He knows who our relatives are, even if we don't.

A slightly different strain of HIV, found in central Africa, is also descended from SIV, and by the same route. In that area both humans and chimpanzees eat monkeys. Infected chimpanzees do not have mild symptoms like the monkeys; they suffer full-blown AIDS like their human cousins

And what of the self-appointed prophets who falsely warned us of their idea of the "sin" that caused AIDS? How has God rewarded them? Jerry Swaggart exposed extramarital affairs by Marvin Gorman and Jim Bakker. Both were defrocked, and Bakker was sent to prison for fraudulent use of donated funds. Swaggart himself was caught several times patronizing prostitutes. He was defrocked, and his $150 million annual income decimated. Oral Roberts' homosexual son committed suicide. Jerry Falwell lost a series of lawsuits to persons he had slandered, and tried to recoup his losses by selling his soul to Sun Myung Moon, who claimed to have replaced Jesus as the Messiah. Pat Robertson was denounced as a traitor by creationists when he said that "dinosaurs lived before the events described in the Bible".

And the homosexuals, on whom the blame was put – did God punish them? They were so enraged and emboldened that they "came out of the closet" by the hundreds, showing the public what kind of people they really were, and demanding more respect. Homosexuals are now treated as a protected minority under civil rights laws. Thirty-eight states now recognize same sex marriages, and the number is growing. This sort of reaction was engendered by intemperate, gay-bashing hate mongers. ***Blessed are the meek for they shall inherit the earth.***

§

Charles Darwin published *On the Origin of the Species* in 1859. The Theory of Evolution had been published before, but never with such compelling evidence, and it had attracted little attention. It could have been just another blip in the growing antagonism between scientists and clerics. Scientists considered it a brick in their beautiful

Charles Darwin

↑
As the media showed him.

←As he was.

edifice that would soon be topped by the result of the Michelson-Morley Experiment. Churchmen were suffering from their loss of authority during the Enlightenment. And millions of willing recruits would soon be brought to the scientific cause by the threat of universal education.

§

The Industrial Revolution required millions of skilled workers in all the new factories. Industrialized countries upgraded their educational systems to meet the demand. In the United States education is a responsibility of the states. Some states were more advanced than others. In some universal education had had arrived with++ the first settlers. In others widespread illiteracy persisted into the Twentieth Century.

By the 1920s every state required at least some high school for every child. In those states where the jump from illiteracy to mandatory high school was made in one generation, trouble loomed. Teenagers were telling their parents that some of their cherished superstitions were wrong. Such insubordination could not be tolerated, and had to be stopped at its source.

The State of Tennessee, in 1925, outlawed the teaching of any theory of human origin that disagreed with the supposed biblical account. The law was patently unconstitutional, violating both the freedom of religion and the freedom of speech clauses. It also contradicted an existing regulation that required the use of a textbook (Hunter's *A Civic Biology*) that included the Theory of Evolution.

Teachers and prosecutors, alike, ignored the impossible situation into which they had been put. The American Civil Liberties Union advertised for a teacher willing to admit teaching evolution, and a prosecutor willing to charge him with that crime, offering to provide expert legal defense.

A group of business men in economically depressed Dayton, Tennessee decided that such an unusual trial would bring publicity to their community, and improve their fortunes. They recruited local volunteers to prosecute and to be prosecuted.[157] At that point the ideals of religious faith and scientific truth were lost. The creationist cause became, and still is, motivated by money, votes, fame, and vanity.

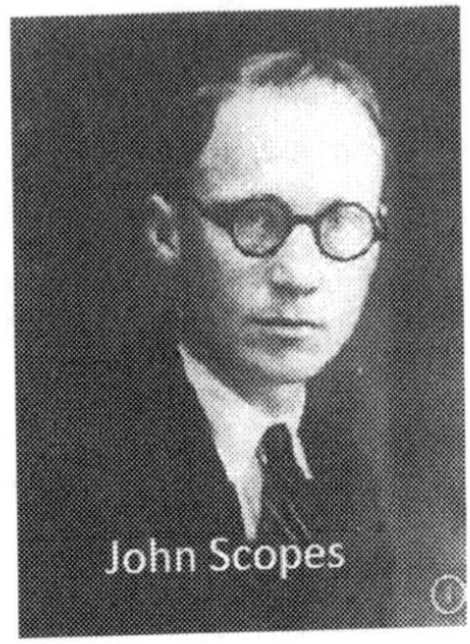

The prosecutor, the defendant, and the judge were in on the ACLU's scheme. But the judge handled the case like any other, and committed judicial errors, which rendered the verdict null and prevented testing the constitutionality of the law. But those lapses were insignificant compared to the furor caused by the shenanigans of a high-profile interloper.

William Jennings Bryan, three-time-losing Democratic presidential candidate, smelled political blood. He offered to assist in the prosecution. His charisma was too much to refuse. Journalists from all over the United States and around the world flocked to Dayton. The money they brought rolled

157 High school biology teacher John Scopes, after whom tne trial was named.

into local cash registers. After the judge had disallowed expert scientific testimony,[158] Bryan took the stand as an "expert on the Bible". He displayed a phenomenal ignorance of the Bible and a willingness to contradict himself under oath. But onlookers loved his bombastic performance, and the crowd grew so large that the trial was moved out of the courthouse onto the lawn. The audience became even larger, and the carnival atmosphere was observed by hordes of reporters, many of them from overseas. America's vaunted educational system and religious freedom took black eyes, from which they have never recovered.

The judge instructed jurors to ignore all testimony except Scopes' "confession". The guilty verdict was a foregone conclusion. Creationists said, and many still say, that was the end of the affair. Hardly! The appeals courts, the major Christian denominations, the general public, the teaching profession, the scientific community, and, most of all, God, were still to be heard from.

The first, and most spectacular, side effect: came five days later: William Jennings Bryan was struck dead by heart failure. Then the Tennessee appeals court reversed the verdict because of judicial error. This exonerated Scopes, but denied him the chance to test the law's constitutionality. The ACLU's purpose in starting the action was thwarted.

The Catholic, Methodist, Presbyterian, and Episcopal Churches have all issued official statements favoring the teaching of evolution.[159] The Methodists added that they oppose the teaching of creationism or intelligent design, The Mormon, Nazarine, Lutheran, and Orthodox Churches have all stated that they are not opposed to evolution, but that their members

[158] Since that time no reputable scientist has agreed to testify in any creationist trial. The attitude seems to be "if they're going to treat us like pagans, let them wallow in their ignorance".

[159] Catholic – Pius XII, Encyclical 1954, *Humanis Generis* Methodist – *Official Statement on science and Technology* Presbyterian – GA Minutes 1970, 59-62 Episcopalian – Resolution 1983 D090

may follow their own conscience. Thus, churches representing the vast majority of American Christians do not <u>not</u> support anti-evolution laws. Those who sincerely believe that teaching evolution is sinful are little more than a cult.

§

The Butler Act remained the law of Tennessee, though all authorities carefully refrained from enforcing it. Many conscientious teachers routinely violated it. They, and their students, learned that sometimes it was better not to obey the law. Politicians elsewhere saw the advantage of supporting an unconstitutional law that was not meant to be enforced. Respect for the Law, its enforcers, and teachers, among young people dropped.

In 1968 the school board at Jacksboro, Tennessee fired Gary Scott, a teacher they disliked, for teaching evolution. They did not endanger their law by prosecuting him, but that no longer mattered. Congress had just passed the Civil Rights Act. Scott went straight to federal court, and sued for religious discrimination. Faced with both a large tort payment and an unconstitutional ruling, the State of Tennessee rook only three days to repeal the Butler Act and reinstate Scott. That quick action preserved anti-evolution laws in other states.

The following year, one courageous teacher, outraged by the low moral tone being promoted in the schools, took direct action and brought down the entire house of cards. Susan Epperson of Little Rock, Arkansas, with the support of the Little Rock Ministry Association, the ACLU, the National Education Association, her own employers, and the parents of her students, announced publicly that she was teaching evolution, and <u>demanded</u> that she be prosecuted. The publicity could not be ignored, and the court reluctantly indicted her. She testified that she had violated the law. There was no other testimony. She was found guilty. Her already-prepared appeal was filed instantly in federal court, and that court quickly declared that all anti-evolution laws throughout the United States were unconstitutional.

Consternation reigned among creationists. But their motives were too disparate for any unified response.

Those who sincerely believed that the Theory of Evolution violates their religion became the Young Earth Creationists. They believe that God created every existing species at the same time, and that no other species have appeared since then, nor have any disappeared. (They teach that dinosaur fossils are a hoax.) They support anti-evolution politicians, though they disagree with their current tactics. They actively propagandize for their philosophy, and have lately adopted electronic and other social media. About one-third of the American public accepts that philosophy, although many of them belong to churches which have officially rejected it.

§

Politicians and businessman were not motivated by faith; they had vested interests to protect. They quickly prepared a backup position to preserve those interests. Intelligent Design was almost the same as Creationism, but didn't mention God or the Bible, just an unnamed Creator. Purist Creationists were outraged by this "compromise" with their faith.

Intelligent(?) design! Chickens, ostriches, and penguins have wings, though none of them can fly. That's not very intelligent. A whale has, within its body, a full set of leg bones, right down to ten tiny toes, though it has no legs. That's a pretty stupid design. Humans have tail bones, but no tails. Whatever designed these parts certainly had no brain. (Of course not! The Bible says they were brought forth by the earth and its waters.) To blame such stupidity on God is downright blasphemy!

In 2005 a group of students' parents sued the Dover, Pennsylvania School Board in federal court for violating their religious freedom by presenting Intelligent Design as an alternative to the Theory of Evolution. The court ruled that teaching any alternative to a proven scientific theory is unconstitutional. This is now the law of the land.

But anti-evolution laws are still being introduced into state legislatures. Politicians have found that introducing bills and failing to pass them get votes as surely as did passing laws and failing to enforce them.

Business has not suffered from taking Creationism out of the schools. Dayton, Tennessee remains a tourist attraction ninety years later. Some of their advertising refers to "Monkey Town". In 1978 the town spent a million dollars to restore the old courthouse to its 1925 appearance, and to add amenities for tourists. It was a good investment.

The Creation Museum in Petersburg, Kentucky takes in $5 million a year just in admissions. It also operates a gift shop, a book store, and a restaurant. It solicits donations from individuals and churches, and claims to be a religious and educational organization. Strategically located near the intersection of two Interstate Highways, it was laid out by Hollywood designers. The exhibits blatantly ignore the Biblical story of creation, and cater to superstition and sensationalism. The most popular exhibit shows human children cavorting among dinosaurs. That is an absolute perversion of both science and the Bible, and heresy to pure Creationists. But who cares? It's what brings in the money!

§

Another group of former creationists, the Theistic Evolutionists, is growing rapidly. They accept fully the Theory of Evolution and other well-established scientific theories, with only the proviso that that God set the whole thing in motion. This group includes many scientists and other well-educated persons. Atheism among scientists is becoming rare as the meaning of the advanced discoveries of the Twentieth Century gradually sink in.

§

The first chapter of Genesis outlines the progress of evolution on the Earth in some detail. It specifically contradicts the teachings of Creationism. It states, without equivocation, that natural agents, lacking intelligence, brought forth all living beings.

The Bible predicts that sinful man would refuse to believe that he was made in the same manner as God's other creatures. Ecclesiastes 3:18-21 says:

I said in mine heart concerning the estate of the sons of men, that God might manifest them, and they might see that they themselves are beasts. For that which befalleth the sons of men befalleth beasts; even one thing befalleth them; as the one dieth, so dieth the other; yea they have all one breath; so that a man hath no preeminence above a beast; all is vanity. All go into one place; all are of the dust, and all turn to dust again. Who knoweth the spirit of man that goeth upward, and the spirit of beast that goeth downward to the earth?

So the belief that we are somehow better than the other animals is vanity.

Vanity is first among the Seven Deadly Sins.

QUANTA

If quantum mechanics hasn't profoundly shocked you, you haven't understood it yet.
— Niels Bohr

If the Theory of Relativity shook up the world of physicists, what followed put it into a tailspin from which it has yet to recover.

In 1927 Werner Heisenberg published his Uncertainty Principle, based on mathematical work similar to that of Einstein. It states that, in wave systems, there are pairs of conjugate properties each of which affects the accuracy with which the other can be measured. When the precision of one measurement is increased, the error in the other measurement necessarily increases.

In classical physics energy is a massless wave system. But matter consists of particles which have mass and obey the laws of motion and gravity. Relativity equated matter and energy, and suggested that one could be turned into the other. When light waves responded to solar gravity, they were acting like particles. Those hypothetical particles were named photons, and they were supposed to have zero mass. It didn't make any sense.

But then Louis de Broglie postulated that some small particles might behave like waves. This was later proven when a beam of electrons was diffracted. The intuitive difference between matter and energy seemed to be disappearing before our eyes.

Relativity had told us that matter and energy were the same, just two aspects of something more fundamental. When the atomic nucleus was finally split, a huge amount of energy appeared in place of a small amount of matter. But something else appeared, too: A virtual zoo of previously unknown infinitesimally small particles that didn't obey the laws of physics. They appeared and disappeared suddenly and unexpectedly. They decayed into other types of particles. They had unrecognizable properties that couldn't even be defined.

These tiny packets of matter and/or energy are called quanta, and the scientific discipline that studies them is quantum mechanics. Listing and describing all these quanta, and discovering the laws under which they exist, is the main effort of modern physicists.

The difficulty of their undertaking is illustrated by the fact that, when Albert Einstein was told of their early findings, he dismissed the whole idea out-of-hand with the comment, "God does not play dice with the Universe."

§

1. The classical laws of physics applied equally to all known objects, ranging in size from an atom to a galaxy. The sub-atomic particles known to chemists, the proton, the electron, and the neutron, seemed to fit well into this scheme. Then the photon was discovered. It and the electron had characteristics of both waves and particles. Was there more to it than that?

A recent listing shows seventy-six kinds of particles that have been identified, and their properties determined, more or less. They can be classified in various ways, but the significance of these classifications is unclear.

Electrons, and all other particles of their mass or less, are leptons. The heavier particles, hadrons, are divided into baryons and mesons. Each baryon, a proton, an anti-proton, or a neutron, consists of three quarks. There are up-quarks and down-quarks, and each comes in three colors. (Not the kinds of colors we see with our eyes, but something entirely different, for which no better name has been found.)

Most mesons have two quarks, and they come in six flavors. (Again, not flavors that we taste.) Leptons have less mass – some of them zero, though they have something that acts like mass.

Known parameters of each particle are: mass, charge, spin, polarization, and lifetime (before it decays into something else).

A most difficult concept of quantum mechanics is "entanglement". Two particles at a distance, sometimes a very great distance, from one another complement one another's characteristics. If one particle changes, the other changes too. This has been verified experimentally, although the universal speed limit (speed of light) absolutely forbids it. Einstein called this "spooky action at a distance".

In a search for some kind of law that these quanta follow, some physicists have developed String Theory, in which particles are located along strings of various shapes, either open or closed, rather than at a point. This gives more satisfying mathematical formulations, but also introduces some unimaginable concepts. We can perceive only four dimensions, but String Theory tells us that there are at least eleven. Those extra dimensions could hold untold myriads of things we will never find. For example, we can't find Heaven in four dimensions, but it could still easily exist in some of those other dimensions. We hear of "worm holes" through which something might pass from this universe into another. Black Holes have been observed. Any object which crosses the "event horizon" of a black hole is doomed to a one way trip into the Hole's center. Could the Big Bang have been the explosion if a Black Hole which had eaten too many previous universes?

All this is nonsense to the public. But one item from quantum mechanics has fired the popular imagination. "Schrödinger's cat", in a closed box, is both dead and alive. Whatever the poor animal's condition, he doesn't deserve the scorn and hilarity heaped upon him.

Are you thoroughly confused by quantum mechanics? Welcome to the club!

§

A brief Internet search turned up several dozen recently published papers on quantum mechanics. Two-thirds of them mentioned either God or spirituality.

The authors of those papers are the most brilliant young scientists we have. Their names will be in the textbooks of the Twenty-second Century. They believe in God, but they reject all dogma and much religious tradition. Some churches welcome them, and their ideas. Other churches treat them like agents of the Devil.

The uncertainty inherent in quantum mechanics can suggest a solution to the difference between Deism and Theism. Deists say that God wrote the laws under which the Universe operates, and then set it into motion. Theists agree, up to this point, but add that God is still fine-tuning His handiwork, and may interfere with those laws at any time. And this point of view imparts increased value to prayer. A Deist prayer brings a person the spiritual strength to solve the problem himself. A Theist prayer also does that, but God Himself may also provide physical help.

The unsolved mystery of entanglement casts doubt on both Sir Isaac Newton's deterministic universe and John Calvin's predestination.

Scientists have touched the edge of spirituality. Who will help them go on from there?

CREDO

Put your creed into the deed.
— Ralph Waldo Emerson

I believe in one God only, the Almighty Creator and Ruler of the Multiverse. God and His Multiverse are infinite, the Universe, which can be perceived by the human mind, is finite.

I believe that God created this Universe with the intention that it would harbor life, which would testify to His glory.

> *Wherever a planet follows a nearly circular orbit at a suitable distance from its star, living beings will appear on portions of that planet that are not subject to, or are shielded from, harmful radiation. If favorable conditions last long enough, some of those beings will evolve into sentient beings, and eventually into intelligent beings.*

I believe that, in response to God's command, the Earth brought forth living beings; and that, in accordance with His laws, they evolved into many different forms, including humans.

I believe that the soul is a bit of the Holy Spirit, which is God's presence on Earth, placed by Him in the body of an animal, to remake that animal into His image, so that it may better serve Him.

I believe that every person is born with an immortal soul, which has been inherited through the generations, beginning with those first parents to whom God endowed His spirit. The quality of a person's life depends on how well he protects and nourishes that soul.

I believe that Jesus Christ, and Jesus Christ alone among humans, received the totality of the Holy Spirit. In that unique relationship, He is One with God, and has the power to save those who seek His help.

I believe that Jesus' taking human form, and with it all the suffering of life and death, was the ultimate act of humility, and that such humility is the first requirement of those who look to Him for salvation. I believe that, in emulating Jesus; actions and in following the concepts of His teachings, one magnifies his own soul, that it may grow to be accepted into the realm of eternity.

I believe that, in deliberately ignoring the precepts taught by Jesus, one diminishes his own soul and weakens his connection to God. Through deception and/or violence, he may even completely destroy his soul, and revert to the status of the animals that his ancient ancestors were before God endowed them with souls.

I believe that the Holy Bible contains the revealed Word of God. That Word was received by His messengers, who were charged with transmitting it to us as accurately as they could. I believe that nearly all of them did their sincere best, but that their limited worldview sometimes allowed them only a partial understanding of the greatness of God's wonders, that some of their languages were inadequate to convey God's full meaning, and that translations into other languages have sometimes introduced errors. I believe that God has also spoken through other messengers, whose writings are not included in the Bible. Those writings can be accepted only after prayer and meditation.

I believe that the Universal Church is a spiritual association of all those who follow the teachings of Jesus Christ, and look to Him for personal salvation. I accept all such persons as my brothers and sisters in Christ. I will not criticize any person's religious belief or moral standards, unless they cause harm to another person.

I believe that tradition, liturgy, and festivals enrich our culture and foster meaningful worship, but they must never be allowed to interfere with the free and conscientious religious practice of any individual.

I believe that all things physical will come to an end. Each person will die. The human species will become extinct. The Earth will be destroyed. The Universe will disappear. God has given us some limited control over our destiny. We can prolong our individual lives by healthful habits. We can extend the survival of our species through proper care of the planet that God has given us.

MANIFESTO

The world is heading for another major crisis, that is being called, even by the secular world, Armageddon.
— Billy Graham

Pope Sylvester II said the world would end January 1, 1000. It didn't.

William Miller said the world would end May 21, 1844. It didn't.

Bishop James Ussher said the world would end October 23, 1997. It didn't.

Jerry Falwell said the world would end January 1, 2000. It didn't.

The Mayan Calendar said the world would end December 21, 2012. It didn't.

But it will, someday!

§

The evidence that global warming is taking place, that it is doing serious harm to people, and that it is caused by people is no longer deniable. No one can reasonably claim that global warming is non-existent, that it is a hoax, that it is exaggerated, that it is a natural phenomenon, that it is harmless, nor that it is necessary to protect jobs. It is, plainly and simply, a monstrous crime against God and Man!

It is far too late to argue about who caused global warming. It is even too late to stop it. Our only recourse now is to try to learn to live with it. This is a major change in the environment. As always, in environmental upheavals, the fittest will survive, the less fit will perish. That is God's Law of Evolution. You can refuse to believe it, but you can't escape its consequences. God's laws are self-enforcing. Unbelievers are among the least fit to survive.

The survivors will be those with the greatest flexibility and mobility. Some of the most valuable and densely populated lands on Earth will become worthless, due to inundation, desiccation, or other changes. The total productive potential of the Earth will be less affected, because some other lands, now worth little, will become valuable.

Those who try to protect their investments in the physical assets that God is destroying are in great peril. There will be new, unimaginable, and dangerously unpredictable investment opportunities. Both the wisdom and the morality of seizing those opportunities are questioned. Much wealth will disappear. New wealth will be created. (Let us not forget that whatever wealth any of us have ever had has been a gift from God.) When global warming has finished redistributing and revaluing the Earth's resources, will we be able to give everyone equal access to what he needs? Our history does not suggest a favorable answer to that question.

Climate changes in the past have often led to migration, and conflict was a frequent result. It might be necessary for 50 million Americans to move to Canada. That could probably be accomplished peaceably. But what will happen if 400 million Chinese move to Siberia? Or if the entire Arab nation has to move to Europe?

The effect of civilization has been to protect humans, especially the weaker members of society, from the many dangers that surround them. Human evolution has been slowed down by our charitable impulses. Our technology and our institutions try to assure the survival of everybody, not just the fittest. Our hubris tells us that, since we are already perfect, we cannot evolve into an even higher form.

But a higher, or at least an altered form may be required for comfortable survival on the radically changed Earth of the future. When that time comes, will *Homo Superiorensis* treat the remaining *Homo Sapiens* any better than *Homo Sapiens* treated the last *Homo Neanderthalis*?

§

We are so comfortably resting in our cocoons that, as individuals, we may not even notice an approaching catastrophe. The world is uncomfortably warm? - Adjust the thermostat. The lawn is burning up? – Turn on the sprinkler.

Wild animals can't do things like that. They have to deal with the new environment immediately. How are they faring? Their fate foreshadows our own.

Over fifty species of frogs have already become extinct. Polar bears and several species of penguins depend of floating ice to carry them to their food. When the ice melts, they starve. The number of polar bears is plummeting. The chipmunks of Yellowstone Park are retreating to isolated mountain tops, where the lack of genetic diversity will probably spell their doom.

Nearly all wild animals who can are migrating poleward. They are often stopped by water or mountain barriers. Interstate highways are especially difficult for them to cross. Plants are also migrating, but much more slowly. Animals who outrun their food supply will suffer, and may steal the food of another species.

Thirty-seven species have been officially declared extinct since 1950. In most cases no one cause could be determined for the extinction. But three were due to ruthless hunting, three were due to loss of habitat, and two were due to global warming. None of those causes were natural disasters, they were all man-made. How long is God going to put up with this?

In the Great Extinctions of the past, some species have proven that they are among the fittest to survive, and despite the odds, they are still here. They may well do it again., Cockroaches will probably survive. So will dandelions. Humans? There is good reason for doubt.

Why should we care about species of animals or plants disappearing? That's not a problem for humans, is it? It will hurt only those humans who eat meat, fruit, vegetables or grain products. BON APPETIT!

§

The Republic of Kiribati has acquired a large tract of land in the Fiji Islands, to resettle those of its citizens who have already lost their homes or their livelihoods to the rising sea level. That entire nation is expected to be flooded out of existence in thirty to sixty years.[160] Other small island nations – the Maldives, Marshall Islands, Nauru, and Tuvalu – are seeking solutions to the same problem.

The Village of Shishmaref, Alaska has already been moved inland from the seashore. The ice sheet that once protected that shore from wave erosion during winter storms is no longer there. Should we worry about the relocation or abandonment of remote villages? Each time it happens, we're one step closer to facing the same problem in Miami, Boston, and New York,

[160] Caramel, Laurence, *Kiribati buys land in Fiji,* The Guardian, June 30, 2014.

§

The Earth has become a messy, dirty place, hardly fit for life. God didn't make it that way! We did! God's creation was amazingly beautiful and intricate. Every little detail as part of His plan. But man decided that he could do better by eliminating, rearranging, or "cleaning up" a few things that didn't fit his idea of a perfect world.

We have invented a special vocabulary to describe our ideas of "unclean". A "weed" is one of God's plants growing where we don't want it. "Vermin" is a group of God's animals living in space for which we have other use. "Dirt" can be almost anything fulfilling God's purpose in a place for which we have another purpose. And an "undesirable" is one of God's children whose nearness offends our sense of superiority

Dutch folklore tells of a housewife who was so clean that she swept her front step several times a day. Her step was always admirably clean, while each of her next-door neighbor's steps often appeared dirty, although they were swept daily. Cleanliness is next to godliness, but it isn't very godly to keep yourself clean by dumping your dirt on the neighbors.

Whenever we clean up or rearrange anything, we bring into effect God's Laws of Thermodynamics. Most of us are not familiar with those Laws, but they are just as strict and inexorable as His Law of Gravity. The First Law of Thermodynamics states, "Matter-energy can be neither created nor destroyed." It can be converted from one form into another, but all the matter-energy there is, or ever will be, was created by God at the moment of the Big Bang.

Any change, either natural or manmade, immediately invokes the Second Law of Thermodynamics: "An increase in orderliness in one part of a closed system is accompanied by increasing disorder in (an)other part(s) of the system, such that the total disorder (chaos) of the system always increases".[161]

Piles of trash (landfills), wastewater outflow, and smoke all represent entropy. All are increasing rapidly. They are the results of our attempts to keep our personal space clean and orderly. But they extract a terrible toll from God's natural environment.

Each American adds about 1400 pounds of trash to landfills every year, and sends about 15,000 gallons of dirty water through the sewers. Even all that is almost literally a drop in the bucket of our total discharge of polluted water. If we add the water fouled by the industrial and agricultural enterprises that produce the good things of our lives, and the runoff from our filthy streets, then each one of us is indirectly responsible for a billion gallons of contaminated water dumped into the natural environment each year.

[161] Scientists refer to the measure of chaos as "entropy". The entropy of the Universe is always increasing. The amount of entropy can be considered a measure of time. When entropy reaches its maximum value (which is unknown) time, and the Universe, will end.

Ironically, some of the most damaging and hard-to-remove water pollutants are detergents and other cleaning supplies, personal care products including cosmetics, garden and lawn fertilizers, and insect repellants. Many people apply these in excessive amounts in order to be "extra clean". The call-to-arms of the environmental movement, "The Silent Spring[162]", pointed out that the use of the pesticide DDT was driving songbirds toward extinction.

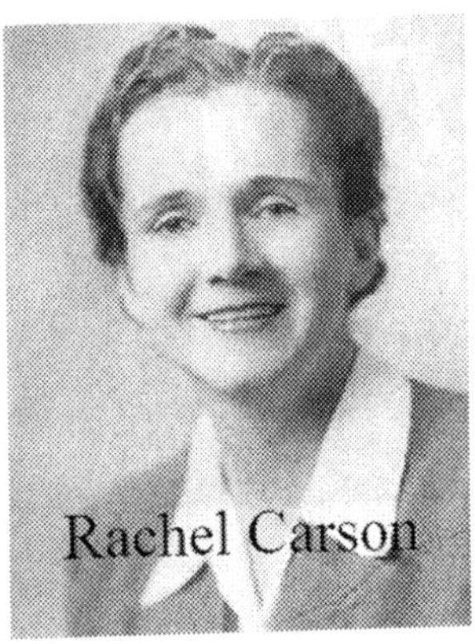

The concepts of recycling and "grey water" have entered our culture. They are doing some good, but woefully too little, to slow down the ruination of the planet. Most people are simply not interested, and participation is minimal. Public authorities often promote recycling only as long as they can make a profit from it.

The City of Chicago originally discharged its raw sewage into Lake Michigan, which is also the source of its drinking water. The result was not pleasant. So it reversed the flow of the Chicago River, and sent the sewage down the Illinois River. Downstream communities didn't like that. So the sewage was treated, and compacted sludge was dumped into abandoned strip mines. (It actually improved the appearance of that despoiled landscape.) Some irreverent prankster threw some seed corn onto the sludge piles. The plants that sprang up had the most vigorous and robust ears of any around. Squeamish legislators quickly outlawed the sale of such corn for human consumption. So it was fed to hogs. The resulting pork chops were enjoyed by many who had no idea of their origin,

§

162 Carson, Rachel, *Silent Spring*, The New Yorker Magazine, June 16,23,30, 1962.

Once a community hired an air pollution engineer and a water pollution engineer to clean up its environment. The clean air expert said, "Run the smoke through a baghouse, and when the bags become clogged, wash them out and send the dirty water down the sewer." The clean water expert said, "Filter the water, and when the filter becomes clogged, scrape off the gunk and burn it." It's just a high tech version of the old Dutch step-sweeping story.

You cannot escape pollution by shoving it aside. What can you do?

1. You can minimize your production of pollutants, and

2. You can turn them into something useful.

God does both! He does not intend for one of His favorite planets to become sterile before its time.

One of the most powerful tools of modern weather forecasters is the isentropic chart. ("Isentropic" means "with no change in entropy".) The complex processes of the atmosphere always adjust themselves so that there is little or no increase in total entropy. This is one of Nature's ways of prolonging the life of this planet. The assumption that Nature (God) will act in this way gives good scientific results,

A dead, decaying dinosaur would be a nasty thing to have around. It is amusing to speculate what a sanitation engineer might do with it. What did God do with them? He turned them into petroleum. Of course, it took Him many millions of years to do it. Perhaps that's the kind of patience we should have if we hope to survive.

It is the richest nations that still produce the most pollution. Most of those nations are also making some, though not enough, effort to clean it up. The recently industrialized nations are still trying to increase, rather than decrease, their output of contamination. Many pre-industrial nations would like to join them. Can that be tolerated?

Blessed are the poorest of the poor. They take little from Nature, and they return to her only that which is rightfully hers. Blessed are they, for they shall inherit the Earth, when the prosperous have perished in their own trash.

§

Virtually all[163] the energy in the Solar System is produced by nuclear fusion in the Sun. The outward flow of energy radiating from our star is $3.35x10^{26}$ Watts. This flow of energy has been nearly constant for over five billion years, and it is expected to remain so for several billion more. A small amount of this energy falls on each planet.

The energy density decreases with distance from the Sun according to the inverse cube law. The distance from the Sun to the Earth averages $149.6x10^{9}$ meters, so the flow of energy across the Earth's orbit is 1.37 Watts per square meter. The Earth's cross section is $127.4x10^{6}$ square meters, so the amount of solar radiant energy falling on the Earth is $1.74x10^{17}$ Watts. The Earth's albedo[164] is about 30%, so the amount of energy the Earth has available to operate all its processes, both natural and cultural is $1.12x10^{17}$ Watts. That is the amount that God has allotted to this planet. It would be most presumptuous to expect or to ask Him to increase it.

Only a minimal amount of the Earth's energy allotment is absorbed in the atmosphere, and much of that is used to ionize the outer air layers, including the ozone shield. The larger amount falls on the surface, where most of it evaporates water or supports photosynthesis. The latent heat of water vapor drives the atmospheric circulation that produces weather and runs the hydrologic cycle. Photosynthesis converts the radiant energy into the chemical energy of the food that nourishes all living creatures.

The latent heat carried by the evaporated water and the heat conducted into the air by

---

163 Insignificant amounts of energy are produced by nuclear fission and by tidal action in certain planets and planetesimals. Tiny amounts of radiant energy are also received from distant stars.

164 The percentage of received radiation that is reflected immediately out into space. That is the light by which inhabitants of other planets might see the Earth,

the planet's surface add up to $3.3x10^{16}$ Watts, This produces the worldwide weather.

The energy that is not used in these processes goes to warm the Earth and its oceans. The Earth itself radiates energy into space (in addition to that which had been reflected). The wave-length of terrestrial radiation is different from that of solar radiation, and the atmosphere is not as transparent to it. Greenhouse gasses (water, carbon dioxide, methane, etc.) capture some of the Earth's radiation, and send it back. To maintain a steady temperature, a planet must emit the same amount of heat that it receives. The Earth' heat budget is now slightly out of balance, and it is warming.

§

If all the arable land on earth were put to the production of plant food for humans, and all the solar energy available were used to produce such food, the earth would be able to permanently support 10 billion humans.[165] All those people would have to be vegetarians to survive. The present meat-and-vegetable diet of the American people takes about four times as much energy per capita to produce. That means that, if all the people in the world achieve the hoped-for American standard of living, the maximum sustainable population will be 2.5 billion. The present population is 7.3 billion, and growing. Think about that for a while before you read any farther.

Don't expect technology to pull us out of the dilemma. The vaunted Green Revolution of the mid-Twentieth Century was a tremendous technological achievement. It saved millions from starvation. But it also (1) used vast quantities of ground water which has not been and cannot be replaced, leaving many areas vulnerable to imminent desertification, (2) introduced destructive fertilizers and pesticides into the environment, (3) used up non-renewable resources, (4) contributed to global warming, (5) decreased the genetic diversity of several important food crops, making them vulnerable to extinction

[165] Wilson, Edward O. *The future of life*, Knopf2002.

by unexpected diseases, and (6) more than doubled the rate of human population increase.

The beneficial aspects of the Green Revolution were immediate, obvious, and politically popular/ The destructive aspects were slow-acting, obscure, and ignored, but inexorable. As usual, we ascribed a noble motive to achieving immediate human gratification rather than cooperating with God's long-range plan.

Continuance of human life on this planet requires getting the population under control. We cannot even maintain the present population unless we

1. Drastically lower the standard of living in the industrialized nations, or

2. Establish, by force if necessary, an even greater wealth gap between rich and poor nations.

§

God has a simple formula for extending the duration of a species existence on earth.

Number of Births = Number of Deaths

When He gave man dominion over the Earth, He commanded us to follow the same rule.

...., be fruitful, multiply. And replenish the earth… — *Genesis 1:38*

That simple phrase has been widely misinterpreted, with tragic results. To be sure what it means, let's define its key word.

Replenish 1. Fill up again.

2. Restore to a previous level.

--*Oxford Dictionary*

The Word of God does not command a growing population, and there is no way it can be twisted to permit the runaway exponential growth we are now experiencing. That is a human idea – a vain, selfish, and sinful idea.

So, how should we control our population? Again, God has shown us how.

§

Animals cannot control their destiny. Cod does it for them. When God gave us free will, He expected us to control our destiny just as He controls the destiny of animals.

God has allowed many, actually most, of the species He created to become extinct. There are three principal processes by which that has happened: (1) overpopulation followed by starvation, (2) over-predation,[166] and (3) lack of genetic diversity leading to defective progeny. God certainly does not want the creature He made in His own image to disappear in such a way.

We must get our population under control or we are doomed. It's up to us. God won't do it for us, but he tells us what is permissible, by allowing some of his other creatures to step back from the brink.

Animals have no technology and no free will. The methods by which some species have saved themselves must be in accordance with God's will, though some of them may be offensive to human sensibilities.

The population of lemmings is extremely unstable. When it rises well beyond the available food supply, lemmings by the thousands march together to a communal suicide. They have survived many episodes of overpopulation.

Much of the food supply of the giant panda has been destroyed by human exploitation. The panda has lost its sex drive, and its birth rate is so low than extinction by lack of genetic diversity threatens.

The moose population on Isle Royale in Lake Superior grew so large that it was facing collapse. An unusually cold winter permitted wolves to cross the ice from the mainland. Now stable populations of moose and predator wolves live together on the island.

Lions kill the cubs of prides competing for scarce food resources.

[166] Humans are, by far, the most dangerous predators. The dodo's only sin was that it was delicious.

Ant colonies make war on one another, with huge numbers of deaths. One bloody war has been observed between chimpanzee troops.

Alligators eat the weakest of their own young. This assures that they will have strong descendants, but not too many.

All these population control practices are loathsome to humans. Except war, of course. That's right up our alley.

§

None of the species of great apes has an overpopulation problem, though some of them are endangered by human intrusion into their environments. How do they do it? They, and their culture, were created by God, so He can't object too strongly to their methods of fulfilling His plan. Each species does it differently, and all are succeeding. Humans are similar to apes, but smarter. Perhaps we can save our species by emulating them.

The Asian gibbon is the epitome of sexual propriety. Gibbons mate for life, and the male and the female are absolutely faithful to one another. Their sex drive and, consequently, the birth rate is low. When a gibbon dies, its mate also dies.

The orang-utan is a solitary animal. It seldom encounters another orang-utan of either sex. A meeting of two orang-utans of opposite sexes, both in a romantic mood, is a rare event.

Most male gorillas are celibate. A silverback male has a harem of five to ten females. He pays so little attention to them that the entire group produces only about one child per year. He will kill any bachelor male who tries to mate with or steal one of his females.

The chimpanzee is the most promiscuous of animals. During the brief period when a female is in estrus, she mates with every adult male in the troop, except her own brothers. A male who tries to establish an exclusive relationship with a female is killed by the other males.

The bonobo is never mentioned in polite human society. He

is promiscuous, homosexual, bisexual, incestuous, and even pedophilic. But the peaceful, sociable, idyllic life he enjoys is a sure sign that God loves him.

The apes do things that make us uneasy. But each species has achieved a stable population without resorting to violence. If they can do it, we can do it too. And if we don't do it, soon, they are going to outlive us.

§

The human population remained very low for thousands of years. Then the agricultural revolution raised it modestly, but did not destroy the balance between births and deaths. What got it badly out of whack was modern medical technology, which has drastically lowered the death rate, especially the infant mortality rate.

We don't like death. We don't like taxes either. But they are both inevitable. Attempts to avoid taxes put us in both legal and financial trouble. Similarly, attempts to avoid death put our species in danger of extinction.

The entirety of medical science and medical practice is, in reality, death control. To keep God's equation in balance the same effort, and the same respect, must be given to birth control. There are only two possibly ways to balance that equation: increase deaths, or decrease births. Which do we want? Which does God want?

World population will peak in the late Twenty First Century, and then will begin to fall. How fast? That depends on us. The population is already well above what the planet can sustain at the American standard of living. We can enjoy this high life, even in the United States, only by drawing down irreplaceable resources, <u>and</u>, by keeping the rest of the world in relative poverty. How long will our technology, or our conscience allow us to do that?

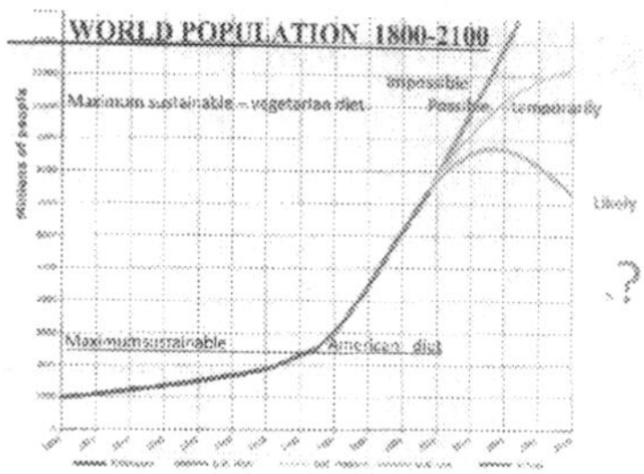

There are three possibilities:

(1) We will reduce our population to, and maintain it at, a sustainable level;

(2) A small group of humans will evolve into another species, better adapted to our despoiled planet, and the rest will die; or

(3) Homo sapiens will become extinct.

The Bible tells us how it will end, but not how soon or how fast.

...behold a white horse; and he that sat on him had a bow; and a crown was given to him; and he went forth conquering, and to conquer. And there went forth another horse that was red: and power was given to him that sat thereon to take peace from the earth, and that they should kill one another: ...And I beheld lo a black horse, and he that sat on him had a pair of balances in his hand. And I heard a voice ... say, a measure of wheat for a penny, and three measures of barley for a penny; and see thou hurt not the oil and the wine. ...behold a pale horse: and his name that sat on him was Death, ... *— Revelation 6:2-8*

Interpretations of the story of the Four Horsemen of the Apocalypse are varied and eerie. Seen in the light of the population crisis, the white horse carries a dictator who tries to hold together a decaying society, the rider of the red horse destroys all restraint and starts universal warfare, the black horse's rider controls distribution of disappearing food supplies, and the pale horse brings death itself.

§

The only way to save mankind from early extinction is birth control. Several methods have proven effective:

Celibacy,
Unorthodox sex,
Sterilization,
Contraceptive barrier,
Hormone treatment,
Abortion, and
Infanticide.

Each of these is offensive to someone, and there are those who insist that all are wrong. But something must be done, or we are doomed. Producing babies that are not loved, or cannot be properly fed, is a greater sin than any method of birth control. And forcing others to do so involuntarily is surely the work of the devil. That would be the most effective way for Satan to destroy God's most beloved creation.

An effective contraceptive barrier was described in hieroglyphics on an Egyptian stele. The ancient Greeks wrote of the silpium plant, whose extract prevented pregnancy. They rendered it extinct by by overharvesting.

If we continue to live by our culture of greed and vanity, humanity will be extinct in two or three centuries. On the other hand, if we can manage to consistently live up to our highest moral standards, and at the same time make the best possible use of our present science and technology, we can probably stretch our survival time to a million years. By exerting a maximum effort to improve our faith, our love, and our knowledge, we just might make it a billion years. God has done His part to make that possible. Can we walk closely enough with Him to make it happen?

THANKS

L'appréciation, c'est une chose merveilleuse.
Il fait ce qui est excellent d'autres nous appartient aussi bien.
— Voltaire

(Appreciation is a wonderful thing
It makes that which is excellent in others belong to us as well).

Ideas received from the following free-thinkers are gratefully acknowledged.

Jesus taught that worship of God does not require us to recite liturgy, to obey authority, or to believe in magic.

Jesus Christ

Born 2 BC Bethlehem
Died 31 AD Jerusalem
Crucified

MARTYRS

Fossey Galileo **Gandhi** **Hus** **Kennedy** **King** **Palissy**

Dian Fossey	1932-1985	American	Zoologist	Murdered	37
Galileo Galilei	1564-1642	Italian	Astronomer	Died in Prison	8,90
Mohandas K Ghandi	1869-1948	Indian	Civil Leader	Murdered	114

Jan Hus	1369-1415	Czech	Clergyman	Murdered	135
John F Kennedy	1917-1963	American	Statesman	Murdered	122
Martin Luther King	1929-1968	American	Clergyman	Murdered	81
Bernard Palissy	1510-1589	French	Hydrologist	Died in Prison	23

HEROES

Nicholas Copernicus	1473-1543	Polish	Clergyman	Censored	8,12
Charles Darwin	1809-1882	English	Naturalist	Demonized	152,153
Albert Einstein	1879-1955	German	Physicist	Exiled	7,9,13,14,157
Richard Leakey	1944-	Kenyan	Anthropologist	Maimed	37,51
Nelson Mandela	1918-2013	South African	Statesman	Imprisoned	127
Alfred Wegener	1880-1930	German	Geologist	Reviled	19
John Wycliffe	1331-1384	English	Clergyman	Desecrated	126,133

CONTRIBUTORS

BIBLIOGRAPHY

Books from which ideas are used.

ROSTER

Biblical persons mentioned in the text.

GAZETTEER

Places mentioned in the text.

INDEX

C

D

E

F

G

H

I

J

K

L

M

N

O

P

Q

R

S

T

ABOUT THE AUTHOR

Bob Snider is a scientist and a Christian. He has often faced skepticism from both his church friends and his working colleagues that he could sincerely believe in both his work and his religion. Carefully examining their arguments, he found them almost always based on emotion, and rarely on reason. He finds such emotions deeply ingrained in or society. They interfere in our political process, and degrade our educational system.

Bob was raised a Methodist in a formerly Mennonite family. He attended a Lutheran college, was married by a Baptist minister and assisted a Baptist missionary. In later life he has been a Presbyterian, and is an ordained elder in that church. He has served on the Advisory Board of the Salvation Army, and as Governor of a Kiwanis District. He now attends Catholic mass once or twice a month, and has worshipped God (the same God everywhere) in synagogues, mosques, and Buddhist temples.

Bob has academic credits from twenty-three colleges and universities, and has taught courses in four of them. His degree in geophysical sciences is from the University of Alaska. He has pursued advanced studies in a variety of sciences at the U S Navy Postgraduate School, the University of Chicago, and the University of Michigan.

A World War II veteran, Bob was ninety-one years old when he started working on this book. He is now crippled, deaf, and legally blind, but he is working on another book.